RIO

Edited by Edwin Taylor
Directed and Designed by Hans Hoefer
Photography by H. John Maier Jr.

APA PUBLICATIONS

THE INSIGHT GUIDES SERIES RECEIVED SPECIAL AWARDS FOR EXCELLENCE FROM THE PACIFIC AREA TRAVEL ASSOCIATION.

RIO

First Edition

APA PUBLICATIONS

Publisher: Hans Johannes Hoefer
General Manager: Henry Lee
Marketing Director: Aileen Lau
Editorial Director: Geoffrey Eu
Editorial Manager: Vivien Kim
Editorial Consultants: Adam Liptak (North America)
Brian Bell (Europe)
Heinz Vestner (German Editions)

Project Editors

Helen Abbott, Diana Ackland, Mohamed Amin, Ravindralal Anthonis, Roy Bailet, Louisa Cambell, Jon Carroll, Hillary Cunningham, John Eames, Janie Freeburg, Bikram Grewal, Virginia Hopkins, Samuel Israel, Jay Itzkowitz, Phil Jaratt, Tracy Johnson, Ben Kalb, Wilhelm Klein, Saul Lockhart, Sylvia Mayuga, Gordon MaLauchlan, Kal Müller, Eric Oey, Daniel P. Reid, Kim Robinson, Ronn Ronck, Robert Seidenberg, Rolf Steinberg, Sriyani Tidball, Lisa Van Gruisen, Merin Wexler.

Contributing Writers

A.D. Aird, Ruth Armstrong, T. lerence Barrow, F. Lisa Beebe, Bruce Borger, Dor Bahadur Bista, Clinton V. Black, Star Black, Frena Bloomfield, John Borthwick, Roger Boschman, Tom Brosnahan, Jerry Carroll, Tom Chaffin, Nedra Chung, Tom Cole, Orman Day, Kunda Dixit, Richard Erdoes, Guillermo Gar-Oropeza, Ted Giannoulas, Barbara Gloudon, Harka Gurung, Sharifah Hamzah, Willard A. Hanna, Elizabeth Hawley, Sir Edmund Hillary, Tony Hillerman, Jerry Hopkins, Peter Hutton, Neil Jameson, Michael King, Michele Kort, Thomas Lucey, Leonard Lueras, Michael E. Macmillan, Derek Maitland, Buddy Mays, Craig McGregor, Reinhold Messner, Julie Michaels, M.R. Priya Rangsit, Al Read, Elizabeth V. Reyes, Victor Stafford Reid, Harry Rolnick, E.R. Sarachandra, Uli Schmetzer, Ilsa Sharp, Norman Sibley, Peter Spiro, Harold Stephens, Keith Stevens, Michael Stone, Desmond Tate, Colin Taylor, Deanna L. Thompson, Randy Udall, James Wade, Mallika Wanigasundara, William Warren, Cynthia Wee, Tony Wheeler, Linda White, H. Taft Wireback, Alfred A. Yuson, Paul Zach.

Contributing Photographers

Carole Allen, Ping Amarand, Tony Arruza, Marcello Bertinetti, Alberto Cassio, Pat Canova, Alain Compost, Ray Cranbourne, Alian Evrard, Ricardo Ferro, Lee Foster, Manfred Gottschalk, Werner Hahn, Dallas and John Heaton, Brent Hesselyn, Hans Hoefer, Luca Invernizzi, Ingo Jezierski, Whilhelm Klein, Dennis Lane, Max Lawrence, Lyle Lawson, Philip Little, Guy Marche, Antonio Martinelli, David Messent, Ben Nakayama, Vautier de Nanxe, Kal Müller, Günter Pfannmuller, Van Philips, Ronni Pinsler, Fitz Prenzel, G.P. Reichelt, Dan Rocovits, David Ryan, Frank Salmoiraghi, Thomas Schollhammer, Blair Seitz, David Stahl, Bill Wassman, Rendo Yap, Hisham Youssef.
While contributions to Insight Guides are very welcome, the publisher cannot assume responsibility for the care and return of unsolicited manuscripts or photographs. Return postage and/or a self-addressed envelope must accompany unsolicited material if it is to be returned. Please address all editorial contributions to Apa Photo Agency P.O. Box 219, Orchard Point Post Office, Singapore 9123.

Distributors:

Australia and New Zealand: Prentice Hall of Australia, 7 Grosvenor Place, Brookvale, NSW 2100, Australia. **Benelux:** Utigeverij Cambium, Naarderstraat 11, 1251 AW Laren, The Netherlands. **Brazil and Portugal:** Cedibra Editora Brasileira Ltda, Rua Leonidia, 2-Rio de Janeiro, Brazil. **Denmark:** Copenhagen Book Centre Aps, Roskildeveji 338, DK-2630 Tastrup, Denmark. **Germany:** RV Reise-und Verkehrsuerlag Gmbh, Neumarkter Strasse 18, 8000 Munchen 80, West Germany. **Hawaii:** Pacific Trade Group Inc., P.O. Box 1227, Kailua, Oahu, Hawaii 96734, U.S.A. **Hong Kong:** Far East Media Ltd., Vita Tower, 7th Floor, Block B, 29 Wong Chuk Hang Road, Hong Kong. **India and Nepal:** India Book Distributors, 107/108 Arcadia Building, 195 Narima Point, Bombay-400-021, India. **Indonesia:** Java Books, Box 55 J.K.C.P., Jakarta, Indonesia. **Israel:** Steimatzky Ltd., P.O. Box 628, Tel Aviv 61006, Israel (Israel title only). **Italy:** Zanfi Editori SRL. Via Ganaceto 121, 41100 Modena, Italy. **Jamaica:** Novelty Trading Co., P.O. Box 80, 53 Hanover Street, Kingston, Jamaica. **Japan:** Charles E. Tuttle Co. Inc., 2-6 Suido 1-Chome, Bunkyo-ku, Tokyo 112, Japan. **Kenya:** Camerapix Publishers International Ltd., P.O. Box 45048, Nairobi, Kenya. **Korea:** Kyobo Book Centre Co., Ltd., P.O. Box Kwang Hwa Moon 1 658, Seoul, Korea. **Philippines:** National Book Store, 701 Rizal Avenue, Manila, Philippines. **Singapore:** MPH Distributors (S) Pte. Ltd., 601 Sims Drive #03-21 Pan-I Warehouse and Office Complex, S'pore 1438, Singapore. **Switzerland:** M.P.A. Agencies-Import SA, CH. du Croset 9, CH-1024, Ecublens, Switzerland. **Taiwan:** Caves Books Ltd., 103 Chungshan N. Road, Sec. 2, Taipei, Taiwan, Republic of China. **Thailand:** Asia Books Co. Ltd., 5 Sukhumvit Road Soi 61, P.O. Box 11-40, Bangkok 10110, Thailand. **United Kingdom, Ireland and Europe (others):** Harrap Ltd., 19-23 Ludgate Hill, London EC4M 7PD, England, United Kingdom. **Mainland United States and Canada:** Graphic Arts Center Publishing, 3019 N.W. Yeon, P.O. Box 10306, Portland OR 97210, U.S.A. (The Pacific Northwest title only); Prentice Hall Press, Gulf & Western Building, One Gulf & Western Plaza, New York, NY 10023, U.S.A. (all other titles).

French editions: Editions Gallimard, 5 rue Sébastien-Bottin, F-75007 Paris, France. **German editions:** Nelles Verlag GmbH, Schleissheirner Str. 371b, 8000 Munich 45, West Germany. **Italian editions:** Zanfi Editori SLR. Via Ganaceto 121 41100 Modena, Italy. **Portuguese editions:** Cedibra Editora Brasileira Ltda, Rua Leonidia, 2-Rio de Janeiro, Brazil.

Advertising and Special Sales Representatives

Advertising carried in Insight Guides gives readers direct access to quality merchandise and travel-related services. These advertisements are inserted in the Guide in Brief section of each book. Advertisers are requested to contact their nearest representatives, listed below.
Special sales, for promotion purposes within the international travel industry and for educational purposes, are also available. The advertising representatives listed here also handle special sales. Alternatively, interested parties can contact Apa Publications, P.O. Box 219, Orchard Point Post Office, Singapore 9123.

Australia and New Zealand: Harve and Gullifer Pty. Ltd. 1 Fawkner St. Kilda 3181, Australia. Tel: (3) 525 3422; Tlx: 523259; Fax: (89) 4312837.
Canada: The Pacific Rim Agency, 6900 Cote Saint Luc Road, Suite 303, Montreal, Quebec, Canada H4V 2Y9. Tel: (514) 9311299; Tlx: 0525134 MTL; Fax: (514) 8615571.
Hawaii: HawaiianLMedia Sales; 1750 Kalakaua Ave., Suite 3-243, Honolulu, Hawaii 96826, U.S.A. Tel: (808) 9464483.
Hong Kong: C Cheney & Associates, 17th Floor, D'Aguilar Place, 1-30 D'Aguilar Street, Central, Hong Kong. Tel: 5-213671; Tlx: 63079 CCAL HX.
India and Nepal, Pakistan and Bangladesh: Universal Media, CHA 2/718, 719 Kantipath, Lazimpat, Kathmandu-2, Nepal. Tel: 412911/414502; Tlx: 2229 KAJI NP ATTN MEDIA.
Indonesia: Media Investment Services, Setiabudi Bldg. 2, 4th Floor, Suite 407, Jl. Hr. Rasuna Said, Kuningan, Jakarta Selatan 12920, Indonesia. Tel: 5782723/5782752; Tlx: 62418 MEDIANETIA; Mata Graphic Design, Batujimbar, Sanur, Bali, Indonesia. Tel: (0361) 8073. (for Bali only)
Korea: Kaya Ad Inc., Rm. 402 Kunshin Annex B/D, 251-1 Dohwa Dong, Mapo-Ku, Seoul, Korea (121). Tel: (2) 7196906; Tlx: K 32144 KAYAAD; Fax: (2) 7199816.
Philippines: Torres Media Sales Inc., 21 Warbler St., Greenmeadows 1, Murphy, Quezon City, Metro Manila, Philippines. Tel: 722-02-43; Tlx: 23312 RHP PH.
Taiwan: Cheney Tan & Van Associates, 7th Floor, 10 Alley 4, Lane 545 Tun Hua South Road, Taipei, Taiwan. Tel: (2) 7002963; Tlx: 11491 FOROSAN; Fax: (2) 3821270.
Thailand: Cheney, Tan & Van Outrive, 17th Floor Rajapark Bldg., 163 Asoke Rd., Bangkok 10110, Thailand. Tel: 2583244/2583259; Tlx: 20666 RAJAPAK TH.
Singapore and Malaysia: Cheney Tan Associates, 1 Goldhill Plaza, #02-01, Newton Rd., Singapore 1130, Singapore. Tel: 2549522; Tlx: RS 35983 CTAL.
Sri Lanka: Spectrum Lanka Advertising Ltd., 56 1/2 Ward Place, Colombo 7, Sr Lanka. Tel: 5984648/596227; Tlx: 21439 SPECTRM CE.
U.K., Ireland and Europe: Brian Taplin Associates, 32 Fishery Road, Boxmoor, Hemel Hempstead, Herts HP 1ND, U.K. Tel: (2)215635; Tlx: 825454 CHARMAN.

APA PHOTO AGENCY PTE. LTD.

The Apa Photo Agency is S.E. Asia's leading stock photo archive, representing the work of professional photographers from all over the world. More than 150,000 original color transparencies are available for advertising, editorial and educational uses. We are linked with Tony Stone Worldwide, one of Europe's leading stock agencies, and their associate offices around the world:
Singapore: Apa Photo Agency Pte. Ltd., P.O. Box 219, Orchard Point Post Office, Singapore 9123, Singapore. **London:** Tony Stone Worldwide, 28 Finchley Rd., St. John's Wood, London NW8 6ES, England. **North America & Canada:** Masterfile Inc., 415 Yonge St., Suite 200, Toronto M5B 2E7, Canada. **Paris:** Fotogram-Stone Agence Photographique, 45 rue de Richelieu, 75001 Paris, France. **Barcelona:** Fototec Torre Dels Pardais, 7 Barcelona 08026, Spain. **Johannesburg:** Color Library (Pty.) Ltd., P.O. Box 1659, Johannesburg, SOuth Africa 2000. **Sydney:** The Photographic Library of Australia Pty. Ltd., 7 Ridge Street, North Sydney, New South Wales 2050, Australia. **Tokyo:** Orion Press, 55-1 Kanda Jimbocho, Chiyoda-ku, Tokyo 101, Japan.

With *Rio de Janeiro*, APA Publications adds another exciting destination to its new and fast growing *City Guide* series. The addition of *Rio de Janeiro* to the APA catalogue is a perfect marriage, uniting one of the world's most beautiful cities with the publishing of world's most beautiful guidebook series. The result is an eye-popping variety of spectacular photos of a spectacular city.

Hoefer

Taylor

Rio de Janeiro follows the same imaginative and innovative style that has brought international acclaim to the *Insight Guide* series. Since the series began in 1970 with the now classic *Insight Guide: Bali*, APA has turned out over 60 guides, each with its own distinctive personality blended artistically into the APA format. That format was designed and perfected by APA founder and publisher **Hans Hoefer**, a disciple to the Bauhaus tradition of graphic arts. Put together under Hoefer's watchful eye, each *Insight Guide* provides a sensitive portrayal of the cultural and human side of travel destinations, combining superb color photography with highly informative text. Based in Singapore, Hoefer and APA have over the years accumulated an impressive list of awards for excellence in travel guide publishing.

For *Rio de Janeiro*, Hoefer called in American-based executive editor **Adam Liptak** who traveled from Connecticut to Rio where he brought on **Edwin Taylor** as project editor for the city guide. A long-time resident of Rio, Taylor is an American journalist-writer who has written extensively about Brazil from all its varied angles—politics, economics, history, culture as well as travel. After several years as a reporter and free-lance writer in Miami, Taylor moved to Brazil in 1979 to assume the position of managing editor of the *Latin America Daily Post*, a daily English-language newspaper that Taylor helped to found. Four years later, Taylor started the first English-language information service on Brazil, called *Brasilinform*, which today publishes what is recognized as one of Brazil's most authoritative and influential newsletters. In the travel area, Taylor has written dozens of articles for travel publications in the United States, Europe and Brazil. He is co-author and editor of *Fodor's Guide to Brazil*, editor of *Fodor's South American Guide* and in 1988 launched the first English-language travel newsletter on Brazil called *Brazil Travel Update*. Over the years Taylor has written for such prestigious publications as *The Wall Street Journal*, *The New York Times*, *Newsweek* and *The Miami Herald*. In addition to his writing and publishing activities Taylor serves as a consultant on Brazil to several multinational companies.

To produce APA's *Rio de Janeiro* guide, Taylor put together a team of experienced, professional writers and journalists, the majority of them past or present residents of the city. **Tom Murphy**, an American journalist from New Jersey, used his expert knowledge of the city's hidden charms to write about Rio's lesser known attractions—the historical downtown area, the charming Santa Teresa neighborhood and the city's out of the way viewpoints. Murphy spent long hours chasing down facts for his portrait of Rio's romantic past plus his all-inclusive look at the greatest show on earth, carnival in Rio. Murphy is a former UPI correspondent for Brazil who has written for numerous publications including *The Wall Street Journal*, *The International Herald Tribune*, *The Christian Science Monitor* and

Pan Am's *Clipper* magazine. He has also researched the *Berlitz Guidebook to Rio* and currently writes for the *Brasilinform* newsletter and the Knight-Ridder Financial News Service.

The task of capturing the spirit of Rio's famed neighborhood, Copacabana, went to **Christopher Pickard**, who left his native England for Rio in 1978. Since then, Pickard has established himself as an unmatched authority on virtually anything of interest to the foreign visitor or resident. As Brazil correspondent for *Screen International*, *Down Beat*, *Cash Box* and *Music Week*, Pickard is a bona-fide expert on Brazilian song, dance and film. He is best known, however, for his *Insiders Guide to Rio*, winner of a Thomas Cook award for excellence. In 1988, Pickard published his second book, *The Insider's Guide to São Paulo for the Business Executive* and joined Taylor in the launching of *Brazil Travel Update*.

Another expatriate British journalist, **Moyra Ashford**, drew on personal experience to describe the unique sensation of dancing down the avenue in a Rio samba school. An art student in London, Ashford, in her words, "fell into journalism," a fall that has been steadied by her obvious talent shown also in her well-documented piece on Rio's Guanabara Bay. Having written for *Euromoney*, *The London Sunday Times*, *Macleans* magazine and *The Chicago Sun-Times*, Ashford is Brazil correspondent for *The Daily Telegraph of London*.

World traveler, journalist, professional musician and admitted full-time romantic, ex-New Yorker **Harold Emert** has been chronicling his love affair with Rio de Janeiro since arriving in the city in 1973. Emert, author of the features on the Beach Lifestyle and the Girl From Ipanema, left New York in 1969, oboe in hand, to discover the world, an adventure that took him to South Africa, Israel and Germany before

Murphy

Pickard

Maier

he accepted a job as first oboist of Rio's Brazilian Symphony Orchestra. Since then he has combined music and journalism, performing and composing in Rio and abroad while also finding time to free lance for a variety of publications including the *London Daily Express*, *New York Post*, *USA Today* and *Compass News Features*.

In theory photographing a beautiful city should be easy. In reality, however, Rio de Janeiro photographer **H. John Maier Jr.** faced an enormous problem—finding new, unusual and spectacular shots in a city that is among the most photographed in the world. Maier, though, was up to the task. Over a four-month period he trekked across the seashores and mountains of Rio as well as surrounding locations, searching out the majority of the book's photos. Looking back on the experience, Maier admits it was a major challenge. "So many photo books have already been done on the city that you have to come up with new ideas for each picture. Somebody once said that Rio was god's gift to the postcard industry and although true, it is not postcards that I was trying to photograph. On the other hand, photographing the people was made extremely easy since *cariocas* are proud of their

Emert

Ashford

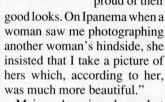

Christensen

good looks. On Ipanema when a woman saw me photographing another woman's hindside, she insisted that I take a picture of hers which, according to her, was much more beautiful."

Maier, American-born but who has lived most of his life in Europe, Asia and South America, works out of the South American bureau of the Time-Life News Service in Rio where he handles writing assignments as well as photography (he contributed the Green Coast feature). His photos have been published in *Geo Magazine*, *Time*, *Fortune*, *Asia Magazine*, *USA Today* and *Runner's World*. He also contributed to the cover for the *1984 Guiness Book of World Records*.

No guide book can succeed without painstaking research, a responsibility that fell to **Kristen Christensen**. An American from Minnesota, Christensen abandoned the cold winters of her hometown Duluth for the tropical sun of Rio in 1971. She has worked as a journalist, translator and English teacher. For *Rio de Janeiro*, Christensen researched and wrote the fact-filled Travel Tips as well as the Sugarloaf box story. She also served as editorial assistant to project editor Taylor, providing invaluable assistance at all stages of the guide.

Special thanks must also go to Brazilian photographer **Vange Milliet**, who provided historical photos, to Kodak of Brazil which developed Maier's photos, and to the officials of the Rio de Janeiro State Tourism Authority (Flumitur) and the Brazilian National Tourism Authority (Embratur). Finally, *Rio de Janeiro* owes its existence to the efforts in Singapore by APA staff members led by Editorial Director **Geoffrey Eu** and Editorial Manager **Vivien Kim**. Assisting in the final stages of the book are APA's editorial team of **Wong Mei Lin**, **Evelyn Chan**, **Audrey Simon** and **Johnny Chng**.

—APA PUBLICATIONS

TABLE OF CONTENTS

TABLE OF CONTENTS

OTHER INSIGHT GUIDES TITLES

COUNTRY/REGION

ASIA
Bali
Burma
Hong Kong
India
Indonesia
Korea
Malaysia
Nepal
Philippines
Rajasthan
Singapore
Sri Lanka
Taiwan
Thailand
Turkey

PACIFIC
Hawaii
New Zealand

NORTH AMERICA
Alaska
American Southwest
Northern California
Southern California
Florida
Mexico
New England
New York State
The Pacific Northwest
The Rockies
Texas

SOUTH AMERICA
Brazil
Argentina

CARIBBEAN
Bahamas
Barbados
Jamaica
Puerto Rico
Trinidad and Tobago

EUROPE
Channel Islands
France
Germany
Great Britain
Greece
Ireland
Italy
Portugal
Scotland
Spain

MIDDLE EAST
Egypt
Israel

AFRICA
Kenya

GRAND TOURS
Australia
California
Canada
Continental Europe
Crossing America
East Asia
South Asia

GREAT ADVENTURE
Indian Wildlife

CITYGUIDES
Bangkok
Berlin
Buenos Aires
Dublin
Istanbul
Lisbon
London
Paris
Rio de Janeiro
Rome
San Francisco
Venice
Vienna

WHAT IS A *CARIOCA*?

Sprawling in majestic disarray across a strip of land between granite peaks and the South Atlantic, Rio de Janeiro is the final victory of fantasy over fact.

Each day, Rio's streets and sidewalks support some eight million persons transported by some one million cars, trucks, buses, motorcycles, scooters and bikes all competing for room in a space designed for one-third their number. This spectacular chaos does nothing to dampen the enthusiasm of the *carioca*, Rio's imperturbable native son. For the *carioca*, all things are relative except for one—the wonder and beauty of Rio de Janeiro.

The *carioca* is a mixture of hedonism and irreverence. He respects nothing and no one, yet he is always searching for someone and something to provide him with pleasure. He is, of course, a Brazilian but above all, he is a *carioca*, an individual of immense resourcefulness, of keen wit, of engaging conversation, of stunning beauty and of worldly knowledge—or so he claims. The *cariocas's* unflagging optimism, boundless confidence and utter self-absorption might be seen as conceit. Nevertheless, *cariocas* are, as their legend says they are, charming.

Altogether, there are 5.6 million *cariocas*, residents of Rio proper, but an additional four million live in suburbs ringing the city. As many as 70 percent are poor, by American or European standards. But there is the beach and the samba and there is carnival and the comforting presence of Rio's extraordinary beauty.

All *cariocas* are passionately in love, 24 hours a day, with their city, the *Cidade Maravilhosa* or "marvelous city". The beach is their playground, *samba* is their music and carnival is their party, a *carioca* party where the poor parade **as** the rich and the rich parade **with** the poor.

Each day, the *cariocas* sit and stare at their beautiful city, at the sea, the forested mountains, the granite monoliths and concoct their dreams. For these tropical Walter Mittys, there could be no better place. Romantics lose their hearts in Rio. Social scientists lose their minds. This is the ultimate land of yellow brick roads.

Preceding pages: Tiny bikinis and beautiful bodies; view from Sugarloaf at sunset; spectacular Carnival float; Sugarloaf guards the entrance to Guanabara Bay. Left, Christ the Redeemer statue.

15

THE DIRTY TRICKS OF HISTORY

The first tourists arrived in Rio in 1502, as part of a Portuguese exploratory voyage headed by Americo Vespucio. The exact date was January 1, 1502 and Vespucio entered what he thought to be the mouth of a river. Hence the name Rio de Janeiro or River of January. Vespucio's river was in reality a 147-sq mile (245-sq km) bay, still known today by its Indian name, Guanabara or "arm of the sea."

Vespucio's voyage was one of a series launched after Portuguese explorer Pedro Alves Cabral discovered the east coast of Brazil in 1500. Portugal laid claim to the colony, including Rio, but concentrated its colonization in the northeast where sugar plantations were set up. Seeing no immediate economic value in Rio, the Portuguese put off settling in the region, an opening that was seized upon by the French.

French colony: In 1555, a French fleet arrived at the entrance of Guanabara Bay with the intention of founding France's first colony in the southern half of South America. Under the command of Admiral Nicolas Durant de Villegaignon, some 500 French settlers disembarked on an island in the bay that today bears Villegaignon's name. A fort was built on the island and the French proceeded with their grand scheme to found Antarctic France for settlement by Calvinists brought from Europe.

Another 1,000 settlers arrived but problems broke out when the Calvinists discovered that the religious freedom they sought in the New World was less than what they had expected. Rumors of religious persecution in the colony reached Europe, bringing further immigration to a halt and dealing a heavy blow to France's plans. In the meantime, Portugal took interest in the southern part of its colony, resolving to drive out the French.

In 1560, a Portuguese fleet entered the bay and after a week of fighting, the French were defeated. Once the Portuguese left, however, the French returned, leading to a second expedition in 1565. This time, the Portuguese were determined to rid themselves of the French and take possession of Rio. After two years of intermittent fighting, Portugal emerged victorious and the French dream of Antarctic France ended.

City founded: From then on, Rio received increasing attention from Brazil's Portuguese masters. In 1567, the city of São Sebastiao de Rio de Janeiro was founded. Named in honor of Saint Sebastian on whose feast day the founding occurred, São Sebastiao de Rio de Janeiro soon became simply Rio de Janeiro. Initially confined to what is today the downtown area facing the bay, Rio's growth was determined by the importance of its port to the colony. By the end of the 16th century, Rio became one of the four main population centers of Brazil. But its port remained secondary to those of the sugar-growing northeastern provinces, particularly the colony's capital of Salvador.

All of this changed when gold was discovered at the end of the 17th century in the neighboring province of Minas Gerais. Thousands of prospectors and fortune hunters many of whom came from Portugal, flocked to Minas to participate in the largest gold rush of its time. Rio, the only port city close to Minas, benefitted immediately. A road was built to link Rio to the gold fields while in the city's port, gold seekers disembarked daily. The enormous wealth uncovered in Minas made Portugal the world's largest producer of gold in the 18th century. Gold became the colony's main export item and all of Brazil's gold went through Rio to Portugal, thus shifting Brazil's economic center from the northeast to Rio.

Boom days also brought problems. Twice, in 1710 and 1711, the French attacked Rio.

Preceding page: Nineteenth-century panorama of Guanabara in oil painting by Nicolau António Facchinetti. Left, portrait of Mario Leopoldina of Hapsburg with her children (the future Emperor Pedro II on her lap) by Domencio Failutti.

NAMES OF RIO

Visitors to Rio de Janeiro's stunning **Copacabana Beach** at the mouth of **Guanabara Bay** might consider that, had a few events been different, they would instead, be sitting on world-famous, Sacopenapã Beach in the heart of São Sebastião near the azure waters of Santa Luzia Bay.

The Tamoio Indians of 1502, the year of Rio's discovery by a Portuguese fleet under Admiral André Gonçalves, called the vast bay *Guanabara*, meaning in their language for the bay. São Sebastião would fall away too, for reasons that are obscure, and residents called their city simply, Rio de Janeiro.

The people living in Rio since 1565 have been called *cariocas*. The name comes from the Tamoio language and probably means "house of the white man" or "white man."

Cidade Maravilhosa or "marvelous city," Rio's nickname among Brazilians, was first used in 1908 by Northeast writer Coelho Netto in his novel, *Os Sertanejos*. The author

"arm of the sea."

But the Portuguese believed they had discovered the mouth of a wide river. Since they sailed into the waters in January, they called the place River of January, or **Rio de Janeiro.**

The bay was called Santa Luzia, in honor of the favorite saint of fleet navigator, Americo Vespuccio.

The city founded years later would be called São Sebastião do Rio de Janeiro. The saint's feast day coincided with the founding. By then, however, most residents had accepted the more logical name, Guanabara

described the "urban marvels" of Rio, then the nation's capital, and showed how they attracted the poor from Brazil's hinterland.

Favela is also derived from events in the Northeast. The battle which ended a bloody war in the 1890s between Brazil's federal government and the fanatically religious settlers of Canudos in Bahia was fought at a place called **Morro da Favela.** When victorious federal troops were discharged, many made their way to Rio de Janeiro where they settled on the **Morro da Providência**. They called their community Favela and, given their low pay and the lack of urban facilities on the hillside, it gradually declined into a slum. Rio's mountainside shantytowns from then on have been called *favelas*.

Copacabana has its origin in the Quechua language of the Indians living around Lake Titicaca on the border of Peru and Bolivia. *Copa* means "luminous place" and *Caguana* means "blue beach." When the Spanish stumbled onto Lake Titicaca in the 16th century they discovered a spot called Copa Caguana which the Indians regarded as

Janeiro. A tiny church on a remote fishing beach called **Sacopenapā** received the image, which attracted the devoted from all over Rio. At first, pilgrims would say "I'm going to Sacopenapā to see Nossa Senhora de Copacabana." Later, they shortened it to "I'm going to see Copacabana" thus saving Rio's most famed beach from being forever known as Sacopenapā, a Tupi name meaning " noise and the flapping of the herons."

Ipanema has a less elaborate origin. It's

sacred. The Spanish erected their own chapel, placing within it an image of Nossa Senhora da Candelária. But the Indians conversion to Christianity, continued referring to it as Copa Caguana, or Copacabana in a later corruption.

Decades later an itinerant silver merchant had a copy of the Lake Titicaca image made and donated it to the diocese of Rio de

Left, view of Niteroi as seen by Henri Nicolas Vinet in the 19th century. Above, the view of Rio from the hills of Santa Teresa in an 1883 oil painting by Jorge Grimm.

simply a Tamoio word meaning "dangerous waters."

Leblon, like many districts in Rio, is named after the first important land owner in the area, Frenchman Charles Le Blon.

Flamengo, on the other hand, received its name following the war to expel the Dutch from the colonial Northeast. Dutch prisoners-of-war, most of them Flemings, or *Flamengos* in Portuguese, were brought to prison camps in the then outlying district. For years, the neighborhood was known as Campos dos Flamengos, later shortened to Flamengo.

On their second try, they broke through its defenses and sacked the city. Blessed with the seemingly unending flow of gold from Minas, the city was soon re-built. In 1763, Portugal at last recognized Rio's new status as the colony's leading city and transferred the capital from Salvador to Rio.

Brazil's preeminent city: For the next 200 years, Rio was to be Brazil's preeminent city. When the Portuguese royal family fled from Napoleon's conquering army in 1808, Rio became the capital of the Portuguese Empire. With Brazil's independence in 1822, Rio became the capital of the Brazilian Empire, changing again in 1889 to capital of

suddenly thrust into a world of courtly manners and elegance which hardly fit its backwoods character. More unusual was the insistence of the transplanted nobles on maintaining their own European court style, including dress, in a fetid port city in the midst of the tropics.

Determined to make the best of the situation, the emperor set about to change the nature of his new capital. Over the next decade, Rio acquired the trappings of European civilization to a greater extent than any other New World capital of the period. Schools, parks, newspapers, banks and a wide variety of imperial government organi-

the Republic of Brazil. Throughout these years, Rio was the economic, cultural and political center of Brazil, home to the pomp of the monarchy and intrigue of the republic.

Among the events that shaped Rio's development during these years, the most remarkable was its sudden and unexpected elevation as the capital of a European empire. The flight of Portuguese Emperor Dom João VI, with an entourage of over 15,000 noblemen, created the unprecedented situation of a colony becoming the seat of government for the mother country. With the arrival of the emperor in 1808, Rio was

zations sprouted across the city, giving it an increasingly European air. Of more immediate importance to both Rio and Brazil was the decision by the emperor to open up commerce which had been previously restricted to Portugal. By stressing trade relations with Napoleon's enemies, principally England, the Portuguese gave a giant boost to Rio's economy and ended its previous isolation. Rio became not only the capital of an empire but an important center of world trade.

Independence: When Dom João finally returned to Portugal in 1821, Rio's population of over 100,000 was more than three times larger than when he had arrived 13 years earlier. The emperor left his son Dom Pedro behind as prince regent of Brazil but Pedro came under the influence of Brazilian nationalists, declaring the colony's independence from Portugal in 1822. Rio now became the capital of the independent nation of Brazil, formally entitled the Brazilian Empire although it had no territorial possessions. With Brazilian noblemen replacing the departed Portuguese dukes and counts, Rio maintained a surface similarity to its former glorious days. But the capital, like the empire itself, was about to go through its most tumultuous period. For the next 20

years, Brazil was nearly torn asunder by constant revolts and regional challenges to the central authority in Rio. Dom Pedro finally abdicated and turned the empire over to his five-year-old son, Dom Pedro II, who ruled through a regency. It was not until the 1840s that Pedro II, by then running the nation, was able to silence the separatist

The old Carioca Aqueduct, left, can still be seen in Lapa near the downtown business district; the "Pedra da Gavea" or "Crow's Nest Rock" (above) before the city spread out to São Conrado.

movements and unite the nation.

What followed were four decades of domestic peace, marked by steady progress and increasing contact with the outside world. Pedro II, a scholarly, well-travelled man, made his capital a South American showcase of the latest marvels of modern science. The city was lit by gas in 1854 and was linked with London by telegraph in 1874. Pedro's greatest coup was the construction of the first telephone line outside of the United States of America between Rio and his imperial retreat, Petrópolis, in the mountains outside the capital.

Military revolt: The tranquil reign of Pedro came to an abrupt end in 1889 when the military, expressing growing republican sentiment, overthrew the monarchy and sent Pedro into exile, scattering the nobility and bringing to a halt Rio's days of titled elegance. In the place of emperors and princesses, the capital of the newly formed Republic of Brazil became the battleground of civilian politicians as Brazil embarked on the first of several attempts at democracy.

In reality, however, the Republic amounted to little more than an exchange of elites. In place of Rio's nobles were the wealthy landowners of the states of São Paulo and Minas Gerais. These new power brokers quickly became the nation's political establishment, deciding amongst themselves the vital issues of the day, including the choice of the president. Their authority remained unchallenged until a 1930 coup brought to power Getulio Vargas, a defender of the urban working class. Under Vargas, populism and nationalism became dominant political themes with the nation's politicians fighting for influence over the masses. As the capital and the country's industrial center, Rio was soon caught up in the urban turmoil that marked Brazil's initial period of industrialization.

During these years, the city underwent rapid urbanization. Its swelling population forced the government to find creative solutions to overcome Rio's chronic lack of space. Establishing a trend that has continued throughout this century, city planners looked south, following the contour of the beaches. At the start of this century, tunnels were drilled through granite mountains to open up the beachside neighborhood of Copacabana and to prepare the way for the later development of Ipanema, the lagoon and the beaches farther south. The first beach front drive was built running from downtown along the bay to Sugarloaf.

Dramatic facelift: Downtown itself underwent a dramatic facelift with the construction of Rio's most elegant avenue. Inaugurated in 1905, Avenida Central was built in response to President Rodrigues Alves' vision of a tropical Paris. Unfortunately, Alves overlooked the fact that downtown Rio, unlike Paris, had no room to grow other than vertically. Through the years, the elegant three and five-storey buildings of Avenida Central, the Champs Elysee of Rio, were replaced by 30-storey skyscrapers. In the process, the avenue suffered a name change, becoming today's Av. Rio Branco. Of the 115 buildings that flanked Avenida Central in 1905, Rio Branco has preserved only ten.

Important as these and succeeding construction booms were for the modernization of Rio, the city paid a heavy price in the loss of much of its architectural heritage. With space severely limited by the topography of Rio, the wrecking ball has done away with much of old Rio. Modern-day landmarks of the city such as the wide Copacabana beach and the splendid Aterro, the giant park that flanks the bay, were made possible by landfill taken from downtown hills. The most tragic case of this came in 1921-22 when the downtown hill of Castelo was carted off together with most of Rio's remaining 16th -and 17th -century structures.

Expansion alternative: While Rio was struggling to find room to expand, its rival to the south, São Paulo, was enjoying a surge of economic and population growth. By 1950, the city of São Paulo had surpassed Rio in population and economic importance, a lead that it has never relinquished. In 1960, Rio suffered the final humiliation when President Juscelino Kubitschek formally moved the nation's capital to the city he had built in the center of the country, Brasilia.

To civil servants used to the physical beauty, lax formality and non-stop pleasures of Rio, the move to Brasilia was seen as a life sentence to Devil's Island. All struggled against it and while most were forced in the end to move, Rio remains home to thousands of federal government employees whose *carioca* creativity won them last-minute pardons.

Since it lost its status, Rio has floundered about, losing also its ranking as the country's leading industrial and financial center, to the upstart São Paulo. Adding to Rio's troubles was government indecision on what to make of the former federal district after the capital was moved to Brasilia. At first, the city of Rio was transformed into the state of Guanabara but in 1975, Guanabara and the existing

state of Rio de Janeiro were combined to join into Rio state, with the city of Rio becoming its capital.

Loss of prestige: This decision solved the question of Rio's administrative identity but did nothing to compensate for the loss of prestige and revenue occasioned by the creation of Brasilia and the consequent mass exit of government bureaucrats and foreign diplomats. Unfortunately for Rio, while the city continues to lose industry and jobs to the fast growing south, it remains a mecca for poor Brazilians from the northeast and the interior states. The steady influx has swelled Rio's infamous shantytowns, the *favelas*, as well as the slums of the northern suburbs.

In the 1980s, with the country strapped by its foreign debt, Rio has been unable to make the investments needed to maintain public services and resolve the housing problem. Downtown Rio, in particular, has suffered a steady deterioration during these years. Visible signs of decay are apparent in the downtown and near-downtown neighborhoods. Even Copacabana has been affected as shown by the increasingly pot-holed streets and littered sidewalks of the famed beach neighborhood.

The problems of today had their origins in federal funding. In a country where the federal government controls the majority of the nation's public sector purse strings, this meant ten straight years of austerity for Rio.

In recent years, however, Rio has begun to make a comeback. Major oil finds off the coast of the state of Rio will provide both the city and state with substantial royalty payments for the foreseeable future. The oil has also generated plans for a major petrochemical complex. The promise of growing tax receipts has encouraged the city government to unveil an ambitious plan to revitalize downtown Rio, turning it into a landscaped area of shops, offices and culture centers.

the last ten years of the 1964-85 military regime when Rio suffered a form of political ostracism. In two consecutive administrations, the state of Rio was governed by politicians in opposition to the military rulers in Brasilia. Although the military did not interfere directly in the administrations of these two governors, it did hold back on

Left, the Rua do Ouvidor was the heart of 19th-century business Rio. Above, a rustic bridge in the gardens of the presidential residence, Catete Palace.

Rio has also been the main beneficiary of a boom in tourism. Although Rio's upper crust refuse to admit it, the city has become increasingly dependent on the tourism trade, the state's biggest money maker today.

For diehard *cariocas*, however, economic gains can never replace the lost glory of the days when Rio was the political eminence of Brazil. But even in the still uncomfortable role of number two, Rio remains a major force in the nation's unending political intrigue. As *cariocas* proudly note, decisions may be made in Brasilia and São Paulo, but plots are hatched in Rio.

ROMANTIC RIO

International reputation: Once upon a time, poker chips circulated in Rio de Janeiro like coin of the realm.

Maurice Chevalier, Tommy Dorsey and Josephine Baker performed on stage while the brother of Brazil's dictator plotted and drank in the back rooms.

International celebrities like Jayne Mansfield and Orson Welles gambled with their love lives and their reputations.

Once upon a time...

The time was the mid-1930s to the late 1950s.

The locale was a string of casinos, night clubs and hotels which gave Rio an international reputation for exotic and sometimes excessive fun.

The map of that exotic Rio still exists. And so do most of the former pleasure domes, some refurbished, others dilapidated like overused Hollywood movie sets.

The map begins at the ice cream-cake facade of the **Copacabana Palace Hotel** half-way down the famous beach. Then it runs down Avenida Princesa Isabel, makes a detour to Urca, continues around downtown to the Rio-Petrópolis Highway, and finally stops at the Grand Ballroom of a spectacular chalet called Quitandinha.

When it was inaugurated in 1923, the Copacabana Palace was the only luxury hotel in South America. It kept the title for more than two decades.

In those days, luxury meant something.

"Guests had everything—pool, theater, gambling casino, the best restaurants in South America and the best service," says Gabriel Catena, a Copa waiter for 39 years. "We weren't allowed to say 'no' when a guest wanted something."

Casino gambling—black tie only—was permitted from the early 1920s until the games were outlawed in Brazil in 1946.

"Some people came to the Copa just to gamble," says Catena, "and some played too much. Portuguese nobleman the Marquês de Pombal came over just to gamble. Then there was an Argentine millionaire, whom everyone knew as Dodeiro, and a Madame Seabra. Nobody ever knew her first name. But the biggest gambler was a landowner from Rio Grande do Sul who came just to drink and gamble. Over the years he sold off more and more of his property to cover

losses until he ended up with nothing."

The Copa had several game rooms, including one called the Morgue, featuring the lowest bet in town. The Morgue was near the main entrance so the croupiers could expel poor losers. But even the Morgue was a black tie affair.

The gambling rage was so great during the 1930s that one columnist wrote "respectable women—really of the very best society—hock their jewelry to pay gambling debts."

But the Copa didn't stop in 1946. In fact, some people say the 1950s were its heyday.

Hardly a celebrity who came to Brazil in

Left, enjoying the spectacular view of Sugarloaf and the bay from Corcovado. Above, a tropical interlude in a hammock.

those years failed to stay at the Copa—the Copa was Rio high society, what they called "cafe society."

"To be a waiter in those days." says Catena, "you had to have personality and speak languages. I was a sad case—I only spoke three. We had a head waiter who spoke 14. At the Golden Room we had the best shows in Brazil—black tie only. Everybody who came to the Copa had class."

John F. Kennedy ("when he was in his 20s, right after the war"), Lana Turner, Tyrone Power, Eva Peron ("with 10 attendants and 100 suitcases"), deposed King Carol of Rumania, who took up residence in the

It took days just for the entourage to install itself comfortably in the hotel. And there were a lot of parties at the beginning. "Five bottles of whisky were sent up to Welles' suite every day," recalls Machado. "Five empty bottles came down every night."

But Welles also worked hard filming slum-dwellers, fishermen and samba schools.

"He spent RKO's money with incredible ease, but the film, a documentary entitled *It's All True*, was never finished," says Machado.

The story of Welles throwing furniture out of the window of his Copa suite is also true,

Copa, Ali Khan and many others were guests. Nat King Cole, Edith Piaff, Tommy Dorsey and many others performed.

And so, in curious ways, did Orson Welles and Jayne Mansfield.

Orson Welles was only 27 at the time of his famous stay in the Copa in 1942.

Says former show promoter Carlos Machado, "Everything they say about Welles in Rio really happened. It's all true."

The director arrived with dozens of technicians, hundreds of pounds of expensive equipment and at least $100,000 in cash after a two-day flight from Washington.

according to Machado. But there are two versions of why it happened.

According to retired Copa doorman Manoel Oliveira, Welles became angry when he heard from actress Dolores del Rio that their on-again, off-again affair was off again, this time for good. That's when the furniture started flying. In the Machado version the cause of Welles' romantic frustration was local showgirl Linda Batista. The furniture flew out of the window in both versions. "Of course, Welles wasn't arrested," says Machado. "He was the honored guest of the Brazilian government."

Jayne Mansfield was at the center of an embarrassing incident in the late 1950s.

It was at the Copa poolside. Someone pulled the string of the actress' famous overflowing bikini top. The top fell to the floor provoking a reaction typical of the American actress—her famous "*ooh*". She was rescued by an admirer who threw her a towel.

At a Copa Carnival ball in 1959, the same thing happened again. This time, Mansfield was dancing with a young reporter named Guimaraes Padilha. A reveller grabbed the neckline of Mansfield's party dress, tearing the material to ribbons and exposing the actress' torso. Newspaper reports the next

more years for the Guinle family, the Copa's sole owners, to get around to it. And even then it was only a government order, making the Copa a national landmark, that prevented the old building from being torn down and a high-rise hotel-shopping complex put up in its place.

Today, the refurbished Copa retains much of its old charm and opulence of bygone days. There are more cars and pollution, of course, but the romance remains. If you listen carefully you'll hear Ali Khan berating one of his wives as the Xavier Cugat Orchestra performs in the background.

Sacha's: Just down the Avenida Atlantica

day said the Copa crowd was "aghast". The actress ran to her suite and was never seen at the Copa again.

Starting in the early 1960s the Copa began a gradual decline. More luxury resorts went up in Rio and, according to Catena, "the Copa became just another hotel."

In fact, by the mid-1970s the Copa was badly in need of a face-lift. But it took 10

Right, the fabled Quitandinha hotel-turned-condominium in Petrópolis, a relic of a bygone era. Above, the ageless elegance of the Copacabana Palace Hotel.

from the Copa, at the intersection of Avenida Princesa Isabel, is another corner of Copacabana where cars and pollution have crept up on traditional night spots.

For decades *Sacha's* was the night club to know in Leme, the elegant beach that stretches from the Meridien Hotel towards Sugarloaf Mountain.

Recalls Machado, "Sacha Rubin was the best musician in the history of *carioca* night life. He used to play all night without a break. Nobody knew how he did it. He would learn the names of regular customers and play a signature tune for each one."

Other bars: There were also other bars clustered around the corner of Avenida Princesa Isabel and Avenida Atlantica, where the Meridien Hotel is today. They had names like The Wonder Bar, The Carlton, The Bolero and The Espanhol. According to Machado, things only got hot around 3 a.m., most nights. There was even one club, the Night and Day, which prided itself on staying open 24 hours.

Carlos Machado: Carlos Machado was a pretty hot property himself in those days.

Starting in the late 1930s, Machado was known as "The King of Carioca Night Life."

He first earned the title because of his dual role as director of a musical group called The Brazilian Serenaders and promotional manager of the famed **Casino da Urca**, located on narrow Urca Beach in the shadow of Sugarloaf Mountain.

After a decade of bumming around four continents working as a dancer, actor and promoter, Machado returned to Brazil in 1939 to produce the Casino da Urca floor show.

Joaquim Rolla: His boss, Urca owner starting in 1937, Joaquim Rolla, was one of the great eccentrics of *carioca* night life. Says Machado, "Rolla was barely literate. He kept saying 'exactly' all the time, especially when he didn't understand what people were saying. (Society photographer and later show promoter) Oscar Ornstein used to act as Rolla's interpreter."

A singer of the period attested to Rolla's lack of savoir-faire: "Once I asked him why he didn't put gondolas in the pond in front of his Quitandinha Casino (in Petrópolis) and he said 'I already tried but they all died.'"

But Rolla understood show business very well and became, in the years just before World War II, Brazil's leading purveyor of night life, using Carlos Machado's talents to the fullest.

As back-up for the casino's regular performers, Machado formed his own group, The Brazilian Serenaders. One critic wrote, "Carlos Machado ably directed his Brazilian Serenaders even though he knew absolutely nothing whatsoever about music."

But music was not Machado's gift. Promotion was.

Says samba musician Luciano Peroni, "For Machado everything had to be the best, including the best international entertainers."

As Urca impresario, Machado contracted Maurice Chevalier, legendary American black singer Josephine Baker and the Xavier Cugat Orchestra among others. (Baker, who escaped U.S. racism to make her career in Paris in the 1920s and 1930s, fled France when the Nazis invaded in 1940. She spent the war years in Rio.)

Machado also made sure there was glittering decor, seductive lighting and lots of dancing girls. He believed in packaging and

public relations. He was the first Brazilian band leader to make his musicians wear the same outfit, to play signature tunes and to change his band's repertoire periodically.

Nor did Machado himself miss out on the good times. Many casino employees participated in an active social and gambling life along with the idle rich. Says Machado, "Casino employees were allowed to gamble and we did gamble. Most of us lived right in Urca. There was so much gambling going on, casino tokens were used as money in Urca and parts of Copacabana."

Decline of gaming: Many observers thought

the April 1946 decree prohibiting gambling in Brazil would mark the death knell of gaming and the high life.

In fact, the Casino da Urca and other Rolla properties experienced a rapid decline. The glittering casino was sold to the Tupi radio and television network. But when the network failed in the 1970s, the garish old building, featuring an archway over Avenida João Luis at the bottle-neck entrance to Urca, was abandoned. Today, it retains the air of a haunted castle, dark, dusty and teeming with the ghosts of long-gone nobility.

But other gambling establishments

games included a future Brazilian president, João Goulart.

Now an office building, the monumental Serrador, with its glittering chandelier and red carpets, still presides elegantly over Rio's Cinelandia district.

During much of the 1950s the illegal gaming was tolerated by lax officials. The Monte Carlo even had top performers headlining in the main room and featured a risque revue.

Another famous spot was the Casablanca, evocative of the sultry, smoke-filled night clubs of Hollywood movies. Located on Praia Vermelha next to the Sugarloaf cable

merely experienced a change in venue, as did showmen like Machado and Ornstein.

At the appropriately named Monte Carlo near the Jockey Club in Gavea there was an illegal baccarat game nearly 24 hours a day, while at the Hotel Serrador downtown, officials of the Brazilian Labor Party played poker and drank through the night in a back room. Participants in the all-night card

car platform, the club was designed to look like Mr Rick's Cafe Americaine, the gin mill owned by Humphrey Bogart in the film *Casablanca*. The long, low building, now owned by the Army, can still be seen.

But the masterpiece of exotic Rio was Joaquim Rolla's ill-fated Quitandinha hotel-casino complex in Petrópolis.

At the time of its construction in the early 1940s, Quitandinha (named after the Petrópolis neighborhood of Quitandinha, meaning Little Green Grocer) was the most elaborate resort hotel in South America. (Today, it is a social club-cum-condominium).

Left, inspiration for lovers, a romantic sunset stroll on Ipanema beach. *Cariocas* have no qualms about public displays of affection, above, at a beachside snack stand.

Quitandinha was built between 1941 and 1946 to rival the Copa. It cost the then unheard-of sum of $10 million and at one time employed 10,000 people. The unfortunate fact, for Rolla and his army of employees, was that Quitandinha probably would have been a success except for the 1946 decree ending gambling in Brazil.

Says Machado, "Joaquim Rolla was born in the wrong country."

Following the decree, which came only 15 months after Quitandinha's opening, occupancy rates plummeted and the hotel began to lose money.

Rolla tried to recoup his losses by selling Quitandinha to the U.S. hotel group, Eppely Hotels, but the Americans backed out at the last minute. Next, the state government tried its hand with a management contract. But the state lost money and handed the complex back to Rolla.

Finally, a private company purchased the property in 1963, turning it into a condominium. Since then it has retained its stately facade but lost most of its former glamor.

Although Quitandinha failed as a business proposition, its architectural splendor lives on.

Wooden balconies and shuttered windows still grace its facade. There are great arching doorways and peaked towers, like something out of Camelot.

The massive structure was planned by Brazilian architect Luiz Fossati and built with the aid of German engineers. The style is Normandy and the emphasis is on wide, gleaming corridors, overstuffed furnishings and exaggerated decoration.

Today's Quitandinha, which can be visited with permission from the condominium manager, closely preserves the 1940s feeling with most of the original fixtures and much of the original furniture still in place. A visit to Quitandinha is like a walk into a Fred Astaire movie. The old Hollywood feeling is especially poignant in Quitandinha's huge Grand Ballroom dripping with red curtains and elaborate light fixtures. You can imagine Harry James on stage and the Marx Brothers stumbling around the plush anterooms, knocking over cocktail tables and falling over the pin cushion-pink armchairs. Today the roulette wheels are out of sight but not out of mind. They have been stored away, just in case.

Petrópolis Tennis Club: But Quitandinha was not the only 1940s hot spot in Petrópolis. There was also the elegant, highly selective Petrópolis Tennis Club nearby. The club catered to cafe society and the nation's political elite. It maintained its own casino (members only paid their gaming debts at

the end of the summer season) and floor show.

One habitual guest was tough-talking Rio de Janeiro Police Chief, Benjamin Vargas, who also happened to be the brother of Brazilian dictator Getulio Vargas.

Recalls Machado, who often performed at the club, "Benjamin Vargas used to send word from the bar to tone it down during the floor show. He would send somebody in to say 'the chief is treating important matters of state in the bar, so tone it down.'"

Says samba musician Peroni, "it was the *Belle Epoque* of Brazilian entertainment."

Left, motorcycle has become a favorite mode of tranportation for Rio's youth. Above, nothing like a cool drink especially on a very hot day.

THE BEACH LIFESTYLE

"The beach is the last backyard left for a carioca who dwells in a city of highrises and congested traffic. Watching the ships sail on the Atlantic Ocean, he tans his skin and meditates on his good luck in only having to cross a few streets to find this marvelous blend of peace, saltwater, sex and beauty."
—Rio journalist Joaquim dos Santos.

Take a good look at the beaches of Rio de Janeiro and you will discover how this city really works. Don't just pay attention to the golden-tanned, sunbathed beauties on the sands. Look closer at this metropolitan sun-deck and you'll see the customs, habits and amusements of the *cariocas*.

The beach, or *praia*, is the place to read, gossip, flirt, jog, work out, dream, think and even close business deals. The beach is everything at once a nursery, schoolyard, reading room, soccer field, volleyball court, singles bar, restaurant, rock concert hall, exercise center and office. Occasionally, someone will also go into the water but only for a refreshing dip before returning to more important activities.

Weekend day: On a glorious weekend day, nearly the whole of Rio spends some time on the beach, which is not to say that they are not there during the week as well.

Sit calmly on one of the stone benches along the beach sidewalk on a Sunday morning, the best day to observe Rio's "zoological" garden, and poise your binoculars. The day begins with the arrival of the beach "employees". These are lifeguards, vendors, gymnastics, professors, swimming teachers and a handful of entrepreneurs who earn their keep by setting up volleyball nets, chairs and lounges of those fortunate *cariocas* who live in beachfront apartments across the street. These employees are true beach historians, some of whom have had decades of service on the sands.

Then there are the buxom, coffee-colored sunbathers, strapped into, but just barely, what *cariocas* call the "dental floss" bikini

Left, mother and daughter enjoy a morning on the beach.

and prominently displaying their tight bottoms in worship of the sun. Sitting nearby on one of the world's most democratic stretches of land may be jet-set socialites or slum dwellers from the hillside shantytowns.

Volleyball games: It may be a day of scorching 100° heat, but the weekly (or daily for some) volleyball games on the hot sands continue. Those agitated, barefoot, bald and paunchy players may appear to be beach bums but during normal working hours, they're bankers, stockbrokers and executives of multinational companies.

Other entertainment on the city's beaches includes soccer played by the Peles of tomorrow, incessant paddleballing ("*frescobol*") and samba or *pagode* music-making and dancing. *Chopp* or tap beer sold in paper cups by barefoot hawkers on the sands, is part of the colorful jigsaw puzzle of *carioca* beach life. For teetotalers, coconut juice is readily available at nearby stands on the sidewalk.

Music lovers will immediately note that each and every vendor has his own rhythm and melody to contribute to a polyphony of tropical beach sounds. Visually, to counterpoint the agitation on the sands, fishermen are out at their post at the tip of Copacabana beach and rowboats from deeper waters bring in a net's catch for sale at the marketplace located across from the Hotel Rio Palace. Late in the afternoon, lone fishermen set their poles in the sand where the multitudes had earlier sunbathed, to try their luck.

Treasure hunters: In the morning, noon and evening, treasure hunters comb the sands in search of valuables left by forgetful bathers, sometimes stumbling across earrings, watches, rings and other items which can include anything from women's panties to leftover chicken wings. Oblivious to the romantic clinches of earnest beach lovers, they are, like many *cariocas*, optimistic that today will bring new rewards.

For the uninitiated, there are surprising and often unforgettable scenes on the beach: beautiful young women who slip into and

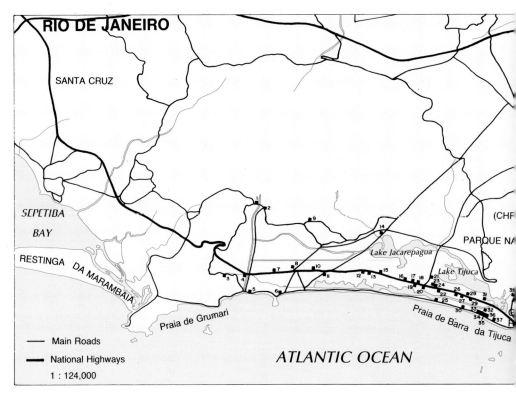

out of their bikinis as if they were in the privacy of their homes; the down-and-out entertainer who displays photos of the days he appeared with Frank Sinatra and sings on the sands for coins; the offerings left by followers of *macumba*, (Brazil's version of voodoo) to the mythical goddess of the sea, Iemanjá; tattoo artists looking for prospective customers; security guards of luxury hotels watching over their hotel guests to protect them from petty thieves.

This magical world of Rio beachlife was not always so. At the start of this century, the beach scene was confined to the bay where a more formal and sedate society dabbed at

on weekends, often forming part of a neighborhood clique that has its own reserved spot on the sand. On the beach, infants nurse, children play and make friends, boy meets girl and on it goes with the elderly walking hand in hand down the beach sidewalks.

New Year's celebration: On New Year's Eve, the *carioca* beach becomes a giant movie set with *macumba* ceremonies presided over by women smoking hefty cigars to obliterate the evil spirits. While drums beat out a pagan rhythm along the length of Copacabana and Ipanema, thousands of *cariocas* and tourists, dressed in white in homage of the sea goddess Iemanjá, mingle

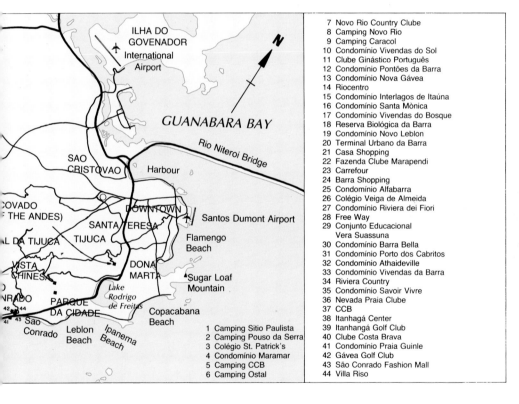

picnic lunches or gently wet their feet and possibly legs in the water. Liberal ideas, population growth and the opening up via tunnels of Copacabana, changed all that. With the passage of time, a day on the beach evolved from tranquil family outings into an all-encompassing cradle-to-grave lifestyle. Today, the beach is not part of the life of Rio, it *is* the life. Entire families flock to the beach

and gaze in awe at the cult ceremonies that fill the beach in what is certainly one of the most distinctive and fascinating New Year's Eve celebrations in the world.

Fireworks, pop music shows, free movies and even political campaigns form a part of beachlife at different times of the year. Advertisers know where their best public is and when to find them—Sunday on the beach. Campaigns to promote films, shows, language schools and new products are often launched in the air by planes carrying streamers to entertain beachgoers.

Even the nation's air force gets into the act for bathers occasionally, with a display of their best pilots and newest jets. For the newcomer it seems as if a *coup d'etat* is beginning but during the last coup in 1964, many *cariocas* were sunning themselves on the beach when the tanks rolled by.

João's tick: Legend has it that Rio's beach craze began on an odd note: João VI, king of Portugal was forced to flee to Brazil in 1808 when Napoleon invaded his country. Bitten

able libraries will be set up on the city's sands, in line with a campaign called "Read on the Beach."

Popular songs: The beach lifestyle has become an important subject for Brazilian culture including popular songs like Tom Jobim's "Wave", paintings, plays and literature. The beach is also a favorite subject for Rio's intellectuals, most of whom can be found on or near the beach at anytime of the day.

Carioca sociologists claim that the beach is Rio's great equalizer in addition to being its great escape valve. According to this theory, the majority of the city's residents,

by a tick, João was advised by a doctor to bathe in the waters of Rio's Flamengo Beach. Thanks to João's tick, a tradition was born.

That tradition now extends to a time schedule which on weekends and during vacation season, is referred to as "before" and "after" the beach. For instance, no local impresario will schedule a musical show or concert on a weekend afternoon at the customary 2:00 or 3:00 p.m. but rather 4:30 or 5:00 p.m., long after beachtime. In the latest admission of beach superiority, the state Secretary of Culture announced that port-

the poor inhabitants of its mountainside *favelas* and northern slums, have equal access to the beach and are therefore satisfied with their lot.

Surprisingly, there is some truth to this romantic notion although a rising crime rate in the 1980s indicates that not all of the poor are satisfied. The beach, though, remains

Above, each summer begins with a basic concern—getting the perfect tan as soon as possible. Right, sunbathers must always keep an eye out for stray volleyballs.

open to all and is free.

While democratic and integrated, Rio's beaches are not entirely classless. A quick walk along the sands of Copacabana will take you past small "neighborhoods" of bathers, each congregating its own social type or group. In Ipanema, near the Country Club, the cream of Rio's high society sunbathe while the gays' favorite areas are near Rua Miguel Lemos in Copacabana and also in front of the Copacabana Palace Hotel. Celebrities favor the crystal waters of São Conrado where at Pepino, fruit salads and cold grapes add a "natural" touch to the usual beer and ice cream bars. Intellectuals gather

at Ipanema in front of Rua Farme de Amoedo. In Leblon, muscle boys and their admirers cavort while the upwardly mobile residents of Ipanema migrate to the Barra da Tijuca. Foreign tourists occupy the sands in front of their hotels in Copacabana, Ipanema, Vidigal and São Conrado. If you return the next day, you will find the same groups in the same places, a "beach corner society" that has become a permanent characteristic of Rio life.

The waves which usually overwhelm the foreigner by their often frightening power, are objects of play for most of the locals who grew up splashing and diving into them. Whereas in most parts of the world a pregnant woman will stay far away or at least covered up on the beach, locally it is very "in" for the mother-to-be to parade about in her bikini.

Topless bathing: Despite a brief attempt to introduce it at the start of the 1980s, topless bathing has never become popular. Ipanema remains virtually the only city beach where women will sometimes remove the tops of their bikinis but only when surrounded by friends.

Bars along the beach drive, especially in Copacabana, on hot, sunny weekends tend to be an extension of the beach. It is common to see men in nothing but their swimming trunks and beach things and women with tiny shorts pulled over their bikinis or with a colorful *canga* tied around their hips enjoying drinks or a meal along Av. Atlântica.

Not everyone who lives in Rio is privileged to live near the beach. An entire north zone of the city exists, far from the waters of the Atlantic and its cooling breezes. The governor of Rio de Janeiro state from 1983-1987, Leonel Brizola—a presidential hopeful—tried to appease the masses during his term by inaugurating a bus system which shortcut the route from the north to the south of the city. The reaction of the inhabitants of the city's southern zone was predictably outrage. They accused the "northerners" of dirtying their beaches, to no avail. The buses have kept coming, turning parts of Ipanema and Leblon beaches into southern outposts of the north zone dwellers.

Common to the *carioca's* vocabulary is the question, "Will tomorrow be a good day to go to the beach?" For most of the past 400 years, the answer has been a resounding "yes".

Even if you are by nature a workalholic, the sight of people sunbathing, swimming, singing, dancing, flirting and drinking beer by the refreshing waters of the Atlantic Ocean on a hot summer day, would make you wonder whose lifestyle is "correct".

Above, "mate" ice tea vendor takes a break. Right, the samba is an integral part of life in Rio, extending to the beach.

More than in any other city, the colors of Brazil are the colors of Rio de Janeiro.

The nation's characteristic racial tricolor—black, brown and white—is displayed on every street corner and, in its most attractive variations, along every sandy beach of Brazil's second largest city.

Statistically, Rio comes closer than any other metropolis in reflecting Brazil's overall racial balance. The 1980 census portrayed a nation 55 percent Caucasian, 38.5 percent mulatto and 5.9 percent negro. The census described Rio's 5.1 million inhabitants as 62.7 percent white, 27.5 percent brown and 9.8 percent black.

Rio was almost as black-and-brown (37.3 percent) as Brazil (44.4 percent) but not nearly as much so as the Afro-Brazilian Holy Land of Salvador (71 percent) in Brazil's Northeast. Brazil's biggest city of São Paulo, however, was exaggeratedly white (74.6 percent), even boasting a 2.8 percent Oriental population, part of the city's melting pot of ethnic groups. Rio, by contrast, was only slightly whiter (62.7 percent) than Brazil as a whole (55 percent). Yet Rio—the former federal capital and still Brazil's chief entertainment center—often seems as cosmopolitan as the big megalopolis to its southwest.

Part of Rio's charm is precisely its racial co-mingling and harmony. This has given rise to the theory of the "mulatto solution," the notion that Rio, like Brazil, has resolved racial tension through an increasing mix of black and white, resulting in the "browning" of the population.

In Rio the white-brown-and-black tricolor takes shapes and hues rarely seen even in other multiracial cultures. The white negro, for example. Some *cariocas* possess all the marks of the African—all except skin color. Others are black *only* in color, with Caucasian features and perpetual tans.

Left, few cities in the world have the racial mixes that characterize Rio.

Indeed, a tropical beach city with five million sun worshippers whose population is more than one-third black and brown to begin with, Rio often seems happily mulatto in its racial and even cultural identity.

Origin: Much of Rio's racial variety is due to internal migration. Bantu-origin slaves of colonial Rio mixed with Nagô Nation Africans migrating from Minas Gerais after that state's gold rush collapsed in the 19th century. Starting in 1877, when a drought devastated Brazil's Northeast, Iorubá-origin blacks from Bahia poured into Rio.

The mix of colors and cultures is most intriguing when it comes to religion. The beliefs of African *umbanda* are present among many of Rio's white residents while European practices, such as faith healing, have penetrated the African religions. And most *cariocas*—embracing spiritism or not—are still nominal Roman Catholics.

Characteristic elements of Brazil's African religious heritage—the figure of an elderly, pipe-smoking black woman as medium surrounded by chanting spiritists in flowing gowns and loaded down with charms—were elegantly exploited in Marcel Camus' 1959 film, *Orfeu Negro,* set during Rio's Carnival. Camus' black Orpheus speaks with the spirit of his dead Eurydice through the sly intervention of a black medium. The noisy, smoke-filled session is one of the movie's climaxes.

Experienced mediums accept possession from a number of spirits, who settle in like old friends from other centuries to chat with "clients." The clients get advice and prophecies. Sometimes they seek favors—the spirit's intervention in a love affair or help in getting a job.

There are few social distinctions among clients. Machado de Assis opens his turn-of-the-century novel, *Jacob and Essau* with an *umbanda* session attended by the wife of a wealthy aristocrat. The black medium predicts her pregnant white client will give birth to male twins who will perpetually quarrel over money and women. The rest of the novel shows how the prophecy comes true. In Rio's suburbs, white working and even middle class couples often marry in two separate ceremonies, first at an interminable *umbanda* ritual and later at a Roman Catholic mass.

The most colorful showcase for Rio's mulatto solution, however, is the annual Carnival parade. Samba composer, Dorival Nery says "the parade is homogeneous. You see rich and poor, black and white, slum dweller and medical doctor, side by side."

Originally an all-black affair, the parade widened its appeal and themes during a half century to become the centerpiece of today's

The female mulatto: The samba parade also highlights an even more heart-thumping aspect of Rio's mulatto phenomenon—the *mulata* or female mulatto.

The very word sends expectant shivers down the spines of almost all Brazilian males. In most cases, foreign males take between 24 hours and, at most, a few days to feel the same symptoms—a weakening of the knees and hot and cold flashes along the backbone.

Mulata is a word that graces a hundred popular songs and is the theme of a million daily commentaries by *carioca* men. Poised, nearly naked, atop the glittering samba pa-

Carnival. The original black element is honored by the mandatory *Ala das Baianas*, featuring hundreds of elderly but incredibly agile black women dressed in the flowing gowns of Bahia. But modern Brazil's materialistic, white-dominated culture increasingly defines the parade's main themes. Rio's, and Carnival's, bourgeois aspect probably reached its zenith a few years ago when one samba group dedicated its entire program to *High Society* newspaper columnist Ibrahim Sued, the rough equivalent of Cholly Knickerboker being honored at a Preservation House benefit for the NAACP.

rade floats or developing intricate, suggestive dance routines on the pavement below, the word becomes flesh and dwells among us, even if only for a few glorious moments.

The *mulata's* allure is not easy to define. Perhaps it's the caramel skin tones—the image of a shapely woman with a perpetual tan. But others see a less aesthetic element.

Black rights activist Percy da Silva says "fascination with the *mulata* is a manifestation of racism. It is part of the image of blacks as destitute of intelligence and with only a precarious hold on conventional morality. The *mulata* may have an exotic, alluring side but she also suffers from a double stigma—as a negro and as a woman."

In fact, nearly all *carioca* blacks and browns suffer a double stigma—that of poverty and that of race.

Says da Silva, "In Rio the black population is segregated in the suburbs and the hillside slums. Foreigners don't see it."

Statistically, he may be right. Rio's population becomes darker as its sprawling suburbs stretch away from the famous beach neighborhoods. Copacabana is 85.7 percent white. Middle and working class Meier, about 12 miles (20 km) from downtown, is only 64.8 percent white. Another nine miles

work force earning one minimum salary (about $65 per month) or less was 11.7 percent. But 15.6 percent of the mulatto work force and 22 percent of blacks in the work force earned one minimum salary or less.

Prejudice abides. And at all levels of society. Says Maria D'Aparecida, a black carioca who left Brazil in 1960 to pursue a successful singing career in the Paris Opera, "the fact is you can't sing the leading roles in the Rio de Janeiro Opera Company if you are black."

"Brazilian blacks are considered good for samba and soccer," she adds, "but little else. Carnival is the public expression of black

(15 km) along Avenida Brasil to Bangu, the white population is a bare majority of 52.5 percent. Six miles (10 km) beyond Bangu is the distant working class suburb of Santa Cruz, 46.7 percent white and 52.7 percent black and brown.

The 1980 Census also confirmed the inferior economic status of Rio's blacks and browns. The proportion of whites in the

Left and above, the faces of Rio show the city's racial mosaic, a mix of black Africans with European immigrants and the native indians.

culture but when it's over, blacks go back to being low-paid, uneducated workers living in slums. Carnival is a paradox."

In recent years, black leaders have become increasingly vocal in their citicisms of discrimination. For them, the mulatto solution is a myth that clashes daily with the harsh reality of the city's black population. Despite this, however, a black movement has not appeared. Sociologists say that for Rio's blacks, the majority of whom are on the bottom of the social ladder, the onus of being poor obscures any onus attached to being black.

Everything in Rio has status, of one sort or another. Ideas, people, things, places, from the insignificant to the sublime, nothing escapes the *carioca* passion for cataloguing. What is out is unspeakably out and what is in is marvelously in.

The following is an "in" and "out" guide to the status symbols of Rio:

Cars—In a city of sharp social divisions, a car is a symbol of relative affluence. The poor don't own cars. But while having a car is positive, some cars are obviously better than others. **The** car is a Mercedes Benz and if possible a late model, red convertible. Since the government keeps out imported cars to protect the local industry, the price tag of a Mercedes is three to four times that in the USA or Europe. For this reason, any imported car is a status symbol but nothing quite matches a Mercedes.

Beach homes—*Cariocas* never get tired of the beach. While they live beside the sea, those who can, build their weekend retreats on the beaches of nearby towns and cities. Those with real wealth also build mountain homes. The number one site for a beach house is the vacation idyll of Buzios with Angra dos Reis in second place. The absolute status symbol, though, is to own an island, for which permission from the Brazilian navy is required.

Penthouses—for Rio proper, status is living on the beach but the ultimate goal is living in a beachfront penthouse. Virtually any beach will do in Rio although for property values nothing comes close to Ipanema's multi-million dollar penthouses. Wise to the *carioca* penchant for penthouses, developers now design apartment buildings with up to four on top: if you can't have a penthouse, then next best is a duplex or, even better, a triplex—but always with a beach view.

Left, making it in Rio means flaunting it and there's nothing better than a hillside mansion overlooking the sea.

Neighborhoods—Rio is divided into two parts, the north zone and the south zone. In terms of status, there is only one—the south where from Copacabana to the Barra da Tijuca, Rio's monied classes predominate. **Ipanema** still retains its top ranking which it wrested from Copacabana in the 1960s, but isolated pockets of status have surfaced in **Gavea**, **São Conrado** and **Leblon**, (actually Upper Leblon, reflecting. The latter reflects a tendency for old neighborhoods to receive new names as their prestige climbs). A special case is the Lagoon, which is really an extension of Ipanema and Leblon, but is so strikingly beautiful that it deserves its own name and high status. Neighborhood status follows property values which in turn depend on population density, convenience of living, proximity to the beach and overall physical beauty. Overcrowded Copacabana is now definitely out while Ipanema is quickly filling up, opening the door for **Barra da Tijuca** whose openness and unspoiled, beautiful beach assure its future as a Rio status address.

The international lifestyle—just as Brazilians don't really consider themselves Latin Americans, status conscious *cariocas* don't really consider themselves Brazilians. Like their city, they are international, sophisticated and worldly. International travel is in, travel inside Brazil is out. Imported goods are in, Brazilian goods are out. Foreign books outsell Brazilian books and for pure status, you can't beat owning a private satellite dish tuned in to American, French and British television.

English—A look around shows that English is spoken here. Fashionable shops, restaurants, boutiques, hairdressers all show a preference for foreign names, with English the obvious winner. In their speech, *cariocas* throw in English words and phrases for which Portuguese equivalents either are non-existent or considered inferior. "Performance" is a must (as is "must"), bars offer "happy hours", businessmen enter into "joint ventures", the stock markets trade "blue chips", computers are "hardware" and operate with "software", consumers go to "malls" and "shopping centers". English is clearly in.

Carnival—Although leaving Rio to spend carnival at a beach or mountain retreat is considered chic, there are definite rewards, for those who stay behind. Watching the s*amba* school parade from a private box with catered meals is a top-rated status symbol. Also in is to be invited to the carnival *feijoada* by highly regarded party-giver Ricardo Amaral who is the owner of the city's most exclusive private club, the Hippopotamus. A special treat awaits those

ness of the parade is shown by the number of *carioca* socialites who dance with the schools.

Samba—Just as the carnival parade has become "in" of late, so also has the *samba* cult. Once viewed as the domain of the lower class, the *samba* world has come into fashion as a type of adventurous, bohemian lifestyle—slumming as it were (disco, meanwhile, is out and for sophisticates, jazz is in with the hot spots being **Jazzmania**, **People** and **Mixtura Fina**). Besides the *samba* school rehearsals, there are *samba* clubs located downtown in the Barra da Tijuca and in the northern neighborhoods. In addition,

who join up with one of the *samba* schools to parade down the avenue (members of Rio's foreign community have long been participating in the parade but now, some travel agents are putting together packages for tourists who wish to join the fun). This involves buying a costume and attending one or two rehearsals of the *samba* schools. Traditionally, the rehearsals (in reality, an excuse for all-night parties) have been held in the poor neighborhoods where the schools are located but as the parade gathered status, some schools have begun staging rehearsals in the south zone of Rio. The increasing in-

there are *pagodes* which are casual jam sessions where *samba* musicians play and onlookers dance and sing. First time visitors to Rio can experience the *samba* phenomenon at Sugarloaf on Monday nights when the **Beija Flor** *samba* school puts on a show, or at the **Scala** and **Plataforma** nightclubs where elaborate productions depict carnival and *samba*.

Food and drink—For this as with almost everything else, the highest ratings go to imports. With the exception of the excellent Brazilian beers (tap is preferred over bottled and always served bitterly cold), and fruit and *aguardente* concoctions called *batidas* (the favorite is a *caipirinha*), *cariocas* prefer foreign brands. Imported scotch, vodka and gin head the list, with rum accepted if nothing else is available. Real snobs may pull out a bottle of Jack Daniels or Southern Comfort although in reality bourbon has never caught on in Brazil.

Tourists should be wary as all imported spirits carry heavy import duties which push bar prices up sharply. Brazilian wines, long considered inferior to imports, are now gaining in status as well as quality. White wine is preferred over red. Brazilian cuisine, however, is as out as ever. In all of Rio, there are

setting. The in spot for Rio's *feijoadas* is the **Caesar Park Hotel** but experts favor the **Sheraton**.

New Year's Eve—Parties are always in but few excel those that usher in the new year. An absolute must is the fireworks display on Copacabana beach which accompanies the *macumba* (Brazilian voodoo) ceremonies at the water's edge. Top honors go to the annual celebration at the Meridien Hotel's posh **Le Saint Honore** restaurant. Real status belongs to those fortunate souls who get invited aboard a millionaire's yacht to see the spectacle from the water. Not only do they have the best seats for the show, but

more restaurants specializing in French cuisine than Brazilian. *Nouvelle cuisine* remains the dominant force, Brazilian cuisine is as out as ever. An exception is the *feijoada*, the closest thing to a national Brazilian dish. Devoured over several hours on Saturday afternoons, the *feijoada* is as much a social event as a meal and thus requires a proper

if they are on the right yacht their names will appear in the column of social columnist Zozimo who is Rio's final word on status. Millionaire yachts are obvious status symbols but there are few. Rio has only two marinas, the more exclusive being the Rio de Janeiro Yacht Club which prides itself on having rejected three times an application for membership by Brazil's leading pop singer, Roberto Carlos.

Women—When not talking to them, *carioca* males seem to be always talking about them. Women are a classic status symbol of the macho society. To be just right

Left, the exclusive and very private Gavea Golf Club. Above, the goal of all status-seeking *cariocas*, their very own Mercedes.

(for the male, that is), a *carioca* woman must be young, alluring, sensual, fashionable and unquestionably faithful. Intelligence is optional. Among the young, professional set, however, this image is changing. The burden of maintaining a middle class lifestyle has pushed the wife out of the home into the job market. In turn, the new woman concept (assertive and career oriented) has acquired a certain rebellious status of its own. Among these groups, the macho man image is out. But even for the more liberal *cariocas*, it is an almost sacred obligation for the woman to maintain her beauty regardless of pregnancies, careers, child caring, etc. Important and shaping and the process of maintaining what has been built and shaped are full-time commitments for *cariocas*. Exercise clubs are in. The teachers and the methods used, are the real key to status. However, jogging is in but even better is running in a marathon. Unmatched for status is having run in the Boston or New York marathons. At the moment surfing is out but body boarding is in. Hang gliding is also losing its status to ultralights. Playing squash is overtaking tennis in popularity.

Beaches—Beach status depends on the quality of sand and water but more importantly, on the quality of the bathers. Copaca-

powerful men insist on being accompanied by beautiful women as part of their image. American feminists have been rejected by *carioca* women, not so much for their ideas but because they are considered physically unattractive. No matter how successful and independent Rio's women may be, they **must** be beautiful. To help them out, the city has a host of plastic surgery clinics. Status may be claimed by those who have been operated on by the king of plastic surgeons, Ivo Pitanguy.

Fitness—Staying in shape is more than in, it is a total obsession. Body building and bana is out on all counts. Ipanema has been in for two decades but is beginning to age. New arrivals are **Pepino**, on the southern end of São Conrado beach, **Grumari**, **Prainha** and the **Barra da Tijuca**. Outside the city, **Buzios** and the island beaches of the **Angra dos Reis** area garner all awards for status. Buzios is also the only beach area where topless bathing is in. Although topless bathing is still practiced by a well-endowed minority in Ipanema, it has never really caught on.

Restaurants and bars—Each year sees a life or death struggle by new entrants into the bar and restaurant category to acquire status and thus ensure their survival. Some go to extraordinary means to attract the "right" people who will then spread the word to other "right" people. If successful, all this will culminate with a favorable mention in Zozimo's column, the next best thing to immortality. Unfortunately, as each year's bar and restaurant obituaries show, few make it to Zozimo. Even for those who do, the war is not over—a slip in quality, the exit of a prized chef, margarine in place of butter in the *sauce bernaise*, any other small error can be fatal for a restaurant's hard-earned status.

literally worshipped by their fans who cite the liturgy of their heroes' conquests with the same ease with which they repeat prayers in church. The top team in recent years has been Flamengo whose colors of black and red tee-shirts are everywhere. The erstwhile challengers to top-ranked Flamengo are Vasco and Fluminense with a fourth club, Botafogo, filling the role of sentimental favorite and perennial doormat. The giant stadium of Maracana which can seat 180,000 is the temple of Rio's *futebol* mania. On days of so-called "classic" matches between Flamengo and Fluminense, the stadium is a war zone with

Soccer—*Futebol* or soccer falls in the category of mixed status. For the lower classes, it is an all-encompassing passion while for the upper classes, it is one of those unfortunate "things" that must be tolerated when living in Brazil. With Brazil essentially a one-sport country, all of the fervor of the country's sports fans is concentrated on soccer. In Rio, the city's leading teams are

Left, good living also means luxury dining. Above, keeping up with top fashion is another must for those who want to be "in".

firecrackers exploding and the huge banners and flags of the teams waving madly throughout the grandstand.

Tourists—Popularly known as *gringos*, foreign tourists are, sad to say, devoid of status. Some, however, are less "out" then others. More favored are fellow Latins, the French and Italians. South Americans are out and Argentines are eternally out. Americans, Canadians, the British, Germans, Swiss, Scandinavians and Asians all occupy the middle ground i.e. out but not aggressively so while Australians and New Zealanders are almost "in".

Along the curving seashore of Rio de Janeiro stands the pride of this city's affluent citizens, a phalanx of luxury highrise apartment buildings attesting to the wealth of those who have. But behind this formidable wall of money and status, visible in brief glimpses down the streets that separate the blocks of wealth, are the homes of those who have not: hillside shantytowns hanging like tarnished ornaments from the forested granite mountains of Rio.

Called *favelas*, they have become a part of the folklore of Rio. Out of the *favelas* come the *samba* schools that march in splendid costumes down the parade route on the second and third days of carnival. Out of the *favelas* comes the *samba* itself, the seductive rhythm that is both song and dance. And out of the *favelas* come the construction workers who built the high rises of the wealthy, the employees of their firms and industries, the waiters who serve them in luxury restaurants and private clubs, the chauffeurs who drive their cars, and the maids, cooks and nannies who tend to the needs of their homes and families.

The wealthy: Each morning in Rio, the residents of the city's beachfront apartments open their eyes to the play of sunlight off the South Atlantic. All see the early morning beach life, the joggers, the fishermen, the arrival of the lifeguards. Some see Guanabara Bay and Sugarloaf while others have views of offshore islands and passing ships. A few, very few, live in penthouse pleasure domes with a 360 degree view, capturing the mountains behind as well as the beach and ocean in front.

Their apartments are encased in marble to protect the owners from the stains of tropical mildew, often occupy entire floors—duplexes and triplexes are not uncommon. Inside, the furnishings reflect expensive tastes and the means to satisfy them. Marble is popular as are rare woods. High tech has recently won a place, from automated security systems to private satellite dishes. To maintain these apartments and to service the

people who own them, there are staff composed typically of two to three maids (one of them a cook), a chauffeur, possibly a handyman or boy and if there are young children, a nanny.

These privileged *cariocas* are proud of their status and feel that they are the equal of any American or European millionaire. Their possessions are indeed very impressive and many also own equally luxurious beach and mountain homes outside of Rio.

All of this is part of the reward, obviously substantial, for those who reach the top of the *carioca* pyramid, itself a smaller version of the Brazilian pyramid. What truly adds distinction to the rich people of Rio is the fact that there are so few of them compared to those at the bottom of the pyramid. Even for the middle class, there is a sense of elitism born of the distance that separates them from the "others." In Rio, only seven percent of the households have annual incomes in excess of $15,000, another 11 percent earn between $7,500 and $15,000. The remaining 82 percent, bring home $7,500 or less with 47 percent surviving on under $1,600 a year.

The inequality of income distribution is just one dividing line between the two Rios. The 18 per cent of *carioca* households enjoy a middle class or higher standard of living have access to quality health care, proper nutritional intake, good schooling for their children and adequate housing. Their Rio is a city of modern consumer goods, of shopping centers and fashionable boutiques, authority. There are white collar crimes in Brazil but there are no white collar criminals. Rio's business elite, the top layer of the upper crust, does not wash its dirty linen in public nor does it have to. Cases of fraud or corruption are in general handled quietly and if possible behind closed doors. The elite is careful to protect its members.

The daily expression of this power, however, involves far more mundane subjects. The elite resolves its daily problems through

highrise apartment buildings, medical clinics, chic restaurants, late model cars, private schools and university education.

What distinguishes Rio's wealthy from their counterparts in other countries, though, is not their means but their power. The elite-driven nature of Brazilian society means those on top have nearly unchallengeable the use of influence. Friendships at the top and family ties through the extended Brazilian family usually are sufficient to handle normal difficulties of day to day living. The middle class also avails itself of this system. When facing a financial or professional crisis, the middle class looks to its more successful friends and relatives to provide a helping hand. Usually they do.

The poor: Each morning, the *favelados*, the dwellers of the hillside shantytowns, awake to a view that is not unlike that of the wealthy along the beach. For many of them, it is actually better, encompassing mountains as

Preceding page: The sprawling Rochina *favela*, largest in Brazil and a city within the city. Left, the precarious hillside existence of Rio's have-nots contrasts sharply with the seashore splendor of the haves (above).

well as the sea. Their homes, though, have none of the opulence of the apartments of the rich nor even the practical convenience of the middle class. They are, however, better than they once were. The tumble-down shacks hammered together out of scrap pieces of wood that first characterized the *favelas* are now being replaced by more durable dwellings. While shacks still exist, their place is increasingly being taken over by structures of brick and concrete. Most of the homes have electricity and some, a minority, have water. But there is rarely any garbage collection and there is no sewerage.

For those on the hillsides, the day begins

shore. For them, education, when available, is through the underfinanced and over-crowded public school system. Health care is through a precarious public health system. Housing conditions are deplorable and mal-nutrition is widespread. There is also no influence other than at election time when politicians routinely re-discover the *favelas* and their inhabitants only to quickly forget them again after the votes have been counted.

The *favelas* have been part of the Rio scene since the start of the century when federal troops, after putting down a rebellion in the northeast, were discharged and came

with a walk down steep, often precarious staircases. When it rains heavily, as it does each summer, the paths down the hillside become torrents of water. Mudslides are common and rarely a year goes by without a disaster striking at least one of Rio's *favelas*.

There are, according to the government, 480 *favelas* in Rio with a population esti-mated at 1 million out of the city's total population of 5.6 million. They are growing at the rate of five percent a year, double the growth rate of the city.

For these *cariocas*, there are none of the advantages of those who live on the sea-

to the city, setting up shacks on a hillside near downtown. At first confined to the downtown area, the *favelas* began to expand with the expansion of the city. They sprouted on the mountains behind Copacabana when that neighborhood underwent its boom years through the 1950s, moving on next to Ipanema and most recently to the Barra da Tijuca and São Conrado, always following the steady southward movement of con-struction sites and jobs.

Attractive mosaic: While those on the mountainsides are the most prominent with the colors of their shacks creating on oddly attractive mosaic in the midst of the gray rock and green forest, the *favelas* have also spread in recent years to the flatlands of the northern and southern suburbs of Rio.

Their existence is graphic evidence of the pressures of population growth on a city whose topography drastically limits its physical expansion. Since colonial times, Rio's residents have chosen to live close to the sea with the mountains to their backs, an aesthetically correct choice that has made Rio a city with clear boundaries between social classes as well as an unending nightmare for city planners. Land values have constantly risen for the downtown area and

ues, pushed up by a chronic housing shortage, are steadily forcing the poor farther north and farther away from the sites of their jobs, the majority of which are downtown or in the south zone. At the same time, new waves of immigrants from the backward states of the northeast and the underdeveloped interior of the state of Rio create rising demand for housing and public services which a cash-short government cannot meet. It is estimated that there is a housing shortage equivalent to 60,000 units for the middle class and 440,000 for the poor in Rio de Janeiro.

Northern flatlands: This situation has led to

on to the southern beaches, making the south zone, as it is called, the home of the monied classes—the middle class and the wealthy.

At the other extreme, the north zone and the northern suburbs, far from the beaches, are the working class neighborhood, a constantly growing maze of slums, housing projects and outright *favelas* with pockets of middle class housing. Even here, land val-

Left, living in a *favela* means a daily struggle to satisfy common necessities. Above, black is the predominant color of the *favelados*.

a population explosion in the northern flatlands, an area called the *baixada fluminense*. It is home to 2.6 million persons, the majority of whom are living in abject poverty. Here, the incidence of infectious diseases and the infant mortality rate are close to the levels of the Northeast of Brazil, the poorest area of the country, and far from the levels of the neighboring city of Rio. In the *baixada*, 150 out of every 1,000 newborn infants will die before reaching the age of one while in the city of Rio the rate is 34.5 for every 1,000. In Rio, there is a doctor for every 250 inhabitants but in the *baixada*, one hour away from downtown Rio, the figure is one doctor for every 3,500 inhabitants. Lacking sewerage and potable drinking water and awash in garbage, the *baixada* is a public health disaster where diseases such as meningitis, typhoid fever and tetanus are common as well as a wide variety of intestinal infections, especially among the children.

Compared to this, a hillside *favela* in Ipanema or Copacabana is a veritable paradise. While the residents of the *baixada* each morning face a two-hour bus ride to reach their jobs, for the south zone *favelados*, work is often only a few minutes away. In addition they have spectacular views and immediate

evident than in the *favela* of Rocinha, Rio's largest and possibly the largest in South America. Rocinha began in the 1940s when a group of squatters took over vacant land on a south zone hillside. By the 1960s, the *favela* had become a permanent feature of Rio although its size was still restricted. During these years, several of Rio's larger *favelas* were removed by the city government and their inhabitants forcibly relocated in distant housing projects.

Rocinha, however, escaped this fate. Since the 1970s, the *favela* has undergone its own population explosion, first with a construction boom in the nearby Barra da Tijuca

access to the beach. These factors have now made the south zone *favelas* the status address for Rio's lower class majority. For most, even this progress is out of reach. Growing demand and the improved housing of these *favelas* have produced an inevitable by-product, rising rents.

When they first appeared, the principal attraction of the *favelas* was their proximity to jobs and the fact that they were rent free. Today, the proximity remains but inhabitants of the south zone *favelas* now pay rents, increasingly to absentee landlords.

Rocinha: Nowhere is this process more

neighborhood. More recently, it received immigrants from the *baixada* who seek to move closer to their work plus the overflow from other, crowded south zone *favelas*. Sprawling across a mountainside, Rocinha today is a city within a city, looking down at five-star hotels, luxury condominiums and a golf course, its unwilling neighbors in São Conrado, a popular, upper income beach area where hang gliders float serenely overhead.

The most urbanized of Rio's *favelas*, Rocinha has a thriving commerce of its own—clothing shops, grocery stores, bars, lunch counters, drugstores, butcher shops, bakeries and a bank branch, all of them providing jobs to the *favelados*. Squatter's rights give ownership after five years but in reality few of the properties in Rocinha have been legalized although the size of the shantytown makes removal unthinkable. In addition, Rocinha supplies the doormen, maintenance crews and other auxiliary help for the hotels and condominiums of São Conrado as well as providing cheap labor for Ipanema and other nearby south zone neighborhoods. It is also the main source of illicit drugs, especially cocaine and marijuana, for the area's high rollers, a fact that has trans-

tion from petty criminals who inhabit the shantytowns and also spread some of the profits from the drug trade among the population. These cocaine Robin Hoods have become folk heroes for the slum dwellers.

Autonomy: In the process, the *favelas* have also gained a certain autonomy. Fear and bribes keep away the police and efforts to resettle the *favelados* have now been abandoned. But despite endless promises by politicians to complete the urbanization of Rocinha and other major slums, little has been done. They continue to face serious difficulties with water supply. Health conditions are for the most part, deplorable.

formed Rocinha into a highly profitable center for Rio's drug trade.

Drug trafficking has also spread to other *favelas* where, as in Rocinha, the economic power of the traffickers has made them the dominant force. Gangs of drug dealers now control the majority of the large south zone *favelas*, including Rocinha. In return for the support of the *favelados*, they offer protec-

Left, middle-class apartment buildings in the Barra da Tijuca. Above, pleasure domes along the water.

Rocinha with its city-size population has only one poorly-equipped health clinic and there are no schools in the slums. There is the constant danger of landslides and even the protectors of the *favelados*, their Robin Hoods, are unreliable—gunfights between rival gangs often claim innocent victims.

It remains a precarious life on the hillsides of Rio but still, the *favelados* are close to work, they have their view, the nearby ocean and bad as things may be, they are seldom as bad as in the flatlands of the northern suburbs. For the hillside-dweller, this is the bottom line.

SENSUAL RIO

Rio de Janeiro is a sensuous city, a feminine personality in a macho society. The sensuality of Rio is expressed not only by its people and their nature but also in the geography of the city. The shore line bends and curves in expressive sensual lines that sometimes make it difficult to understand exactly where you are.

The city is divided into two zones, the north and the south but for tourists, there is only the south, home to Rio's scenic wonders—Sugarloaf, Corcovado, the Tijuca Forest, the lagoon—as well as the famed beaches of Copacabana, Ipanema and the newly "discovered" beaches of São Conrado, the Barra da Tijuca and Grumari. Life for the residents of Rio and the tourists revolves around the beach which is the starting and ending point of any weekend day. Fortunately Rio has enough beaches to go around, each with its own personality, its distinctive quality and, as always, its status.

But Rio is more than the sum of its beaches and mountains. As befits a city with a 400-year history, there is also a historical side to Rio, concentrated in its downtown area, the storied hillsides of Santa Teresa and the vast Guanabara Bay, all of which merit a long, reflective look.

Rio also is the capital of the state of Rio de Janeiro, replete with attractions of its own. Day trips from the city take visitors into the nearby mountains, and to the refreshing coolness of the mountain resort cities of Teresópolis and the former summer residence of Brazil's emperors, Petrópolis.

The coastline of the state of Rio contains formidable rivals to the city's beaches. For many *cariocas*, the beach resort of Buzios is unmatched anywhere in Brazil while others insist that the archipelago of Angra dos Reis with its hundreds of tropical islands is number one. Both are within hours of Rio.

At night, Rio comes alive a second time. With beach lounging or sightseeing now past, natives and tourists flock to Rio's world class bars and restaurants many blessed with spectacular and romantic views of Rio just outside the window.

Preceding pages: Landscaped parks of downtown Rio with Sugarloaf in the background; catching up with the news *carioca*-style; jumping in at an isolated beach near Buzios; the Gloria Church, a priceless relic of colonial days. Left, diving off a schooner.

DOWNTOWN RIO

Every old city has a story to tell. Rio de Janeiro's downtown tells its own colorful story, and much of Brazil's, like an illuminated manuscript.

Museums and landmarks: The tale begins at **The Museum of the Republic**, former residence of Brazil's presidents, in the Catete District.

Purchased by the federal government in 1896, the palace served as presidential residence until 1954. (It was closed after then-president Gutúlio Vargas committed suicide in an upper chamber but reopened as a museum in 1960.)

The museum highlights presidential memorabilia of every period from the 1889 proclamation of the Republic to the military regime that ended in 1985. But its atmosphere is the main attraction. A first floor meeting room displays the cabinet table used by Deodoro da Fonseca, Brazil's first president. Each place is marked with the dispatch book of one of Fonseca's ministers.

The second floor features an elegant diplomatic reception room where Brazil's presidents received newly appointed ambassadors. On the third floor were the private quarters of Brazil's presidents. It was in the Vargas Bedroom that the ex-dictator shot himself in the heart on Aug 24, 1954. The room is preserved as it was that day.

One subway station north of Catete, on a hill overlooking Guanabara Bay, is picturesque **Nossa Senhora da Glória do Outeiro Chapel**. Designed in 1720, the multisided church with its curved ceiling and gleaming white walls is Brazil's first important example of baroque architecture. Blue-and-white tiles highlight the interior.

One more subway stop brings visitors to bustling **Cinelândia**. Emerging in **Praça Floriano** visitors are surrounded by public buildings and spacious movie houses. Just across broad Avenida Rio Branco is Brazil's Na-

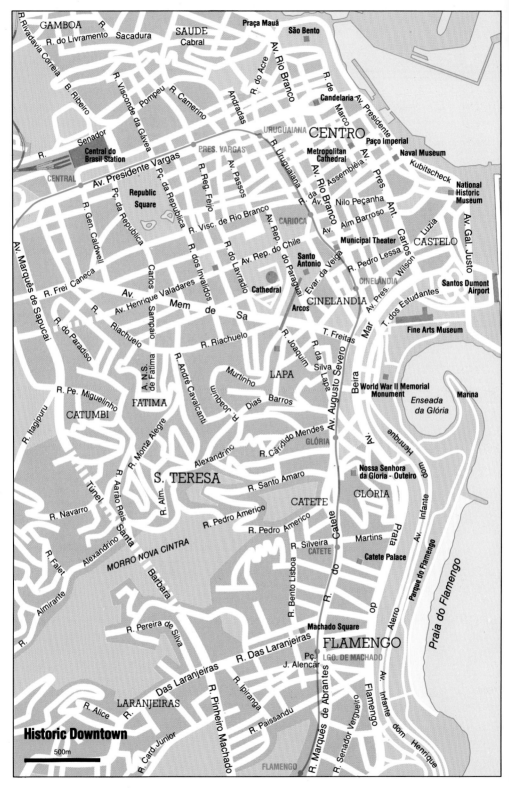

Historic Downtown

500m

tional **Library**, a gaudy Victorian structure completed in 1910. The library possesses a Latin Bible printed in 1462.

Fronting Praça Floriano is the august **Municipal Theater**, a two-thirds replica of the Paris Opera inaugurated in 1909. Nijinsky danced there in 1913, Pavlova four years later. Maria Callas slapped Director-General Barreto Pinto in the face one night in 1952 when he told the great diva she "stank" in *Norma*. The theater's "Golden Age" was the 1920s, when tuxedoed waiters served champagne and program cards were sprinkled with perfume.

Across Avenida Rio Branco from the Municipal Theater is Rio's French neoclassical **Museum of Fine Arts**, completed in 1908.

Brazilian artists: The museum's most popular display is **Pedro Américo's** overblown *Batalha do Avaí*, an immense panorama depicting a forgotten, and forgettable, engagement of the 19th-century war against Paraguay. Américo was Brazil's most popular painter in the last century. His lush landscapes and pompous court portraits had a reverse influence on colleagues, who felt they could learn how *not* to paint studying Américo.

One such artist was **Victor Meirelles**. Once a student of Américo, Meirelles' work featured realistic figures and a sharp appreciation for character. His *A Primeira Missa no Brazil* (The First Mass in Brazil) is almost as large as Américo's battle scenes, but displays a more subtle touch for anatomy and color.

Twentieth-century Brazilian art also enjoys a place of distinction in the Fine Arts collection. **Agostinho da Mota's** still lifes, perfectly wrought compositions noted for expert coloring and detail, represent a step away from overblown patriotism toward artistic unity.

Another artist, **Rodolfo Amoedo**, applied lessons learned from Mota's still lifes to portrait painting. His sensuous *Marabá*, depicting a half-caste Indian girl, combines deft anatomy with sympathetic treatment of character.

Such painters were precursors for Brazil's most important artistic phase since the 18th-century baroque—the new wave of modern Brazilian art. **Cândido Portinari**, probably Brazil's greatest artist, is represented by two major works—*Retrato de Maria* (1932) and *Café* (1934). *The Portrait of Maria* seems conventional at first glance. But a closer look reveals the irreal patterns of shadows, a studied expression and eyes out of proportion to the thin face of the subject. *Cafe* is Portinari at his best, imposing a dominant color scheme—browns and tans—with exaggerated, rounded figures in the foreground. Such works make the Fine Arts archive one of Brazil's most important.

Religious buildings: Just behind the Municipal Theater is sprawling **Largo da Carioca**, with its bustling peddlers, searing subway station walls and aged **Santo Antônio Monastery** atop a low hill.

The monastery complex was completed in 1780 but surviving portions of previous building date from as early as 1608 and are Rio's oldest examples of religious architecture.

The main church's interior is typically baroque. Left of the nave is a curved, windowless vault. Hundreds of crackling candles reflect eerily off its walls as worshippers pray in a monotonous drone.

Next to the main church is **São Francisco da Penitência Chapel**, dating from 1739. Its gold-leaf interior and stark wood carvings make it even more mysterious and darkly stylized than its neighbor. Art critics consider it a precursor of Brazil's 18th-century baroque artistic explosion.

Just north of Largo da Carioca is bleak **Praça Tiradentes**. A center of bohemian night life in the 19th century, the plaza today is a concrete wasteland. Its only saving graces are sparkling

João Caetano Theater and, on Avenida Passos, snug **Nossa Senhora da Lampadosa Chapel**, built by slaves starting in 1748. Revolutionary Tiradentes heard mass there two hours before his 1793 hanging on the square which now bears his name.

Nestled just behind Praça Tiradentes is another square mixing grey decay with signs of renovation—**Largo de São Francisco**. A staging area for buses on one side of the square brings noise, pollution and litter. But the magnificent **Igreja de São Francisco de Paula**, fronting the square's south side, is still impressive behind its manicured shrubbery and rococo façade, begun in 1756.

São Francisco's striking **Vitória Chapel** displays intriguing religious paintings by baroque artist **Mestre Valentim da Fonseca e Silva**. Rows of portraits on the church's east corridor are a gallery of 19th-century Brazilian notables.

A web of shop-filled pedestrian streets stretches from São Francisco back to Avenida Rio Branco and hides some of Rio's oldest churches.

Nossa Senhora da Conceição da Boa Morte, completed in 1735, is one. Located on Rua Miguel Couto at an odd angle to Avenida Rio Branco, the church's ornate, rounded windows, like a ship's portholes, are distinctive. The sacristy houses a collection of tropical birds. They sometimes disrupt mass with their exotic, ear-splitting calls.

One of downtown's busiest churches is Rua da Alfândega's **Santa Efigênia e Santo Eslebão**. The church was the site of the 1817 marriage of Dom Pedro I and the Empress Leopoldina. Work on the structure was completed by black slaves in 1754.

Along the southern margin of downtown, on Avenida Chile near the gaudy **Petrobras Building**, is Rio's new **Roman Catholic Cathedral**. A huge, cone-shaped structure, the cathedral is meant to demonstrate the channeling of human energies to the heavens. It re-

The magnificent movie and municipal theaters.

72

minds some visitors of the first manned space capsules which were making news when its cornerstone was laid in 1964 (the cathedral was inaugurated in 1978). Four enormous stained glass windows put rainbows of light into the towering interior.

Eating places: Some of Rio's most intriguing lunchtime respites are located near Largo da Carioca.

For boisterous atmosphere and generous German cuisine there's **Bar Luiz** on Rua da Carioca. A downtown fixture since 1887, the spot is famous for its polished wood furnishings, *appfelstrudel* and tangy, dark draft beer.

Another venerable lunchtime address is the **Cafe do Teatro**, in the basement of the Municipal Theater. Its dazzling decor, featuring massive pillars and colorful mosaics depicting scenes from life in ancient Assyria, could have been designed by Cecil B. DeMille. The menu varies daily.

Rua Gonçalves Dias, near Largo de São Francisco, is home of one of Rio's most traditional restaurants— **Colombo**. A tea room with turn-of-the-century furnishings dominates the first floor. Tall, jacarandá-wood cabinets display colorfully wrapped delicacies like a 19th-century emporium. Upstairs is the main dining room, featuring a wrap-around balcony with a splendid view of the tea room below, reflected in wall-length Belgian crystal mirrors with rosewood frames installed in 1913. A soft glow emanates from the stained-glass skylight as a piano trills from a cool alcove.

Shrimp, flounder and baked codfish are recommended.

Founded in 1874, Colombo moved to its present location 20 years later. For decades it was the gathering place of intellectuals inspired by its Belle Époque decor and camaraderie.

Restored buildings: Across Avenida Rio Branco, about three long blocks from Largo da Carioca, is an area of restored buildings and pedestrian streets rich in history.

The imposing Candelaria Church, a favorite spot for high society weddings.

Praça XV de Novembro honors the date (Nov. 15, 1889) Brazil's Republic was founded. One of Rio's most historic structures, the recently restored **Paço Imperial**, dominates the plaza's south side. Its straight rows of windows give it marked architectural unity while its intricate iron and woodwork make it pleasingly archaic.

Work on the building was completed in 1743 and, for 63 years, it served as headquarters for Brazil's royally appointed viceroys. King João VI made it his palace in 1808 when he arrived in Brazil, accompanied by the entire Portuguese court, as a refugee from Napoleon. In 1822, Brazil's youthful regent, Pedro I, declared from a palace window that he would remain on Brazilian soil, thus defying Portuguese orders to return home and setting the stage for Brazilian independence.

The former palace now serves as a culture center.

Two churches, on nearby Rua Primeiro de Março, are no less historic.

The larger edifice, **Nossa Senhora do Carmo**, was Rio's Metropolitan Cathedral until 1978. Completed in 1761, its now greying façade was once considered Rio's most architecturally harmonious. The blue-tiled bell towers were added in 1850. Carmo's glittering interior includes rococo carvings by Valentim. Both Pedro I and Pedro II were crowned there.

South America's first Roman Catholic Cardinal, **Joaquim Arcoverde**, governed his archdiocese from the cathedral between 1905 and 1930 and is buried in its crypt. Next to the archbishop are the supposed remains of **Pedro Alvares Cabral**, the Portuguese discoverer of Brazil. Cabral's bones were brought from Portugal in 1913.

Nossa Senhora do Monte do Carmo, dating from 1770, is separated from its larger neighbor by a narrow passageway. The church is noted for its baroque façade with neo-classical touches added in the 19th century.

A half block down Primeiro de Março toward Avenida Presidente Vargas is the imposing **Igreja de Santa Cruz dos Militares** completed in 1811. Much of its rococo decor was executed by Mestre Valentim.

But of all the downtown churches, vest pocket **Nossa Senhora da Lapa dos Mercadores** may possess the most beguiling interior. Located on Rua do Ouvidor near Cruz dos Militares, Mercadores seats only a dozen worshippers at a time. Its tiny dome allows a soft penumbra of light to suffuse the nave, which is crammed with intricate wood carvings. A passageway under the pulpit leads to a miniscule sacristy, where the smell of candle wax mixes macabrely with the scent of aged wood.

The chapel, financed by donations from itinerant merchants, was completed in 1750.

The network of narrow streets and arcades surrounding Praça XV de Novembro forms one of Rio's most fascinating districts, hiding quaint restaurants and high-ceilinged storefronts. Many of the offices fronting the **Beco do Comércio**, for example, are restored 18th-century homes. The most noted is long, low **Edifício Telles de Menezes**, famous for its archway leading to the plaza.

Nearby **Rua do Ouvidor** was once Rio's newspaper street. With its open-sided bars it became, in the 19th century, one of the city's most colorful meeting places. Rio's first commercial telephone line was installed there in 1877—only one year after its invention by Alexander Graham Bell. Newspaper editor Antônio Chaves designed the instrument himself from accounts he read in the foreign press.

A few blocks south of Praça XV is one of Rio's most important landmarks the **National Historical Museum** (due to reopen in 1988 after an extensive renovation).

The museum is a rambling structure reflecting different architectural styles and historical epochs.

Wooden balconies, colorful masonry

Right, downtown Rio with the Praça Paris parkway in the foreground.

and glinting red-tile roofs create an irresistable ice cream cake effect (with tropical flavors). The interior retains a musty air appropriate to its subject.

Among the items on display are murals depicting the death of Tiradentes (next to a macabre exhibit including chunks of wood from the gallows where he was hanged) and the Proclamation of Independence.

Among archive materials is the 1888 document freeing Brazil's slaves. Carriages and antique cars are parked incongruously next to one another in the main courtyard.

The museum building itself is of indeterminant age. Wings and improvements have been added and subtracted since 1603 when a small fortress was first begun at the site. In 1922 the entire conglomerate of 17th, 18th and 19th century sections was remodeled to accomodate portions of the independence centennial fair. Since the end of the fair the building has served as a museum.

About one long block north of the sprawling historical archive is Brazil's attractive **Naval and Oceanographic Museum**.

To protect the wooden floors, visitors must don floppy felt slippers before exploring the two-story museum, constructed in 1899. World War II-vintage torpedoes and mines take up one portion of the display. Other galleries feature maps and paintings of Brazilian naval engagements. But the highlight of the museum is its lovingly detailed ship models, some more than a meter long.

A 15-minute drive from downtown is the National Museum, the former residence of the imperial family in the 19th century. The impressive palace, next to Rio's zoo, houses natural history, archaeological and mineral exhibits. It is located at **Quinta da Boa Vista.**

Four short blocks west of Praça XV, on Avenida Presidente Vargas, is the impressive **Igreja da Candelária**.

Dedicated by King João VI in 1811,

The spectacular and slightly bizarre Assyrius restaurant in the Teatro Municipal.

Candelária is one of Rio's most striking monuments. Its white dome dominates the avenue without overwhelming it. Architects call it one of the most perfectly proportioned cathedrals in the world.

Candelária's Italianate façade was begun in 1775 following frank baroque lines. But construction took so long the interior decor already intruded on the emerging neo-classical style, explaining the towering columns of multicolored marble. The dome was only completed in 1877 and the bronze doors attached in 1901.

Five blocks east, down Avenida Rio Branco toward **Praça Mauá**, is one of Rio's oldest churches—the **Monastery of São Bento**, commanding a magnificent view of Guanabara Bay.

Work on the Benedictine monastery began in 1633 and continued for a century. Its façade shares the flat, thick mannerist style prominent in 17th-century Brazilian religious architecture.

São Bento is noted primarily for the opulence of its interior, highlighted by the familiar gold leaf and an explosion of baroque wood carving. Spires of light from narrow windows are an eerie contrast to the darkness of the aged wood.

The hill on which the monastery stands is one of the few that still survive in downtown Rio. The others which existed during the colonial period have fallen victim to *carioca* progress, a penchant for removing hills to fill in the bay. The Candelaria church which once stood close to the water is now far removed thanks to land fills using dirt from the fallen hills. The most tragic case of this came in 1921-22 when the downtown hill of Castelo was carted off together with most of Rio's remaining 16th- and 17th-century structures.

Praça Mauá itself, located in Rio's port area, is a contrast between the sacred and the profane. Dominated on one side by the monastery, the plaza's southern wing is a row of rowdy strip joints. The clubs feature relatively tame sex shows attracting hordes of sailors and cruise ship passengers.

Another downtown area featuring strip-tease action is the famed **Lapa District**, which acted as a magnet for bohemians in the 1920s and 1930s. Lapa began losing its allure when Rio's money, and nightlife, moved to Copacabana in the 1940s. Today, the strip bars on **Avenida Mem de Sá** are considered seedier than their Praça Mauá rivals and the avenue at night is home to Rio's aggressive transvestites.

However, recent years have seen efforts to recapture Lapa's lost charm with inauguration of classy clubs at its downtown end. The best known is the **Asa Branca**, a vast dance hall featuring top performers of Brazilian Pop and samba tunes but attracting few tourists. The **Assyrius** and the **Café Nice**, on nearby Avenida Rio Branco, offer elegant decor and dancing.

In downtown Rio—even at night—the city that was, dwells in peace with the city that is.

A crowded pedestrian mall.

SANTA TERESA

Old-fashioned gables and trolley cars, decades of green growth, pastel-shaded masonry and zig-zagging staircases make Rio's downtown **Santa Teresa District** a magic mountain.

Santa Teresa is accessible by car or bus from most points in the downtown area. But the best way to visit the picturesque district is by trolley car.

The trolley system: The trolley ride, which starts at the downtown **Petrobras Building Plaza**, the headquarters of Brazil's state oil company, crosses one of Rio's most notable engineering feats, the 18th-century **Carioca Aquaduct** (also called the **Arcos da Lapa**). The aqueduct once brought water from Rio's central spine of mountains to city dwellers. The structure served its original purpose for a century but was then abandoned until the Ferro Carril Carioca Traction Company obtained its right of way in 1896. Since then, the massive arches have conducted trolley traffic from downtown into a zig-zagging network of tracks throughout Santa Teresa—one of the most interesting day trips. (The trollies of late have become targets of petty thieves and pickpockets. Hold on to your purses, cameras and wallets).

In 1988, the state government still possessed 19 of the yellow, open-sided trolley cars. However, parts shortages kept many of them out of service. At one point, only two cars were running, with microbuses substituting on the Santa Teresa trolley lines. The state governor promised a complete renovation of the U.S.-built cars (the newest dates from 1950).

Santa Teresa's residents: According to legend, black slaves used Santa Teresa's mountain trails to escape from their owners during the 18th century when Rio was Brazil's leading slave port. Santa Teresa began to receive more permanent residents when a yellow fever epidemic forced the city's population to flee to the hills to escape from the mosquitoes carrying the disease. The 1896 introduction of the trolleys (or *bondes*, so-called because the system was financed by foreign bonds) opened an era of opulence for hilly Santa Teresa, which, by the early 20th century, had become a center for artistic and literary activities. Writers, artists and musicians built lodgings along its winding streets. Bankers and businessmen followed, constructing elaborate masonry staircases to reach their homes, often built at fantastic angles against the slopes.

Architectural styles: Opulent European ironwork, exaggerated statuary and other adornments were added to the staircases. Much of what Santa Teresa was at the turn-of-the-century, is today retained in its elegant old mansions.

Santa Teresa is characterized by an odd variety of architectural styles. Among its distinct features are a gabled castle, an onion-domed Orthodox Church, at least one Alpine lodge and rows and rows of 19th-century houses notable for their complex patterns of stained glass and wrought iron.

The district offers unexpected views. From the second trolley station, visitors glimpse the vast blue expanse of **Guanabara Bay**. From many of its cobbled streets, public staircases wind in stages to the neighborhoods of **Glória** and **Flamengo**, hundreds of feet below. The 70- and 90-year-old store-fronts display their merchandise in polished wooden cabinets.

Santa Teresa is also rich in neighborhood pride. Virtually all of its public buildings, including the 1750 **Convento de Santa Teresa**, located near the first trolley station, are well preserved. Most residents have added something to their Victorian-era homes without detracting from the district's charm. Flower gardens are everywhere-many seem to pour over the chipped retaining walls. There are few abandoned structures in Santa Teresa.

Left, aging mansions spilling down the hillside of Santa Teresa.

Brazil's best art museum: One of the most surprising highlights of a district noted for surprises is the **Chácara do Céu** (Little House in the Sky) modern art museum. The museum, at **Rua Murtinho Nobre 93**, was once the residence of Brazilian collector, Raymundo Ottoni de Castro Maya.

The **Castro Maya** house is probably the best little art museum in Brazil. Its collection includes samples of the finest in modern Brazilian art, including works by Antônio Bandeira, Iberê Camargo, Volpi, Di Cavalcanti and Cândido Portinari, one of Brazil's greatest artists of all time.

But that's not all. Chácara's breezy, sun-bright galleries include works by modern European masters-Braque, Dali, Degas, Matisse, Modigliani, Monet and Picasso.

All its corridors and anterooms are jammed with objects rarely appreciated in Brazil, such as 17th-century Persian rugs, Indian and Chinese ivory and a white, smooth torso carved by a Greek sculptor more than 2,400 years ago.

The house itself is an ideal setting for an art museum.

One side of the topaz facade is substantially hidden by trees; the other faces a pleasant lawn with a few stone benches, fountains and grassy recesses at its margin. The view from the grounds is spectacular. On one side is the panorama of downtown Rio; quaint trolley cars cross the aqueduct, looking like toy trains in a plaster and plastic artificial city. On the other side is a classic view of Guanabara Bay.

The emphasis of Castro Maya's magnificent collection is on modern Brazilian art, with special attention to works by the collector's life-long friend, Portinari.

Portinari's collection include a portrait of Castro Maya himself, and two large canvasses completed in 1941. A *Barca* (The Boat), and *O Sapateiro de Brodowski* (The Shoemaker of Brodowski), large rounded figures characteristic of much of Portinari's work.

The fight to get a seat on the Santa Teresa trolley.

Also noteworthy is the collection of 36 Portinari color drawings depicting scenes from *Don Quixote*.

Among other Brazilian artists represented are Antônio Bandeira, whose *A Grande Cidade* (The Big City) recalls the splashes and splotches of Jackson Pollack and Emiliano Di Cavalcanti, whose works are crowded with playful human figures against a typical Brazilian cityscape.

Among Brazilian sculptures is the huge, dark as death *Asas* (Wings) by Cesar Baldaccini, dated 1921. The iron figure dominates the entire second floor gallery. Modern French painting is represented better, perhaps, than at any other museum in Brazil.

Modigliani's *Portrait of a Young Widow* is displayed in the room which was once Castro Maya's office, as is Salvador Dali's small but suitably surreal *Two Balconies*. The work, with its bizarre formations—a rock with a human ear, a man's head that seems to melt into the ground—is as representa-

tive of Dali's work as any.

A Matisse (*The Luxembourg Garden*), with its pastel colors and tranquility, is also specially displayed.

The collection includes a Picasso, displayed on the ground floor. *La Dance*, dated 1956, is a few brush strokes and some color background and looks like it was scrawled by the artist in his sleep.

What is perhaps most interesting about the Castro Maya collection is the presence of art objects from distant times and cultures. A pair of Chinese cast iron birds, in excellent condition and fantastically detailed, are more than a thousand years old. A tiny female bust is 7th-century Cambodian.

There is no article of decor or furnishing which is not a precious object of art. The museum represents a lifetime of careful selection by one of Brazil's most astute and public-spirited collectors. Castro Maya, said architect, Lúcio Costa, was "a public man in the highest and best sense of the term."

Bus stop with 1986 World Cup soccer mural.

THE BAY

Like a big buttonhole cut out of the Atlantic coast, the 147 sq mile (380 sq km) **Bay of Guanabara** is a living map of Rio's maritime past.

Its narrow entrance is guarded by two historic forts, the 17th-century **Santa Cruz** on the eastern bank, today's Niteroi, and the 19th century **São Joāo** on the western, Rio de Janeiro side. Their walls were built from solid granite blocks, cemented with whale oil. The surviving forts lie on much older sites dating back to 1555, when the Portuguese realized that they would have to fortify the bay if they were not to lose it to the French.

For 50 years after its discovery in 1502, the bay attracted freewheeling Portuguese and French adventurers. Ships returned to Europe loaded with rare birds, parrots, monkeys, Indian slaves and Brazil wood, the heavy red hardwood from which dye was extracted. The Portuguese made their base on the Rio side of the bay; the French on the eastern shore, clashing frequently in sea skirmishes.

French effort: In 1555, the French launched a definitive effort to conquer *Riviere Guenere*, as they called the bay. A fleet sent by King Henri II took possession of a region on the Rio side, building Fort Coligny on the isle, **Ilha Villegagnon**. But 'Antarctic France', as they called their new territory, was short-lived. Within five years they were driven off by the Portuguese, the survivors taking refuge with the Tamoio Indian tribe in Niteroi.

When surveying the bay today, it is a sobering thought that nothing remains of what the French and Portuguese fought over—no Indians, no Brazil wood trees, no parrots.

Looking upwards at the granite hills, all must be much the same as at the time

Left, the gentle bay, thought at first by the Portuguese to be a river.

SUGARLOAF

Sugarloaf mountain is undoubtedly Rio's and Brazil's best known landmark. Today a symbol of the city, it was at its feet that the original city of São Sebastiao do Rio de Janeiro was founded in 1565. The Indians called this singularly shaped granite monolith guarding the entrance to Rio's Guanabara Bay, *Pau-nd-Acuqua*, meaning high, pointed, isolated peak. To the Portuguese, this sounded like *pão de açucar* (sugarloaf) and its shape reminded them of the clay molds used to refine sugar into a conical lump called a sugarloaf.

Still popular with rock climbers, the first person known to have reached the 1,300-foot (400-meter) summit was Englishwoman, Henrietta Carstairs, who in 1817 placed a British flag at the top. This was soon replaced with a Portuguese flag by a patriotic soldier.

Cable car: In the first decade of this century, Brazilian engineer Augusto Ferreira Ramos envisioned an aerial link that would make the view from the mountaintop accessible to all. Despite general skepticism, he obtained authorization from the mayor for his project in 1909 and the first stage of the cable car line to 705-foot (220-meter) Morro da Urca, the low mountain in front of Sugarloaf, was inaugurated in 1912. The final leg from there to Sugarloaf was completed in 1913. The original 24-passenger German-made cable cars remained in use for 60 years before being replaced in 1972 by larger cars to handle the increased demand.

Now visitors are whisked up in Italian-made bubble-shaped cars that hold up to 75 passengers and offer 360-degree view. Each stage takes just 3 minutes, with a car starting out from the top and the bottom simultaneously, zipping past each other in the middle of the ride. Departures from the Praia Vermelho station where you get your tickets are

A cable car ride to the top of Sugarloaf.

every half hour from 8 a.m. to 10 p.m.

Spectacular views: From both the Morro da Urca and Sugarloaf itself, you have spectacular views on all sides with paths leading to viewpoints. To the west lie the beaches of Leme, Copacabana, Ipanema and Leblon and the mountains beyond. At your feet are Botafogo and Flamengo leading to downtown, with Corcovado peak and its Christ statue behind. Most visitors feel the view from taller Corcovado is more spectacular than that from Sugarloaf, one of the main reasons being that the former also offers the best view of Sugarloaf itself. To the north, the high bridge across the bay connects Rio de Janeiro and Niteroi, with the latter's beaches stretching away towards the east. Bring a map to help you get your bearings.

If you go up Sugarloaf late in the afternoon, you can see the city in the daylight, watch the sunset and the first lights coming on and see the city at night. Or have a leisurely late lunch at the Pão de Açucar restaurant on Morro da Urca which is open for lunch only.

The Brazil Experience, a 45-minute, 2,500-slide audiovisual presentation is shown hourly from 9 a.m. to 8 p.m. on Morro da Urca, with the soundtrack available in English, French, Spanish and Portuguese. Acquainting viewers with Brazil's sights, the show also explains their historic and cultural significance. By outlining the country's evolution from a New World colony to the modern nation it is today, the program offers the foreign visitor a rare insight into Brazil and its people.

Every Monday night, there is a samba show with members of one of Rio's top samba schools performing at the amphitheater atop Morro da Urca. Carnival and New Year's Eve balls are also held here each year. Concerts by popular singers and bands are scheduled periodically, often with dancing. Tickets to the evening events include the cable car ride up and back sometimes dinner as well.

Corcovado
as seen
from
Sugarloaf.

of discovery. But the lower one drops one's glance, from the highrises along the Rio and Niteroi shoreline, the industries and oil refineries, to the silted-up mud flats where lush mangrove swamps once sheltered exotic fauna and the murky water itself, the more one is aware of the toll that predatory development has taken on one of the world's natural wonders. A recent *New York Times* article on the bay was aptly headlined, "The Bay's a Thing of Beauty; Pity It's a Cesspool".

An estimated 1.5 million tons of refuse and sewage find their way into the bay, every day, from 10 million inhabitants along the bay's banks, from Rio proper to the sprawling **Baixada Fluminense**, a slum region that spreads mushroom-like around the shoreline. Residents and ecologists sigh in despair about the prospects of seeing the bay cleaned up, after successive electoral promises evaporate in practice.

Center of recreation: Until the 1930s, when *cariocas* started moving to the ocean beaches, the bay was the main center of recreation. People had picnics on its shores, fished and swam in its waters. The well-heeled built holiday homes on **Paquetá**, the largest of the bay's 84 islands. A ferryboat trip to Paquetá's beaches, lapped by the gentle waters of the bay, so different from the crashing waves of the Atlantic, was a welcome treat.

These days, Paquetá's beaches are fit only for sunbathing, but a boat trip to the island is still a must. There are three ways of getting there: by the ferryboat, leaving from **Praça Quinze**, which costs a few cents and takes an hour and a half; by aerofoil boat, *aerobarco*, a swift 15 minutes; or, the most leisurely and expensive way, by **Bateau Mouche**, a tourist boat that does a round trip, leaving from the **Sol e Mar restaurant**, next-door to Botafogo's Yacht Club.

From half a mile out, the buildings of Rio look like small, neat false teeth, dwarfed by the green and black hills. It

A trip across the bay— evidently a popular activity.

is a sight to file away and retrieve on the streets of Copacabana where the buildings seem overpowering.

Bay islands: Turning into the bay, one passes Ilha Villegagnon, the former seat of Antarctic France, which was joined to the mainland by a 1929 landfill during the erection of Brazil's naval academy. **Ilha das Cobras** (Snake Island), today a port for naval frigates and Brazil's one aircraft carrier, was consecutively, an unloading area for slave ships and a monastery. **Ilha Fiscal**, with its strange spired green palace, which was formerly a barracks for customs officers and where the Imperial Government held its last ball in 1889, is now joined to Ilha das Cobras.

Passing dockland on the left, one goes under the span of the **Rio-Niteroi Bridge**. Once the bridge is behind, one is in the bay proper. A vast panorama of water and islands opens up, although few are the tropical idylls portrayed by French engraver, Debret in the 19th century. Those that have not been turned into promontories by landfills, such as the 17 sq mile (44 sq km) Ilha de **Governador** which houses Rio's international airport, have been given over to oil tanks and armament deposits.

Further into the bay, however, some islands retain a thick crop of wild tropical greenery. One of these is **Ilha de Sol** (Sun Island), where the 1950s cabaret star and striptease artist, Luz del Fuego, set up Brazil's first nudist colony. She hosted parties which attracted guests from Europe but met a mysterious end. Whether she was murdered by her politician lover or by a jealous fisherman, or whether she merely drowned has never been solved.

Paquetá: The island of Paquetá has survived the passage of time well, preserving the sensation of another age when life moved slowly and quietly. This feeling is captured by the island's one-story, flower-surrounded houses and the fact that private cars are not allowed. Transport is by bicycle, which

can be rented, or by a horse-drawn buggy which does a trip round the island at 19th-century pace for US$5.

There are three small hotels, four seafood restaurants, a string of beach-side bars and a small but pleasant park-cum-nature reserve taking up one end of the island. In splendid isolation, on the adjoining island of **Brocoio**, stands one of the official weekend homes of the Rio State Governor.

The Bateau Mouche runs another excursion, in the opposite direction— past Sugarloaf and Copacabana, through the neck of the bay between the forts of São João and Santa Cruz to the **Cagarras Islands**, a tiny archipelago in the Atlantic where the boat anchors for sea bathing. If the Atlantic is too choppy, the boat will anchor in the calmer waters off **Jurujuba** beach in Niteroi. For exploring **Niteroi**, ferries and *aerobarcos* leave Praça Quinze every few minutes.

Niteroi: *Cariocas* generally thumb their noses at Niteroi, claiming that it is a second-class version of their own city. Its only claim to fame, they sniff, is that it offers an excellent view of Rio proper. In fact, Niteroi's charms are quieter and on a lesser scale than those of Rio. But it is because of this paro-chial calm that people choose to live there.

Many of the town's best features lie off the beaten track, such as **Parque da Cidade**, 890 feet (270 meters) above sea level, via a winding road through an unspoilt nature reserve. It offers stun-ning views over the bay and back over the lush hills of the mainland, plus two takeoff platforms for hang gliders.

Many historical monuments, such as the **Rio Branco-Imbui-São Luis** com-plex of forts high up on a rough unpaved road, overlooking Jurujuba beach, re-quire previous permission and private transport to visit. The climb is worth it, not only for yet another stunning view, but for the sense of timelessness im-bued by the old forts nestled in the green hillside. São Luis is in ruins, only its

Ferries and hydrofoils make the passage across the bay.

splendid portico has been preserved.

Indian chieftain: Of Niteroi's many notable churches, the one with the most vivid story to tell is the simple **São Lourenço dos Indios**, where the Indian chieftain Arariboia is believed to be buried. Arariboia, or São Lourenço (an honorary sainthood endowed upon him by the Jesuits), was chief of the Temimino tribe from the other side of the bay. Allying himself with the Portuguese, he led a victorious campaign against the French and the Tamoio Indians in Niteroi in the 1550s and 1560s. The Portuguese first gave him deeds to the region where Rio's port lies today but later transferred him to the Niteroi side where he took possession on November 22, 1573. This date is celebrated today as the founding of the city. Within a century, however, the Portuguese had forgotten their debt to Arariboia and ousted his descendants from Niteroi.

The further one gets from Niteroi city center, the prettier and more unspoilt the beaches: **Sambanguia** with its yacht club, *Jurujuba* with its seafood restaurants and, last of the bayside beaches, the small twin coves of **Adão and Eva** (Adam and Eve).

Santa Cruz fort: Yet it is on the tip of the promontory that Niteroi's *piece de resistence* lies—the **fort of Santa Cruz**.

Well preserved, the fort is a magnificent compendium of three centuries of military architecture. The oldest parts, such as the rough-hewn stone **Santa Barbara** chapel and the torture chamber date back to the 16th century. Garibaldi, the hero of Italian liberation and José Bonifacio de Andrade, Brazil's "patriarch of independence" were imprisoned here. It takes at least three hours to go around the fort's myriad chambers, galleries, dungeons and courtyards. As it is still used as a military prison with weekend prison visits, tours are best confined to weekdays, by previous arrangement with the commanding officer, telephone 711-0166 or 711-0462.

The massive span of the Rio-Niteroi Bridge.

COPACABANA

Most educated travelers know of Copacabana but few can actually pin-point where it is or what it is. Many, quite correctly, think that Copacabana is a beach. Others, quite wrongly, (thanks to a popular song), think it is a nightclub.

Copacabana is one of the world's great beaches. Together with the now demolished church of the Virgin of Copacabana, it has given its name to one of Rio de Janeiro's most populous suburbs, although "suburb" is hardly a just description today.

With a population exceeding 300,000 spread throughout 109 streets, Copacabana can be viewed as a city within a city, rather than a suburb. Its population is a melting pot of class and color, living and working side by side, making Copacabana a classless neigh-borhood, unlike its wealthy neighbor, Ipanema.

Relative newcomer: In historic terms, Copacabana is a relative newcomer to the *carioca* scene. A Republican sub-urb, if you like, as its birth and subse-quent growth at the end of the 19th century, coincided with the end of the Brazilian monarchy in 1889. Its best days were already over by the time Brazil's capital was changed from Rio de Janeiro to Brasilia on April 21, 1960.

Except for the trans-Atlantic tele-graph that linked *Posto 6*, (close to the Rio Palace Hotel) with London, Co-pacabana remained basically un-touched and uninhabited at the turn of the century.

Copacabana owes its development and growth to the Rio Tramway, Light & Power Company of Canada, or "Light" as it is called by the *cariocas,* the same company responsible for the railway which scaled Corcovado. It was Light that invested in the linking of Copacabana with the rest of Rio, a city which was by then, nearly 400 years old. The linkage came by blasting through the rock to make tunnels, thus giving trams the easy access they could not find over the mountains. Then, as now, new areas often received transport, light and gas before receiving a resident population.

The first "breakthrough" was the opening in 1892, of **Tunel Alaor Prata** *(Tunel Velho)*, which links the middle of **Botafogo**, on the downtown side of the mountains, with the heart of Copacabana at **Rua Figuereido Magalhães** and **Rua Siqueira Campos**.

A second tunnel, **Tunel Engenheiro Marques Porto** *(Tunel Novo)*, was added in 1904 to link Copacabana and its extension, **Leme**, via **Av. Princesa Isabel**, with the end of Botafogo Beach where the city's showpiece drive, **Av. Beira Mar**, had just been completed. With these tunnels the Atlantic Ocean suburbs of Copacabana and Leme, and later Ipanema and Leblon, were born.

Center of activities: After 1910, the urbanization of Copacabana picked up pace as houses were built amongst the dunes. The **Copacabana Palace Hotel** which was inaugurated in 1923, quickly became the center of activities in Copacabana. For several decades, it was considered one of the world's "great" hotels.

Blessed with roads, tunnels, gas, electricity and fresh water, and with the help of hotels like the Copacabana Palace, casinos and nightclubs, Copacabana started to attract the world's rich and famous who flocked in, in ever increasing numbers in the 1930s and 1940s.

Copacabana's popularity however, fell abruptly on April 30, 1946 when gambling was outlawed and the country's 69 casinos were closed. But while Copacabana settled back into a less extravagant existence, the war years had seen rapid growth. Houses and apartment blocks sprang up to claim every square inch of building land available, and Copacabana became Rio's most sought after commer-

Preceding pages: The famed crescent curve of Copacabana; burst of colorful bird kites; the big bikini market; topless bathing is still an infrequent sight.

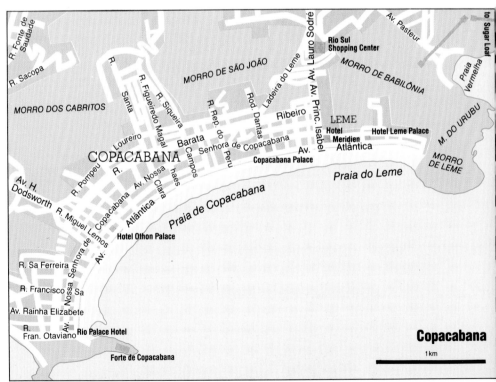

cial and residential center. All the city's best hotels, restaurants and nightclubs were to be found along its streets. Many of the hotels and restaurants of this period have survived the passage of time although their immediate surroundings have changed dramatically.

The original Bife de Ouro restaurant in the Copacabana Palace dates from 1938, while other beachfront eateries include **Lucas**, dating from 1941, on the corner of **Rua Souza Lima**, and **Bolero**, one of the most famous and traditional of Copacabana's thirty-five beachfront bars. Lucas has been operating in the same location since 1945. **Le Bec Fin** is another survivor from the 1940s and remains one of the city's best restaurants.

As early as the 1960s, Copacabana had reached maximum capacity at ground level. The answer was to go up and every year the apartment blocks climbed higher and higher. The beachfront highrises, however, cast long shadows, leaving much of the

beach in shade from mid-afternoon. To resolve this and traffic problems, the beach was widened through landfill. The former two-lane **Av. Atlantica** became six lanes, lined by wide, sweeping sidewalks with their famous mosaic designs.

In the 70s the skyline of newly widened Copacabana was radically altered—several large hotels were constructed in a bid to cope with the city's growing tourism and the demand of the international business community.

Hotel landmarks: The two most obvious landmarks on Copacabana today are the **Meridien Hotel**, which towers 37 floors at the exact spot where Copacabana becomes Leme, and the 27-story **Othon Palace** which stands further along the beach to the west, on the corner of Av. Atlantica and **Xavier da Silveira**. Copacabana almost had a third highrise constructed at its most westerly end but because of building restrictions, the luxury **Rio Palace Hotel** was built much lower than what was

A new beginning: sunrise on the beach on New Year's Day.

the original intention.

The new hotels have brought back much of the life to Copacabana and this is particularly true of the Meridien and Rio Palace Hotels.

The Meridien is a gourmet's paradise and is topped off, literally, with Paul Bocuse's **Le Saint Honoré**, a restaurant that is considered to be among the best in the world, with a view which is hard to beat anywhere. The hotel also boasts a jazz bar, and two other restaurants, including the **Café de la Paix**, a French *brasserie* which is open round the clock.

At the other end of the beach, the luxury Rio Palace has helped bring the glamor back to Posto 6 and the area of the old Atlantico casino. Since its opening, in 1979, the Rio Palace has offered shows by personalities like Frank Sinatra, Julio Iglesias, Bobby Short and has, in one of Brazil's top French restaurants, **Le Pré Catelan**, a menu orchestrated by Gaston Lenotre.

Copacabana and its residents are dif ferent from any other area in Rio. They are more traditional. They are also resigned to the parking problems of Copacabana and therefore like to walk and shop locally. Corner stores thrive as do the beachfront bars which in Copacabana, fill the role of the traditional British pub where a faithful clientele return night after night or lunch after lunch, with the owner's takings boosted by the tourist or visitor who finds his way to the bar.

Street markets: Despite the overcrowding, Copacabana has managed to retain its street markets which bring chaos to their immediate area each week. No visit to Rio would be complete without some time spent examining the exotic fruits and vegetables and the tropical flowers on display in these markets.

The more traditional street markets are **Rua Gustavo Sampaio** (Monday), **Rua Domingos Ferreira** (Wednesday), **Rua Belford Roxo** and **Rua Ronald de Carvalho** (Thursday) and

Flirting with the girls.

the **Rua Decio Vilares** (Sunday).

Recent years have seen Brazil's better fashion stores setting up branches in Copacabana, sited on seven blocks around **Rua Santa Clara** and **N.S. de Copacabana**. The souvenir trade has also moved back to Copacabana to dominate the roads between **Rua Paula Freitas** and **Praça Bernardeli**, behind the Copacabana Palace Hotel.

The early 1980s was a period which saw the establishment of a number of large fashion malls in Rio, one of which, **Rio Sul**, is located just past *Tunel Velho* from Copacabana. The only modern mall located within Copacabana is the **Cassino Atlantico**, below the Rio Palace Hotel, which has a predominance of art and antique stores as well as a good selection of souvenir stores.

Beach life: The beach at Copacabana remains one of Rio de Janeiro's most popular, attracting not only its 300,000 residents but also *cariocas* from all over the metropolis who arrive each weekend on packed buses or by car to park along the beach's crowded 2.4 miles (four km).

The beach has a life of its own, separate from the rest of Copacabana, and only darkness slows the pace. Even at night, joggers are to be found and games of beach soccer continue under floodlights.

In 1948, three Argentine girls caused a storm on the beach by sunbathing in front of the Copacabana Palace Hotel in two-piece swimsuits, the forerunner of the bikini. From then on, Rio de Janeiro, first through Copacabana and later through Ipanema, would lead the world as far as summer fashion, especially swimwear, was concerned.

By the start of the 1960s, it had become clear that Rio's traffic was outgrowing the available road space. Work started on the filling-in of the bay along the beachfront in Flamengo to create Flamengo Park while in Copacabana, work began in 1969 to widen the beachfront street, Av. Atlantica. Beach

A tight fit in one of Rio's ubiquitous beach snack trailers.

lovers, at the time, may have been worried about what would become of the beach but as it turned out, they need not, as the beach's new alignment resulted in a much wider beach than anyone could have imagined.

Copacabana Beach is so wide that it is more a sandy park than a beach. To get to the water's edge, swimmers must cross an expanse that houses full size soccer fields and volleyball courts. In summer, the sand is so hot that it is impossible to cross its expanse without shoes. Watching the *cariocas* at play on the beach gives an idea why Brazil has been a dominant force in soccer and volleyball, both of which, are national passions.

Sitting on a beach in Rio, particularly in Copacabana, is never dull. Live theater surrounds you as the beach becomes a stage for the body beautiful and the unforgettable *carioca* girls in their equally unforgettable bikinis. Youngsters happily share the beach with families and the tourists whose pale white skin is their calling card.

The beach is unfortunately also the stage for most of Rio's petty crime. The problem arises when visitors leave their possessions on the beach, unattended, as they stroll its length or take to the waters of the Southern Atlantic. Rio's sharp-eyed petty thieves are quick to pounce on cameras, personal stereos, and wallets which are left sitting on top of beach towels.

One of the safest locations for visitors is the beach in front of the big hotels as most of these employ their own minders to ensure that their guests go undisturbed.

Strong currents: As the beach of Copacabana is open to the elements of the South Atlantic, it is affected by strong currents which can be very dangrous for inexperienced swimmers. For most of the year, the waters of Copacabana look rougher than they actually are. As the sea breaks over a sandbank further out, it is possible to swim through the waves and stand up. The

Left, paddle ball, another *carioca* passion and right, beach beauty with a tattoo— the latest fad.

key here is to observe what the *cariocas* are doing, especially the surfers, who have the most experience with local conditions.

Accidents usually occur when the victim panics. In Copacabana, there is little need to panic as it has an excellent lifeguard system which places guards on the beach in patrol boats, and in patrol helicopters.

The surfers also take it upon themselves to keep an eye out for inexperienced swimmers, taking them beyond the breaking waves, on their boards, to the calmer, deeper water.

A visiting swimmer should remember that the current off Copacabana takes one down the beach and not away from the shore. The current can cause interesting problems for the nearsighted swimmer when he emerges from the sea, far from his towel and friends.

Copacabana's lifeguard stations, the *postos*, were for many years, a method of directing people around the area.

There is logic to sidewalk mosaics but very little to traffic. Next page, in Copacabana, every Sunday is Carnival.

Posto 1 covered Leme and *Postos* 2, 3, 4, 5 and 6, Copacabana. Today, only *Posto* 6 is referred to and covers the area from Rua Sá Ferreira to the Rio Palace.

The *postos* were knocked down when the beach was widened and new lifeguard stations constructed in the early 1980s. Copacabana's residents, however, continue to refer to locations on the beach in terms of where the old *postos* stood.

Rio de Janeiro, Brazil and Copacabana are synonymous. What happens to Brazil or to Rio, is reflected in the streets of Copacabana, especially Rua Miguel Lemos, which closes for a party at the slightest excuse. The World Cup of soccer is a month-long excuse, win or lose, but if it is a win, there is no more exhilarating place to be than Miguel Lemos and the streets of Copacabana.

Carnival on Copacabana: Carnival is another excuse to party and despite being some distance from the main Carnival parade grounds, at Marques de Sapucai and Av. Rio Branco, Co-

pacabana is one of the liveliest places in the city during the revelries.

Street bands are one of Rio's most traditional carnival activities and Copacabana has some of the best, including *Banda do Leme*, *Banda da Sá Ferreira*, *Banda da Miguel Lemos*, *Banda da Vergonha do Posto 6* and the *Banda do Arroxo*. These bands snake their way through the streets of Copacabana, followed by thousands of revelers. The bands normally go out at around 4 p.m. and continue for as long as they have a following, which can be into the early hours of the next morning.

Copacabana's carnival balls cover the whole spectrum in terms of style, price and content and range from the exclusive hotel balls to simple parties in the smaller bars and clubs in the back streets.

Copacabana also boasts what is probably the world's largest party which takes place every New Year's Eve when more than one million people, the majority dressed in white, crowd Copacabana Beach, the beachfront bars and the luxury hotels to welcome in the New Year.

The celebration also has a religious significance for the followers of *macumba*, Brazil's voodoo. For them, December 31 is the feast of Iemanja, the Goddess of the Sea. Offerings to her are launched into the sea throughout the night, culminating in a mass offering at midnight, when the faithful hope that the third wave after midnight will take their offering.

Thousands crowd the beach for this mystical ceremony enhnaced by the staedy beat of drums in the night.

The New Year celebration in Copacabana is an event that is unequalled anywhere in the world, surprising many visitors who consider it more spectacular than Carnival. A massive fireworks display co-ordinated by the big hotels, at midnight lights up the Southern Atlantic which comes alive with bobbing pleasure crafts out to watch the spectacle from the water.

NIGHTLIFE IN COPA

There is an awful lot of coffee in Brazil, the song tells us, and a lot of that coffee gets drunk in Rio de Janeiro—which may be one explanation for the terrific stamina the *cariocas* exude. For them every night is Saturday night, even without the benefit of a noonday siesta.

While in most cities, nightlife begins after dark, on Copacabana the preliminaries start during daylight hours with the beach serving as a vast singles bar. From the beach it is just a quick hop across Avenida Atlantica to one of the beachfront's numerous sidewalk cafes for a before dinner drink.

The options for the dinner itself are wide and appealing, ranging from an informal meal at a *carioca* steakhouse to the heights of sophisticated dining at one of the neighborhood's several exquisite centers of gourmet cuisine. Afterwards, the best option is to simply mingle with the crowd or crowds. At night, Copacabana jumps with a special nervous energy. Throngs gather in front of discos, tourists browse through the wares of street vendors, couples walk slowly along the beachfront and prostitutes, male, female and indeterminate, prowl the edges of this moving mass.

Historically, since the 1930s, Copacabana has been the center of Rio's night life, taking over this mantle from the downtown area around the Teatro Municipal where, at the time, the city's best movie houses, theaters, bars and restaurants were located and where, close by, was **Lapa**, the Bohemian district of its day.

Center of entertainment: Copacabana's Golden Age as the center for Rio's entertainment was unquestionably from the early 1930s until the start of the 1950s, during which time the **Copacabana Palace Hotel** and the **Cassino Atlantico** attracted the world's rich and famous to Rio to gamble and enjoy the nightclubs and restaurants which had sprung up around them. The Copacabana Palace Hotel still exists today, a regal landmark of Copacabana's seafront drive, **Avenida Atlantica.**

Best restaurants: Copacabana's Golden Age was responsible for many of the area's better restaurants, many of which still survive today to quench the appetite of the *cariocas.*

The Copacabana Palace's **Bife de Ouro**, despite several reforms, dates back to 1938, while close by, in Praça da Lido, is **Le Bec Fin** which has consistently served some of Rio's better dishes since opening in 1948. The small restaurant of the elegant **Ouro Verde Hotel** is another restaurant with an historic past and has been under the command of the same Swiss chef since 1958.

The opening of the luxurious Meridien and Rio Palace hotels in the 1970s gave Copacabana's gastronomic pretensions a further shot in the arm as each hotel inaugurated restaurants which would be the pride of any city in the world,'including Paris.

The restaurants in question are the **Saint Honore**, under the direction of Paul Bocuse, in the Meridien, and the **Pré Catelan**, under the direction of Gaston Lenotre, in the Rio Palace.

Bocuse and Lenotre are both living legends within French culinary circles.

Copacabana does not, however, only cater to the top end of the market, although it is fair to note that the vast majority of Copacabana restaurants are of excellent quality, and three restaurants at the **Leme** end of the beach deserve a special mention.

Mariu's at Av. Atlantica 290, is one of the city's most popular restaurants and is generally agreed to be Rio's best *churrascaria rodizio*. A *churrascaria rodizio* is a barbecue house with a difference. The difference is that the waiters bring to the table every imaginable type of barbecued meat set off by a vast array of accompaniments, many of which are peculiar to Brazil. And the waiters keep bringing the meat until the diner screams for mercy. Eating, without thinking, they say.

Rodizio's offer extraordinary value for money and are therefore popular with residents and visitors alike. Wherever a line of people is seen waiting to get into a restaurant the chances are that it is a *rodizio*. Other *rodizios* in Copacabana include **Carretao** and the **Palace.**

Located along the beach from Mariu's is **Le Fiorentina,** which although not as in vogue as a decade ago, is still a popular bohemian watering hole where a table of artists and actors is likely to be found at any time of the day or night.

On the road behind is another bohemian haunt, though bohemian is hardly an accurate description of the clientele of this hole-in-the-wall eatery called **Shirley**. Shirley's cuisine, a mix of Spanish and seafood, has been well considered for decades and the clientele

invariably includes a number of ex-cabinet ministers and a *carioca* socialite or two.

Many of the restaurants and bars of Copacabana are the equivalent of the British pub in that they cater to their faithful clients who return again and again, the majority of whom live within a short walk of the restaurant.

Most *cariocas* eat late, 9 p.m. still being considered early, and because of this, many of them choose to take in a movie before eating, after which they go on to the shows and night clubs which only start to warm up later in the evening.

Because of the very nature of the residents of Copacabana, there is not one set area for entertainment, the restaurants, theaters and night clubs being split democratically throughout the area's 109 streets.

Movies & theatre shows: Copacabana has nine movie houses, most of which show first run movies that retain their original soundtrack with Portuguese

Strippers liven up the night.

subtitles added. Copacabana's main cinemas include the **Roxy** and **Condor Copacabana** while the art houses are considered to be **Cinema 1**, **Ricamar** and the **Studio Copacabana**.

Live theatre is also popular in Rio and Copacabana offers one of the city's best selection of live drama, the standard of which, is extremely high. Virtually all the plays are in Portuguese and the vast majority feature Brazil's top actors and actresses, many of whom are known internationally for their work in Brazilian films.

It is no coincidence that Brazil won the best actress prize at the Cannes and Berlin film festivals in 1986, a feat they repeated in the Berlin festival in 1987.

Copacabana used to be the site of the majority of the traditional "tourist" shows but since the beginning of the 1980s these have moved on to **Leblon**. Today Copacabana concentrates on live shows which appeal to the residents and those visitors who want to discover the real Brazil.

Although not technically in Copacabana, being through the Tunel Novo next to the popular **Rio-Sul** shopping mall, **Canecão** is Rio's most important showhouse offering the best national and international attractions in the city.

Artists who play Canecao can last for one show or six months, although in recent years Canecão has even managed to stage three different shows in one night, the first show starting at seven in the evening, the next at nine-thirty, and the final attraction going on stage around midnight.

In Rio, Canecão's only competition comes from the **Scala** in Leblon. In Copacabana the competition is from the smaller and less popular **Golden Room** of the Copacabana Palace and the theaters **Raquel** and **Arena.**

More intimate shows are the domain of the hotels with the **Rond Point** jazz bar in the Meridien and the **Horse's Neck** of the Rio Palace dominating.

The hotels also dominate Copacabana's night club and disco-

For the disco crowd, Rio has Brazil's largest disco-theque.

A NIGHT
ON THE TOWN

As the sun begins to set behind the buildings of Copacabana, the thoughts of visitors and residents alike start to turn to the evening, an evening which can be well spent in Copacabana without ever having to move to another neighborhood in Rio.

But even as the sun sets, a visitor should be on the move if he wants to fit a full program of events together.

For the first-time visitor to Rio, a few basic tips: dress comfortably and casually, *cariocas* are avowed enemies of formal wear even at their most chic restaurants and bars; if you are not by now, relax and at ease, Copacabana at night is a fascinating mix of cultures and types; don't be concerned with the wayward figures along the sidewalks—the beggars, street vendors and prostitutes—they are all part of the show.

Pre-dinner drinks can be taken at many varying locations. For the sheer splendor of its views across the open sea to the coast at Niteroi, a table by the swimming pool of the **Rio Palace hotel** is an excellent choice, with the sun, in the early evening, at play on the far-off islands and coastline.

The bar at the top of the **Othon Palace** is another popular choice and gives a full panorama of Copacabana's famous mosaic pavements. From the top of the Othon Palace, it becomes clear that there is some sanity in the madness of the patterns below.

At ground level, any **beachfront bar** is an equally suitable choice and gives the opportunity to observe the resident Copacabana population at play as many of the residents stay on at the beachfront bars for dinner. Among the best are **Cabral, Lucas, La Fiorentina**, and the fish restaurants of **Principe** and **Real** at the Leme end of the beach.

The swimming pool area of the **Copacabana Palace** is also a delightful place at street level, to sip *caipirinhas*,

Brazil's national drink, as day turns to night and a cloak of darkness envelops Copacabana.

For dinner—but not before 8 p.m. please, as most *cariocas* eat late, the most popular time being 10 p.m.—there are a wealth of options.

At the top end of the market are Le **Bec Fin** (traditional), **Le Pré Catelan** (nouvelle cuisine) in the Rio Palace, and **Le Saint Honoré** (nouvelle cuisine with a view) in the Meridien, all outstanding French restaurants. The restaurant of the **Ouro Verde Hotel** is more international in its tastes and offers a *crepes suzzette* that has survived the test of time whilst **Enotria** serves gourmet Italian.

For serious carnivores, Copacabana offers **Bife de Ouro** in the Copacabana Palace and **Café de la Paix**, the pavement *brasserie* of the Meridien, as well as three barbecue houses that keep bringing the barbecue cuts until the diner begs for mercy: no visit to Rio would be complete without a meal at

Convivial piano bars, a mainstay of Copacabana nightlife.

Mariu's, Carretão or the **Palace**. Copacabana's most traditional barbecue house which has been hosting visitors for decades, is **Jardim** in **Rua Republica do Peru**.

For Brazilian food, the choice is split between **Arataca** and the **Moenda** in the **Trocadero Hotel**, while for seafood, Copacabana and Leme offer **Shirley's, Principe, Real** and a **Marisqueira**. The best choice however, is **Grottammare**, which sits between Copacabana and Ipanema.

Bars and clubs: After dinner, it may be the time to catch that movie or play or return to the beachfront bars as the more raunchy aspects of Copacabana and Rio's nightlife start to emerge.

The girls at play can be observed at the bars which stretch from **Bolero** up to the Meridien, with the popular and lively favorite being **Mabs** located on the corner of Av. Prado Junior and Av. Atlantica.

For the boys, the choices are the bars around the **Alaska** gallery located at the other end of the beach.

Nightclubs with the erotic shows start to fill around midnight and carry on through daybreak or at least until there is some business to be done.

For the more up-market, catch some jazz or Brazilian music in the **Round Point** of the Meridien or **Horse's Neck** of the Rio Palace. Both hotels, along with the Othon Palace, have their own chic private nightclubs.

Copacabana's bars, beachfront or otherwise, stay open late, most till 3 a.m. or later, with some like Bolero staying open for that final late night *chopp* (beer) until 6 a.m. Rio is a city that truthfully never sleeps.

And if the night has gone particularly well, you may still be around to see the sun rise in which case, the direction to head is for any of the major hotels which offer the delights of the tropical fruits at their breakfast table. The best suggestions are the Meridien's Café de la Paix or the pool areas of the Copacabana Palace and Rio Palace Hotel.

The night for cariocas starts late and runs until morning.

theque scene with the **Palace Club** of the Rio Palace; **Studio C** of the Othon Palace and, at the time of writing, the Meridien who were set to replace their branch of **Regine's** with another private club.

Copacabana's most famous discotheque, one of the largest and most modern in Latin America, is **Help**, a landmark in its own right in the center of the beachfront which also holds its own lively Carnival ball. Of late, Help has begun to attract some of Copacabana's abundant crop of young and beautiful prostitutes. Tourists should be aware that not all of the disco's attractive habituees are there to dance.

Under the same roof as Help is **Sobre As Ondas** which offers music and dancing at a more sedate pace, a formula which is followed by **Vinicius**, located above the Churrascaria Copacabana.

At the other end of the scale is **Crepusculo de Cubatão** the temple of the city's darks and punks. Crepusculo, which is rarely out of the headlines, boasts as one of its partners, British train robber Ronald Biggs— Brazil's most famed refugee— and stays open and active from late evening to early morning all through the week.

Rio's best red light district: Copacabana would not be Copacabana, however, without its red light district, the best in Rio, if not Brazil, which has gained international fame without the notoriety of Bangkok.

The red light district splits its activity between the heterosexual to the east of the beach and homosexual to the west.

The heterosexual bars and clubs spread through the back roads of Copacabana, stretching from behind the Hotel Lancaster up to the Meridien. As Brazil is the world's largest Catholic country, the "shop fronts" remain discreet, only the names giving any hint of what lies beyond. The **Pussy Cat, Erotika, Swing, Don Juan, New Munich** and **Frank's Bar** are all to be found in the area and all offer some version of erotic show and, for the clients, what are generally accepted to be some of the most beautiful prostitutes in the world.

The homosexual area of Copacabana is based on and around the bars and clubs of the **Galeria Alaska**, at the western end of the beach.

Copacabana offers entertainment and relaxation that appeal to every taste and budget and offers it seven nights a week, 52 weeks of the year. The streets, bars and restaurants come alive around nine p.m. and carry on through until the early morning hours. Most restaurants take orders as late as two a.m. a time when the bars and clubs are only starting to warm up. The majority of the clientele are the residents of Rio de Janeiro and most of them will have to get up early the next morning to look bright and breezy in the office, when they start to plan the night ahead.

Life is too short for *cariocas* to have only one Saturday night a week.

Meat is sliced from the skewer right on to your plate at a *churrascaria*. Right, Rio prostitutes: are they men or women?

VIEWPOINTS

Since Portuguese explorer, André Gonçalves discovered it in 1502, Rio de Janeiro has been taking visitors' breaths away.

Charles Darwin wrote during a visit in 1823, "Guanabara Bay exceeds in its magnificence everything the European has seen in his native land."

Rio's landscape has changed considerably since, yet much of the "magnificence" which impressed Darwin remains and can be spied from strategic points scattered around the city.

Rio's views can be classified into three categories: classic, out-of-the-way and *very* out-of-the-way vistas for adventurers with time on their hands.

Classic views: Among classic views, there is nothing quite like the panorama from the top of **Sugarloaf Mountain.** It's all there—the vast curve of **Copacabana Beach**, the perfect curl of **Botafogo**, the **Rio-Niterói Bridge**, and, on clear days, the jagged **Serra Flumenense** mountain peaks more than an hour's drive away.

As with many of Rio's classic sights, getting there is half the fun. But getting to the top of Sugarloaf may be carrying things too far. Visitors should be prepared for a heart-stopping, six-minute glide in swaying, glassed-in cable cars.

Rio's other "best view" is obtained from a commanding height of 2,340-foot (713-meter) Corcovado (meaning "hunchback", Corcovado is the mountain pedestal of Rio's famed **"Christ the Redeemer" Statue**).

The best way to attain the summit is on the recently-renovated 2.3-mile (3.7-km) Corcovado Railroad with trains leaving every few minutes from a quaint station in **Cosme Velho**. Tunnels of lush foliage and splendid views make the comfortable ride in modern coaches more scenic than a car trip.

Left, sun set behind the mountains of Rio's romantic lagoon.

The railway was originally carved out of Rio's mountainsides by engineer, Pereira Passos in 1884. First trains to chug up the mountain track were foreign-built steam engines. It was a dangerous, smelly, time-consuming trip. In 1912, the Rio de Janeiro Tramway, Light and Power Company electrified the route and it became more popular.

At the summit, visitors are greeted by a dizzying view which includes Sugarloaf, the southern beaches, swank residential districts and shimmering **Rodrigo de Freitas lagoon**.

The Christ Statue presiding over the scene is 99 feet (30 meters) tall. The work of a team of artisans headed by French sculptor Paul Landowsky, it was completed in 1931.

Behind Corcovado is a network of sub-tropical jungle known as **Tijuca Forest**. It includes 60 miles (100 km) of narrow, two-lane roads featuring a number of spectacular look-out points.

One, the **Mesa do Imperador**, offers a "high" view of Rio framed by exuberant foliage. Visitors gaze straight down the spine of mountains leading to the poking head of Sugarloaf. Below is the sparkling Rodrigo de Freitas lagoon.

Another look-out point, **Vista Chinesa**, gives a "low" view of Rio—less breathtaking than Mesa do Imperador.

A third classic view on the Corcovado-Tijuca circuit is the **Dona Marta Belvedere** on the road to the Corcovado summit. From an attractive patio, visitors enjoy a wrap-around look at city, beaches and mountains. Straight ahead is a full view of Sugarloaf, surrounded by the blue basin of Botafogo.

Rio also offers classic views from less dramatic elevations (including sea level). Alfred Hitchcock, in his 1946 classic, *Notorious*, exploited Rio's romantic allure by having Cary Grant and Ingrid Bergman dine at twilight on an apartment terrace in Copacabana. Roughly the same view can be obtained today standing at the corner of **Avenidas Atlantica** and **Princesa Isabel**. Its counterpart—the south-to-

north view of Copacabana with the nub of Sugarloaf rising in the background—is seen from the **Posto Seis** end of the beach. Pleasant bay cruises offer their own intriguing views. Cruise boats venture as far as **Cagarras Islands** for a front view of Rio's ocean beaches with the city and hills floating majestically in the background.

In many cases, Rio's views are two-way. The view of the lagoon from Corcovado is spectacular but then so too is the view of Corcovado from the lagoon. In fact, the lagoon, a refreshing open space amidst the high rise apartments of Rio's south side, is one of Rio's best sites for extraordinary views. From the avenue that surrounds the lagoon, you can see Corcovado, the Tijuca Forest, the **Dois Irmaos** Mountain at the end of Leblon beach and the distinctive flat top of Gavea Mountain. If this is not enough, there is always the lagoon which day or night is a sight that never disappoints.

Directly inland from the lagoon is the **Jardim Botanico** neighborhood whose streets offer the best vantage for a head-on view of the sheer granite cliff of Corcovado, a gray eminence that dominates the horizon.

Another haven for photographers and sightseers is the **São Conrado** neighborhood, home to Gavea Mountain. The drive along **Avenida Niemeyer** from Leblon to São Conrado clings to the cliffside, offering a unique view of Ipanema. The best, though, is saved for last when the road descends to São Conrado and the neighborhood's beach with towering Gavea in the background comes into view. If this doesn't take your breath away, nothing will.

Rio's out-of-the-way views: Visitors seeking out-of-the-way views should head for the **Santa Teresa** trolley lines with cars leaving every few minutes from the **Petrobras Plaza**. The second trolley station, offers a striking glimpse of **Guanabara Bay** framed by quaint houses and rambling gardens. (Unfortunately, petty thieves now infest the

Left, the beach of São Conrado with the imposing Gavea Mountain in the back. Next page, Vista Chinesa, another look-out point.

trolley cars, making it unwise for tourists to carry cameras.)

But the best Santa Teresa view is from the **Chácara do Céu** art museum on **Rua Martinho Nobre**. The expansive lawn behind the museum is a restful setting of fountains, flower beds and benches. At the edge of the lawn, visitors can peek through a frame of hedges and fluttering tree limbs to see the entire panorama of downtown Rio.

One of Rio's most interesting day trips is following the rugged coast road that snakes through the city's outer beaches, starting with remote **Recreio dos Bandeirantes**. The surf is stronger in Recreio than in Copacabana and sometimes shoves a shifting white fog of spray across the road. Between the mountains and the sea are shimmering, tree-lined lagoons.

From Recreio, the road climbs abruptly, revealing a series of spectacular seascapes as it curls around rocky ledges, descending first to **Prainha** and then to **Grumari**, a pair of vest-pocket beaches nestled dramatically beneath verdant escarpments. Both beaches are gratifyingly undeveloped.

From Grumari an even older, more pock-marked road lumbers toward **Barra de Guaratiba**.

Glimpses of Grumari below reveal a Gauguin-like vision of virgin beach, the horseshoe of sand set-off tantalizingly by green-clad hills. At the top of the rise, visitors are rewarded with another breathtaking view—the vast expanse of the Guaratiba flatlands and a limitless string of beach called **Restinga de Marambaia**.

An entirely different set of views awaits visitors to **Niterói**, the city across the bay from Rio. It starts with the ferry ride from Rio's **Praça XV**. The whole panorama of urban Rio with its backdrop of green mountains, takes shape as the ferry leaves the pier.

Once in Niterói, the most noted views are from the city's bayside beaches, starting with narrow **Gragoatá**, about a mile from downtown. The same expan-

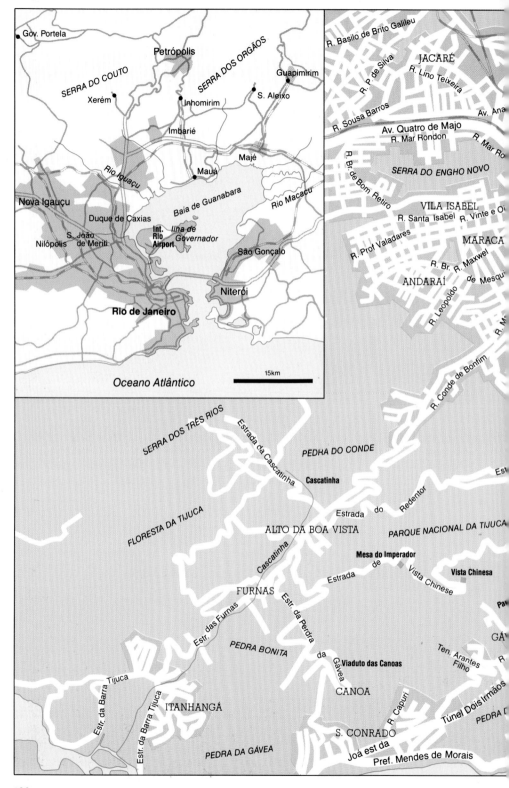

Gov. Portela

Petrópolis

SERRA DOS ORGÃOS

SERRA DO COUTO

Guapimirim

Xerém

Inhomirim

S. Aleixo

Imbarié

Majé

Rio Iguaçu

Mauá

Rio Macacu

Nova Igauçu

Baia de Guanabara

Duque de Caxias

São Gonçalo

S. João de Meriti

Int. Rio Airport

Ilha de Governador

Nilópolis

Niterói

Rio de Janeiro

Oceano Atlântico

15km

R. Basilo de Brito Galileu

JACARÉ

R. P. de Silva

R. Lino Teixeira

R. Sousa Barros

Av. Ana

Av. Quatro de Majo

R. Mar Rondon

R. Mar Ro

R. Br. de Bom Retiro

SERRA DO ENGHO NOVO

VILA ISABEL

R. Santa Isabel

R. Vinte e Oi

MARACA

R. Prof Valadares

R. Br. R. Maxwel

de Mesqu

ANDARAÍ

R. Leopoldo

R. M

R. Conde de Bonfim

SERRA DOS TRÊS RIOS

Estrada da Cascatinha

PEDHA DO CONDE

Cascatinha

Est

FLORESTA DA TIJUCA

Estrada do Redentor

ALTO DA BOA VISTA

PARQUE NACIONAL DA TIJUCA

Cascatinha

Mesa do Imperador

Vista Chinesa

FURNAS

Estrada de

Vista Chinese

Pa

Estr. das Furnas

Estr. da Perdra

GÁ

PEDRA BONITA

da Gávea

Ten. Arantes Filho

R

Viaduto das Canoas

Estr. da Barra Tijuca

CANOA

R. Capuri

Túnel Dois Irmãos

PEDRA [

Estr. da Barra Tijuca

ITANHANGÁ

S. CONRAD0

PEDRA DA GÁVEA

Joá est da

Pref. Mendes de Morais

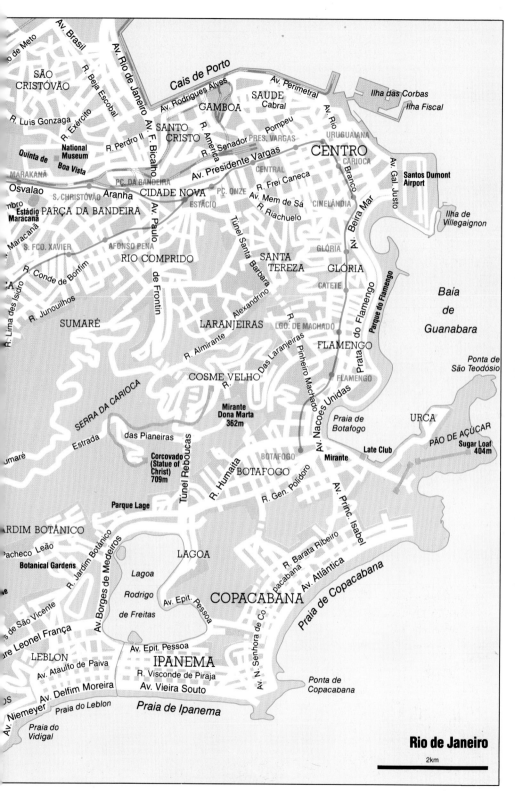

Rio de Janeiro

2km

121

sive, front view of Rio can also be obtained from **Icarai** and **São Francisco**. Apartment buildings, traffic and numerous bars and restaurants make Icarai the mirror-image of Copacabana.

Rio's very out-of-the-way views: Visitors seeking Rio's *really* unusual views have plenty of options too, but should be prepared to expend their blood, sweat, toil and time.

The **Niterói side of Guanabara Bay**, for example, includes a number of sweeping, rarely appreciated views. Continuing along the coast road beyond São Francisco, visitors reach Niterói's rugged ocean-side beaches.

The well-known, **Itaipu**, is a long, low curve of sand separating the Atlantic from a pair of attractive lagoons. The best thing about Itaipu is the panorama of Rio across Guanabara Bay. The view embraces the entire city, from the flat top of **Pedra da Gávea** to the 3,370-foot (1,030-meter) height of **Pico da Tijuca**. An odd juxtaposition, with the southern part of Rio seeming to curve off to the west instead of the south. The effect is startling and majestic.

Backtracking a few miles along the main road leads to the turn-off for Itaipuaçu. Steep, winding **Estrada de Itaipuaçu** climbs through tropical forest until the summit is suddenly attained, it offers the same panoramic view of Rio as Itaipu, but this is framed by the forest. Continuing on to the other side of the mountain, visitors encounter another view—the long, only partially developed beach of **Itaipuaçu** stretching toward the horizon.

Also on the Niterói side, near Gragoatá, intriguing **Boa Viagem** beach hides one of Guanabara Bay's finest "secret" views.

Boa Viagem's tiny curve of sand is naturally decorated by outcroppings that look like meteorites. At the west end of the beach, across a narrow footbridge, is the lush island of Boa Viagem

Right, the Dona Marta viewpoint encompassing Botafogo, Sugarloaf, the Bay and Niteroi.

122

with its charming **Nossa Senhora dos Navegantes chapel**, dating from 1734. The iron gate at the footbridge is usually locked, so visiting Boa Viagem is risky. Visitors lucky enough to find a caretaker, can hike up the 100-odd chipped, sloping steps to a small plaza gracing the rear of the church. Searing white walls of the chapel are striking and the view of Rio from the esplanade is unhindered and spectacular.

One of the most startling views of Rio can only be obtained by driving more than an hour on the **Rio-Teresópolis Highway**. A wide look-out point has been landscaped into the roadside near the turn-off for Teresópolis. On clear days it affords an awesome view of Guanabara Bay, embracing the entire watery basin from behind. The shiny surface seems to belly into a vast white puddle then funnel toward the narrow gates of the bay, guarded by Morro do Cão, on the Niterói side, and Sugarloaf in Rio. The whole mountainous profile of Rio itself strikes off to the right, including Corcovado, Pedra da Gávea and Tijuca Peak.

Adventurous visitors may wish to sample Rio's spectacular, but challenging view—the towering summit of **Tijuca Mountain**. The peak is located deep within the Tijuca Forest Reserve. Cars penetrate only to the **Bom Retiro** picnic ground. Then it's a two-mile hike along often poorly-marked trails to the mountain top. Average time is about an hour and a quarter.

The last few yards of the ascent follow a rocky path to Tijuca's round-head summit. The effect, arriving at the peak, is vertiginous. The tiny plateau towers above everything, even treetops of the forest below. Many climbers feel compelled to cling to the ground as soon as they attain the peak.

But the view is worth it, encompassing the entire city and its surroundings, dwarfing even Corcovado—the last, best view of one of the world's most beautiful cities.

Left, aerial view of a volleyball game.

IPANEMA

Ipanema is Rio's poshest, most cosmopolitan neighborhood where international is "in" and Brazilian is "out". It is the gathering place of Rio's "beautiful people", of artists and intellectuals, the locale of chic discotheques, nightclubs, elegant and intimate restaurants, luxurious beachfront apartments, exclusive art galleries, fashionable boutiques and top cinemas and theaters.

The neighborhood's 65,000 residents live in an area stretching from the end of Copacabana at **Rua Bulhões de Carvalho** to the Dutch-like canal at **Jardim de Alah** (Alah's Garden), including a nook with strong waves at the Copacabana end called **Arpoador**. Seen from above, along the scenic road that passes through the Tijuca Forest, Ipanema, its extension Leblon, and the **Rodrigo de Freitas Lagoon** known to *cariocas* as the *lagoa*, all form a homogeneous unity of apartment buildings, tree-lined streets and wide expanses of water. This is the money belt of Rio, home to a mixture of traditional wealth and the *carioca nouveau riche*.

Land development: Ipanema (an Indian name meaning dangerous waters) began as an adventuresome land development in 1894, marked by dirt roads running through the existing sand dunes with a handful of bungalows along the sides of the roads. Considered a distant outpost on the fringe of civilization, the neighborhood was mostly ignored until the 1950s when the crush of Copacabana became too much for its well-to-do residents. Following the same path that had taken them from the bay neighborhoods to Copacabana, they then moved on South, over to the next beach.

As Ipanema became more prosperous and fashionable, its dirt roads gave way to paved streets and avenues, bungalows were replaced by the homes and apartments of the well-to-do and shopping arcades sprang up where sand dunes once sprawled. From the 1950s to the present day, Ipanema has undergone an extraordinary real estate boom and population explosion. Its early homes were replaced first by four-story apartment buildings, some of which still survive, and since the 1960s, by a surging tide of high rises steadily turning the Ipanema skyline into an updated version of Copacabana with one major difference: Ipanema property values are the highest in Brazil with beachfront apartments fetching up to and sometimes over $1 million.

For long-time residents of Ipanema, the neighborhood's steadily increasing population and building density are seen as crimes against humanity that they have vowed to fight. Forsaking the normal *carioca* attitude of what will be will be, the neighborhoods of Ipanema, Leblon, the lagoon and nearby Gavea and Jardim Botanico have launched Rio's first determined effort to preserve the city's natural and man-made charms. Such action is greatly welcomed in a city that is showing deep scars along some of its most treasured routes.

Wave of liberalism: That this should happen in Ipanema is not surprising. In the 1960s, the neighborhood was swept by a highly romanticized wave of liberalism that achieved international fame. Rio's bohemians and intellectuals gathered at Ipanema's sidewalk cafes and bars to philosophize over the movements of the decade—the hippies, rock and roll, the Beatles, drugs, long hair and free love. Like their counterparts in the United States of America and Europe, Ipanema's long-haired youth were revolting against the values of their time.

Being Ipanema, however, and not San Francisco or London, the movement quickly acquired a romantic strain. A muse was selected. She was Leila Diniz, a free-thinking and free-living actress who scandalized the still-traditional morals of Rio by expressing her independence and doing her own thing, including being the first woman in Rio to wear a bikini while pregnant.

Ms. Diniz lead the march of the Band of Ipanema, a carnival street band, in celebration of this short but vibrant moment. Humor was present in a monthly, satirical newspaper, *Pasquim*, which proudly announced the founding of the Independent Republic of Ipanema. At its highpoint, the citizens of the Republic were capable of such rousingly romantic acts as rising from the tables of a sidewalk cafe to applaud the setting of the sun.

Meeting places: The "capital" of the Republic was divided amongst three bars, the meeting places for intellectuals and other bohemians: the Zeppelin (home to the Band of Ipanema), Jangadeiros and Velloso, headquarters of a companion movement, Brazil's *bossa nova*.

The guiding light of the *bossa nova* and one of the Republic's favorite sons was famed composer ,Tom Jobim, who took *The Girl from Ipanema* in song from the district's streets to Carnegie Hall. Looking back today, Jobim recalls this magical period with nostalgia. "Ipanema used to be a paradise, one of the best places in the world. Between Paris, Rome and New York, I used to prefer Ipanema, always. Not because of man-made things but because of nature and beauty. The ocean on one side, the lagoon on another. It had an abundance of fish, clean water, forest and you could see the mountains. To give you an idea of what Ipanema was, when I first brought my song to the United States of America I had to fight to maintain my title because no one knew where or what Ipanema was. One year later came the tourists and the hotels. Because of *The Girl from Ipanema*, I was once stopped on the street by a furious guy who said I was responsible for rents skyrocketing in the neighborhood!"

This mystical blend of Camelot and Haight Asbury finally ended with the 1964 military coup and a subsequent

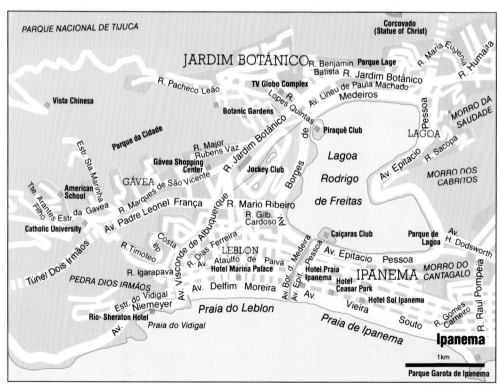

crackdown on liberals in 1968. Particularly affected was the nation's most liberal neighborhood and its left-leaning bohemians, driving many into exile. With this, as writer Heloisa Hollanda remembers, "The neighborhood lost its innocence...a crisis came and the party ended." The final blow came in 1972 when Leila Diniz, muse of the Republic of Ipanema, died in a plane accident.

Modern spirit: Despite its brevity, this period defined the modern *carioca* spirit—irreverent, independent and decidedly liberal towards matters of the flesh and spirit. It also propelled Ipanema into the vanguard in determining *carioca* style, pushing Copacabana back into second class status. In a fad conscious city, the fads of Rio begin and end in Ipanema.

Today, Ipanema is the center of chic and sophistication. If it's not "in" in Ipanema then it's simply not "in". Rio's most fashionable boutiques line the streets of Ipanema and Leblon. Separated only by a canal, these two neighborhoods have different names but an increasingly shared identity. The apartments that line beachfront **Avenida Vieira Souto** and its continuation, **Delfim Moreira**, are the most treasured and disputed in Rio.

The beach itself is a smaller version of Copacabana, both in length and width. At the Copacabana end, **Arpoador** is famed for its surfing and its view. Passionate *cariocas* claim that the best ending to a long night out is to watch the sunrise from Arpoador, looking out at the crashing waves as early rising fishermen cast their lines into the sea.

Imposing mountain: At the far end, standing sentinel is the imposing **Dois Irmaos (Two Brothers) Mountain**, which frames one of Rio's most spectacular natural settings. In the morning, joggers and cyclists fill the sidewalk while exercise classes go through their gyrations on the beach. During the day, the golden youth of Rio frequent the beach and waters. Befitting its image of

Ipanema's popularity is attested to by the invasion of highrises in the neighborhood.

GIRL FROM IPANEMA

Tall and tan and young and lovely, the girl from Ipanema goes walking, and when she passes, each one she passes goes 'ahhh....

In the mid-1960s, that lyric and the mellow, romantic music that carried it exploded on the music scene, immortalized by the tenor sax of Stan Getz and the sultry voice of Brazilian singer Astrud Gilberto. Now a pop classic, *The Girl from Ipanema* was the first big hit to emerge from the *bossa nova* movement of Brazilian singers, and composers. It put Brazilian popular music on the map and brought instant fame to composer Tom Jobim and lyricist/poet Vinicius de Moraes.

But what about the girl, or was there ever a "girl from Ipanema"? There was indeed and in fact, there still is. The song and lyrics were inspired in 1962 by the beauty of then 14-year-old Heloisa Pinheiro. A schoolgirl, Helo regularly sauntered past the Veloso Bar sidewalk cafe on Montenegro Street in Ipanema on her way home from school. Looking on, enchanted, were Jobim and Moraes, two of Rio de Janeiro's more famed bohemians. After several weeks following Helo's daily passage, the two felt sufficiently inspired to turn out the song that made them famous. Today, the street has been renamed after the poet Moraes, and the bar is appropriately called **A Garota de Ipanema** (The Girl from Ipanema).

Looking back with a smile, Helo today, still strikingly beautiful, attributes her immortalization to "being at the right place at the right time." Other observers, however, most notably Jobim himself, insist that Helo at 14, represented **the** image of the stunning Rio beauty. Says Jobim: "She had long golden hair, these bright green eyes that shone at you and a fantastic figure. Let's just say she had everything in the right place."

Composer Tom Jobim with the original girl from Ipanema Helo (left) and her daughter.

The impact on Helo of the Jobim-Moraes team's inspiration was immediate: "One day a Brazilian journalist told me a song had been inspired by me—I couldn't believe it. Before I knew it, I was being interviewed and appearing in magazines and this is still going on. I was glad to be chosen but I must admit I didn't realize at that time what this meant."

The fame of being the girl from Ipanema eventually lured Helo into modeling and television where she appeared in Brazilian soap operas and hosted women's programs. In 1988, at 40 years of age, Helo is a successful businesswoman who, with her husband, owns a stereo shop called Ipanema Som (Ipanema Sound) and a modeling agency in São Paulo where the girl from Ipanema now lives. The mother of a son and three daughters, she is proud to note that her eldest daughter, Kiki, 19, is the newest Girl from Ipanema, having won the title in a 1986 Rio beauty contest.

Today, composer Jobim, who turned 61 in 1988, has become a world-renowned tunesmith. His songs have been recorded by everyone from Frank Sinatra to Sarah Vaughan and with his own youthful, family group, he appears regularly at international stops such as Carnegie Hall.

Moraes, who studied law in Rio and English literature at Oxford, died in 1980. He wrote reams of romantic poems and the lyrics for numerous songs including the score for the film, Black Orpheus (1959). But none of his works ever matched the success of The Girl from Ipanema.

And today, when Heloisa Pinheiro passes, do the men still go 'ahhh?'

"Sometimes, I'll be walking down the street and somebody will come up behind me and start whistling or singing the song. It's very flattering and I still get a kick out of it, even after all these years. It's a beautiful song from a beautiful era when love was something really romantic."

ahhh...those
eauties
rom
panema.

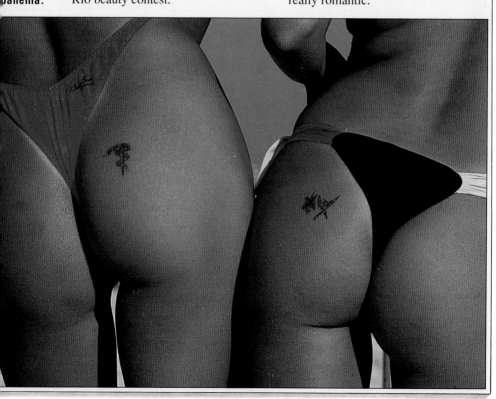

free-spirited youth and daring, Ipanema is virtually the only beach where women go topless, although not many do. Palm trees add to the special, intimate setting of Ipanema which faces offshore islands of the Cagarras chain. At sunset, the sidewalk is crowded with lovers of all ages, walking hand in hand through the crepuscular light of day's end, a timeless ebb and flow that continues into the evening's darkness. Less boisterous and rambunctious than the beachfront of Copacabana, Ipanema preserves the romance of Rio more than any of the city's 23 beaches.

For more practical pursuits, such as shopping and eating, Ipanema is also in a class of its own. Until shopping centers began to flourish recently, the neighborhood boutiques and shops were practically the only options for Rio's discriminating shoppers. The high quality of their goods, however, still attract a significant portion of the city's well-heeled clientele. Ipanema's elegant boutiques also remain the favorite choices of the neighborhood's residents who enjoy the ease of shopping close to home.

The Hippie Fair: A modern tradition of Ipanema is the **Hippie Fair**, on Sundays at **Praça General Osorio**, 9 a.m. to 6 p.m. Started in 1975, the fair is now less hippie and more sophisticated. But it is still a pleasant, open-air bazaar of Brazilian handicrafts where natives and tourists mix easily.

As befits the wealth of its residents, Ipanema has also become Rio's jewelry center. The block of **Rua Visconde de Piraja** between **Rua Garcia d'Avila** and **Rua Anibal Mendonça** is one of the world's leading centers of fine jewelry. Located here are the headquarters of **H. Stern**, Brazil's top-ranked jeweler and one of the most respected in the world. On the same block are branches of **Amsterdam Sauer** and **Roditi**, numbers two and three respectively plus the stores of four other rivals, making a total of seven jewelers on one block. During the peak summer season, hundreds of foreign tourists are ushered each day to this street in buses chartered by the jewelry chains.

Unlike Copacabana, Ipanema's nightlife is not dominated by beach hotels of which the neighborhood has few. In its entire extension, the Ipanema-Leblon beach has only five hotels and three beachside bars, a far cry from Copacabana. Ipanema, however, does have one of the city's finest hotels, the **Caesar Park**, favored by business travelers. Famed for its service, the hotel also offers two of Ipanema's better restaurants, the **Mariko**, considered Rio's finest Japanese restaurant, and the **Petronius**, an elegant dining option serving international cuisine. On Saturdays, the Caesar Park puts out what *aficionados* consider to be one of the city's top *feijoadas* and on Sundays, the hotel serves unbeatable *cozido*, a traditional Brazilian dish that amounts to a mouth-watering combination of pork tenderloin, sausages and vegetables simmered for

A family outing in Rio's Botanical Garden.

hours to capture each disparate taste and accompanied by a wide variety of delicious sauces.

It is beyond the beach, though, that the art of good eating is most evident in Ipanema. There are fast food outlets for a quick hamburger, croissant, crepe or pizza plus fruit juice bars and ice-cream parlors. For meat eaters, the **Porcão**, Rua Barão da Torre 218, is one of Rio's premier steak houses, serving up as much as you can eat via the popular *rodizio* system. An Ipanema landmark is the **Lord Jim Pub**, Rua Paul Redfern 63, an authentic English pub. The pub is a favorite watering hole for Rio's foreign community and is the only restaurant in town that offers fish and chips and Yorkshire pudding as well as darts. The neighborhood's real fame, though, is as the home of intimate, sophisticated restaurants. Among Ipanema's top eateries are:

Le Streghe, Rua Prudente de Morais 129: Excellent Italian food, leaning towards *nuova cucina* although not too far. Sparkling, good and unpretentious. Downstairs is the **Caligula** nightclub, a popular choice among *cariocas* for dining and disco or relaxed conversation around the piano bar.

Satiricon, Rua Barão da Torre 192: an attractive and reasonably-priced home to excellent seafood.

Esplanada Grill, Rua Barão da Torre 600: as Rio's trend setter, Ipanema usually is the site of the city's latest "in" restaurant. For 1988, that term fit this Ipanema-based steak house, easily distinguished by the long lines that form at its entrance.

Negresco, Rua Barão da Torre 348: a small, quiet cove for Portuguese cuisine at its best.

Rive Gauche, Av. Epitácio Pessoa 1484: one of a select few of Ipanema's restaurants located along the banks of the beautiful Rodrigo de Freitas lagoon. Traditional French cuisine, intimate setting, live music and a spectacular view. Downstairs is the **Biblos Bar** one of a handful of singles bars in Rio.

Sipping beer at outdoor cafe.

Antonino, Av. Epitácio Pessoa 1244: another perfect combination of quality cuisine (international) and romantic view.

Leblon: Neighboring **Leblon** is, like Ipanema, a largely residential neighborhood of highrise apartment buildings extending up the side of Dois Irmãos mountain. While it doesn't possess the extensive shopping areas of Ipanema, Leblon is home to the **Rio Design Center** (119 Avenida Afranio de Melo Franco) where the latest in furniture and decorative design is on display.

Nearby on Rua Paul Redfern (named after an American aviator who was lost in the Amazon) is a Leblon landmark, an authentic English pub complete with a call box straight out of London. The **Lord Jim Pub**, built at the whim of a homesick British expatriate, is a popular watering hole for Rio's foreign community and is the only restaurant in town that offers fish and chips and Yorkshire pudding.

Traditionally a quiet neighborhood, Leblon has recently begun to kick up its heels. Two of Rio's best nightclubs, **Scala and Plataforma**, are now located in Leblon. Both of them offer excellent reviews highlighting carnival and samba by the city's most eye-catching showgirls. Scala (divided into two theater-clubs) also offers top Brazilian and international singers and is the venue for some of Rio's liveliest balls during carnival.

Leblon has also made its contributions to the dining out map of Rio. Among the neighborhood's culinary prizes are **Dinho's Place**, a quality steak house at Rua Dias Ferreira 57; **Florentino**, a favored restaurant-bar of Rio's new money set at Av. General San Martin 1227; **Antiquarius**, Rua Aristides Espinola 19, this elegant and expensive Portuguese restaurant is packed with antiques and specializes in cod (*bacalhau*) dishes; **Un, Deux Trois**, Rua Bartolomeu Mitre 123, undistinguished food but a fine upstairs

Left, cold beer on a hot day. Right, an Ipanema artist.

nightclub which presents many of Brazil's top singers; the **Buffalo Grill**, Rua Rita Ludolff, an attractive and top quality steak house.

Hangouts for the young: The Dois Irmãos end of Leblon, called **Baixa Leblon**, is a hangout for Rio's restless youth. Their favorite places to pass the night include the **Luna Bar** (984 Av. Ataulfo de Paiva, open until 5 a.m.) and **Alvaro's** (500 Av. Ataulfo de Paiva, closes at 2 a.m.).

The area is filled with other small bars and restaurants. On summer nights and weekends its streets and sidewalks overflow with young people who come from throughout Rio for the action.

Another enclave for the young has taken hold at Ipanema's **Praça Nossa Senhora da Paz**. The streets surrounding this public square are packed on weekends by cars, dune buggies and motorcycles as well as the action-oriented youth of the south zone. Besides pizza parlors, sidewalk bars and a disco, the square is also the site of one

of Ipanema's most respected restaurants, **Sal e Pimenta** with its lively downstairs piano bar, **Alo Alo**. You can also find Rio's most "in" private club, the **Hippopotamus**.

Following the highrises inland, you will uncover another timeless symbol of Rio's romantic side, the **lagoon**. More than any of the city's beautiful settings, the lagoon has acquired a social function. Thanks to its refreshing presence, this one-and-a-half sq mile space (2,500 sq meters) has been saved from the onward march of apartment buildings. The tranquil, open expanse of water provides a breathing space for the high-density south beaches of Rio.

A natural lake originally part of a 16th-century sugar plantation, the lagoon has proven to be a dogged survivor. Numerous attempts, some partially successful, have been made to fill it in. The lagoon today is roughly one-third its original size, but with the passage of years, **Lagoa Rodrigo de Freitas** has become a sacred appendage of Ipanema

A novel approach to tandem sunbathing.

and the surrounding neighborhoods. The residents of the beautiful apartments that ring the lake consider it their personal shrine, a sort of *carioca* holy place whose beauty they defend with maximum passion and energy. Their latest victory ended the practice of dumping untreated sewage into the lagoon, thus removing a stench that was at times unbearable and is bringing back the fish. The *lagoa* has generated a lifestyle of its own, dedicated to the outdoors and nature.

Mountain scenery: Around its winding shore, joggers, walkers and cyclists beat a steady path, inspired by the very finest of Rio's mountain scenery— Corcovado and the rich green tapestry of the Tijuca Forest, Dois Irmãos Mountain and the distant flat top of Gavea Mountain. From sunrise to sunset, the colors of sky, water and mountains shift and change, sometimes forming solid blues, grays and greens, then into rainbow streaks or suddenly breaking into shapes and colors that draw approving smiles from awed onlookers. In the mornings, lines form for the honor of playing tennis on one of the lagoon's public courts. In the afternoons, the wealthy and near wealthy gather at the private clubs that have sprouted on the banks of the lagoon. At night, an endless stream of cars forms a ribbon of light around the *lagoa*, home to many of Rio's most famous restaurants and bars such as the **Bar da Lagoa**, known for its insulting waiters (a tradition of the house) and **Chiko's Bar**, an "in" spot for drinks and romance. On weekends, picnickers frequent the lagoon or stroll through the **Catacumba Park** across the street, the former site of one of Rio's largest hillside slums.

Botanical garden: On the Corcovado side of the lagoon, close to the mountain is Rio's **Botanical Garden** on **Rua Jardim Botanico**, an area of 340 acres (100 hectares) containing some 135,000 plants and trees which represent over 5,000 species. Created by Portuguese prince regent Dom João VI in 1808, the garden was used to encourage the introduction into Brazil of varieties of plants and trees from other parts of the world. The tranquil garden is a refreshing respite from the heat and urban rush of Rio and deserves a long, studied walk through its myriad examples of tropical greenery. At its entrance is a double row of 134 royal palms, a soaring, majestic avenue planted in 1842.

Nature is also the theme at the **Parque da Cidade**, 116 acres (34 hectares) of relaxing greenery in neighboring **Gavea**. On its spacious grounds is the **Museu da Cidade** (City Museum) with photographs, maps and exhibitions reviewing the birth and growth of Rio de Janeiro.

Another landmark of Gavea is the city's 19th-century race track called simply, **Jockey (Praça Santos Dumont 31)**. Races are held on Saturday and Sunday afternoons and on Monday and Thursday evenings.

Left, afternnon concert in Praque da Catacumba. Right, street sweeper with an ear for music.

SÃO CONRADO
AND THE BARRA

South of Ipanema are the outlying beaches, the most isolated and therefore the most unspoiled of Rio. The first, **São Conrado**, rests in an idyllic natural amphitheater, surrounded on three sides by thickly forested mountains and hills including the **Gavea Mountain**, a massive block of granite more impressive in shape and size than Sugarloaf.

Closing the circle on this small, enclosed valley is the São Conrado beach which is popular among the affluent youth of Rio. São Conrado can be reached from Ipanema by a tunnel underneath Dois Irmãos Mountain but a far more interesting route is **Avenida Niemeyer**, an engineering marvel completed in 1917. The avenue hugs the mountain's cliffs from the end of Leblon to São Conrado, looking at times straight down into the sea with striking vistas of the ocean and Ipanema looking back. The best view is saved for the end where the avenue descends to São Conrado and suddenly, the ocean beach and the towering presence of Gavea emerge into sight. In a city where the spectacular becomes commonplace, this is a view that startles with its suddenness and unmatched beauty.

Vidigal: On the cliff side of Avenida Niemeyer is the neighborhood of Vidigal, an eclectic mix of rich and poor where the mountainside homes of the former have been slowly surrounded by the advancing shacks of the Vidigal *favela*, one of Rio's largest shantytowns. On the ocean side of the avenue is the Sheraton Hotel, one of only two resort hotels in Rio. Although access to beaches is guaranteed by law in Rio, the Sheraton's imposing presence which encompasses the entire width of Vidigal beach, gives it the added distinction of being the city's only hotel with a de facto private beach. Unlike the hotels of

Copacabana and Ipanema, the Sheraton and its fellow resort hotel, the Inter-Continental located down the road in São Conrado, are blessed with ample space. This has permitted the construction of large swimming pools as well as lighted tennis courts, both of which are rarities at Rio hotels. The two hotels also boast excellent dining and two top-rated nightclubs, making them the center of nightlife for this area of Rio.

São Conrado: Space, and the absence of the crush of Copacabana and Ipanema, are the main factors that separate the outlying beaches from their better known neighbors. While compact in area, São Conrado has an uncrowded openness guaranteed by the 18-hole Gavea Golf Course which runs through its middle.

A sugar plantation during colonial times, São Conrado remained largely undeveloped until the 1960s when the construction of the Nacional Hotel on its beach finally brought a spurt of development to the neighborhood. By then, however, the golf course was already in place as were dozens of elegant homes that surrounded the links, thus limiting area available for apartments. Of the original plantation, the main house and its spectacular grounds known collectively as **Vila Riso** are still intact and open to visitors.

One of Rio's more exclusive addresses, São Conrado is also a near perfect microcosm of Rio society. On the valley floor live middle and upper middle class *cariocas* in sometimes luxurious apartments, homes and condominium complexes which line the beach front and flank the golf course. The link's privileged location makes it one of the most beautiful in the world and adds to the dominating presence of green in São Conrado. But as lush as São Conrado is, its beauty is marred by a swath cut out of the hillside vegetation where **Rocinha**, Brazil's largest *favela* spreads like a blight across the mountain from top to bottom. In this swarming anthill of narrow alleys and streets,

Preceding page: Soaring over São Conrado. Below, the Barra da Tijuca, Rio's high growth area.

over 80,000 people live (some estimates are double this), most of them in tumble-down brick houses and shacks, pressed tightly together side-by-side.

Hang gliders: At the end of São Conrado, a highway surges past the massive Gavea, a point where hang gliders soar overhead preparing for their landings on the beach to the left. On the right, another road climbs up the mountainside leading to the takeoff point for the bird men of Rio. This same road leads back to the Tijuca Forest and Corcovado, passing through the thick tropical forest and providing memorable views of the beaches below. For tourists who wish to experience the sensation of jumping off a wooden runway 1,680 feet (510 meters) in the air to glide down to the beach below, several of Rio's more experienced and trustworthy hang glider pilots offer tandem rides for $60. For information call the Rio Hang Gliders Association at 220-4704 or ask at your hotel.

Barra Da Tijuca: From São Conrado, an elevated roadway continues on to the far southern beaches, twisting along the sharply vertical cliffs where the mansions of the rich hang suspended at precarious angles. Emerging from a tunnel, you are suddenly face to face with the **Barra da Tijuca**, Rio's current high-growth area for the middle class. This vast lowland with mountains in the western horizon is Rio's answer to America's suburbia. Low rises and homes fill most of its streets with a growing army of high rises shooting up along the beachfront. The Barra, as it is called, is where Rio's largest shopping center is located, a recent phenomenon that has captured the imagination of *carioca* consumers. Unlike the more traditional beach neighborhoods of Copacabana and Ipanema where shops, supermarkets and stores are all within walking distance, in Barra, distances are greater and the car is king.

The settlement of Barra da Tijuca began officially in 1624 when the area was presented as a land grant to a Por-

Suburbia, Rio style.

tuguese nobleman. At the time composed primarily of marshland (the name Tijuca supposedly means marshy area and was given to the region by African slaves), it was largely ignored by its first and subsequent owners. Its only early claim to fame was the result of an attempt by a French pirate in 1710 to attack Rio by surprise, landing first in the Barra and proceeding overland to strike the city from behind. His scheme, however, failed. In the 19th century, the Barra was divided into small farms and continued unnoticed by the rest of Rio until the 1960s when the construction of new roads improved access to the area. Since then, the Barra has enjoyed a rapid and disorganized expansion. A 1969 urbanization plan drawn up by Lucio Costa, the planner of Brasilia, was never put into practice and till today, the Barra suffers from a lack of basic services. Many of the streets are unpaved and a sewage system is only now being installed.

But despite its growth problems, the Barra is where Rio's future lies, for *cariocas* and tourists alike. This is the only large beach area that has not yet been completely developed and space is Rio's most valued commodity. Coming from Rio's high density neighborhoods, the Barra is like an enormous breath of fresh area. Much of it is still vacant lots, waiting for the city's next real estate boom which will certainly occur here.

Longest beach: The Barra beach, running for 11 miles (18 km), is Rio's longest and during the week its most deserted. On weekends, it fills up with bumper to bumper traffic on the beach drive, Avenida **Sernambetiba**. The beach is now attracting the tourism trade, with several buildings along Sernambetiba converted to apart-hotels, one and two-bedroom apartments with kitchens that are rented as rooms. Most are at rates well below those of comparable hotels in Copacabana, Ipanema and São Conrado. Several of the apart-hotels are part of condomin-

Forested hills surround Grumari Beach.

ium complexes, providing guests with access to swimming pools, tennis courts, saunas and exercise centers.

The condominiums themselves are proof of the *cariocas'* growing desire to escape the urban crush that has claimed the city's more traditional residential areas. In the Barra, there is room to park your car, take walks, grow gardens and engage in a multitude of leisure activities not permitted by the closed-in living conditions in Copacabana and Ipanema. The epitome of what has been dubbed the Barra lifestyle is the condominium, some of them sprawling complexes of highrise apartments and carefully landscaped homes.

What has been missing in the Barra has been an active nightlife but this too, is changing. In recent years, several excellent restaurants have opened up along the beachfront avenue and near the Barra Shopping Center. Highly regarded Barra restaurants include: **Rodeio**, the Rio branch of one of São Paulo's top steak houses, virtually un-beatable for the quality of its char-broiled sizzling steaks, located at **Casa Shopping**, an attractive Barra da Tijuca shopping mall that specializes in home furnishings; Porcão, a *rodizio* all-you-can-eat steak house, Av. Armando Lombardi 591; **Le Petit Paris**, an excellent and unpretentious French restaurant, Av. Sernambetiba 6250; **Nino**, part of a chain of businessmen's restaurants with good food (international cuisine) and a serious, businesslike setting at Av. Sernambetiba 330; **La Mole**, another chain restaurant that has set up a successful Barra branch, good reliable Italian food, including pizzas, for a more than reasonable price, Rua Armando Lombardt, 175.

In addition, Vidigal and São Conrado offer two of Rio's better restaurants. In the Sheraton Hotel, diners will discover what many food critics consider to be the city's best and most luxurious restaurant, **Valentino's**, famed for the creativity of its cuisine. Food lovers all types and ages will be entirely satisfied

Real estate boom in the Barra.

with Valentino's northern Italian, *nuova cucina* dishes, served in an elegant setting with the accompaniment of romantic piano music. Nearby at the Inter-Continental Hotel is another dining treat, the **Monseigneur** restaurant, home to top-quality French cuisine. Leaning towards *nouvelle cuisine* but with a touch of classic French cooking, the Monseigneur combines old and new in a sophisticated setting.

This area of Rio has also become home to the fast food revolution which established its first foothold in the Barra, led by McDonald's which is present at the Barra Shopping Center.

Discotheques, small bars and *samba* clubs have also invaded the Barra but the neighborhood's most distinctive nighttime feature is the myriad trailers that dot Avenida Sernambetiba.

The Barra's trailers: The Barra's answer to Copacabana's sidewalk cafes, nondescript trailers sell cold drinks and hot food during the day to bathers but on weekend nights, they become convivial meeting points for couples and singles. Large crowds gather around the more popular trailers, some of which are converted at night into *samba* centers or *pagodes*. Originally confined to backyards in the city's lower class northern neighborhoods, *pagodes* were no more than *samba* sing-alongs where musicians, professional and amateur, engaged in midnight jam sessions. In the move to the affluent south zone of Rio, the *pagodes* have maintained their purist *samba* qualities but have acquired commercial overtones, becoming in effect open-air *samba* bars. For romantics, however, there can be no quibbling over the splendid image of the Barra's beachside trailers with the sound of the surf crashing behind them, guitar and percussion instruments pounding out the *samba* in the night and scores of fun-seekers singing along—just right for an evening out in Rio de Janeiro.

Romance and the Barra have a more palpable connection in an area where dozens of motels have sprung up over

Roadside vendor offers live crabs.

the years. In Rio, as throughout Brazil, motels are for lovers and rooms are rented out by the hour, replete with such facilities as saunas, whirlpools, and ceiling mirrors. Some of the Barra's love centers outshine Rio's five-star hotels in luxury and sheer indulgence. Originally aimed at providing young couples with privacy for romantic encounters as Brazil's youth tend to live with their families until they are married, the motels have retained this function and added another—serving as meeting places for adult love affairs as well. Because of this, the Barra's motels are usually hidden behind high walls with private garages for each room to protect guests from inquisitive eyes and unfortunate chance encounters with the wrong person. Many married couples also frequent the motels in search of an added sense of adventure.

Recreio Dos Bandeirantes: At the end of the Barra is the **Recreio dos Bandeirantes**, a small beach with a natural breakwater creating the effect of a quiet bay. From Recreio, the road climbs sharply along the mountainside and descends to **Prainha**, a beach popular among surfers, and then to **Grumari**, a marvelously isolated beach where part of the movie, *Blame It on Rio* was filmed. From Grumari, a narrow, pot-holed road climbs seemingly straight up the hillside from the top of which visitors have another of Rio's unforgettable views, the expanse of the **Guaratiba flatlands** and a long, sliver of beach stretching off into the distance, the **Restinga de Marambaia**, an army property that is unfortunately off limits to bathers. Down the hill is **Pedra da Guaratiba**, a quaint fishing village that beckons with the best seafood restaurants of Rio—**Candido's**, **Tia Palmira** and **Quatro Sete Meia**).

All of this—from São Conrado to Guaratiba—adds up to an exhilarating day trip topped by a leisurely two-hour lunch over shrimps or fish dishes at any of the Guaratiba restaurants, the favorites of the Rio "in" crowd.

Seafood repast at Candido's restaurant in Pedra de Guaratiba.

PETRÓPOLIS

Home is where the inheritance is.

The pastel hues and green gardens of **Petrópolis** and **Teresópolis**—Rio de Janeiro's mountain retreats—are a nation's 19th-century imperial inheritance, the material traces left by independent Brazil's first rulers, Emperors Pedro I and Pedro II.

Petrópolis: Petrópolis, especially, is like a warm, antique-cluttered, ancestral home. It could be a village of grandmothers.

Rio de Janeiro State's leading mountain resort and fourth largest commercial center, Petrópolis is chiefly a monument to Pedro II, emperor of Brazil from 1831 until his exile in 1889 (he died in France two years later). Pedro II's 58-year reign put him in a longevity class with the likes of England's Victoria and France's Louis XIV.

Petrópolis was first envisioned in the 1830s by Emperor Pedro I, who purchased land in the spectacular *Serra Flumenense* for a projected summer palace. But it was his son, Pedro II, who actually built the palace and the quaint town surrounding it, starting in the 1840s. The idea was to maintain a refreshing refuge from Rio's wilting summer heat.

Pedroll: Petrópolis, like all good sight-seeing experiences, is as much a state of mind as it is a collection of buildings and natural settings. And that state of mind, like nearly everything about its founder, is friendly, human and modest. Pedro II was a rarity in human history—a wise, scholarly and diplomatic king. During his more than half century on the Bragança throne, Brazil remained comparatively peaceful and prosperous while most of its neighbors seethed with civil strife or settled into austere poverty. During the American Civil War, President Abraham Lincoln told intimates the only man in the world he trusted to arbitrate between North and South was Pedro II of Brazil.

Petrópolis is not as august as its European counterparts. But Brazilians are justifiably proud of the humanity of their kings rather than their grandeur.

Scenic ride from Rio: The city is only 40 miles (65 km) from Rio. The modern **Rio-Petrópolis Highway** is an engineering marvel. Its concrete bridges soar over green valleys and the road curves around mountain walls revealing vistas that seem like aerial photography. From sea level in Rio, the highway reaches 2750 feet (840 meters) during an approximately hour-and-a-quarter jaunt. On the way, visitors can still glimpse traces of the old **Petrópolis Highway**, a perilous cobbled affair that once kept royal road workers busy the year round with repairs. The imperial road is still in use today but only for the intrepid. The one-hour climb up the mountains provides a rare sensation of stepping back into history. The road though, for most of the way is wide enough for only one car at a time.

Streets of Petrópolis: The medium-sized city (population: 270,000) of factory workers and shopkeepers is centered around two busy streets, **Rua do Imperador** and **Rua 15 de Novembro**, the only part of town with buildings over five stories high. The two thoroughfares are divided by a waterway and aged shady trees that shed their leaves in autumn. Temperatures are lower than in Rio and the city's sweater and jacket-clad inhabitants give it an autumnal air during the cool months.

Perpendicular to Rua do Imperador is the city's lush boulevard of kings, **Avenida 7 de Setembro**. The avenue is divided by a slow-moving canal and by shady trees that intertwine with the bushy foliage of the nearby **imperial park**. Its surface is partially cobbled and horse-drawn carriages for rent by the hour form an old-fashioned taxi stand on its sun-dappled stones.

Left, a refreshing bloom of wildflowers on a mountainside near Petrópolis.

The area around the **Summer Palace**, now called the **Imperial Museum**, itself is crowded with tropical and temperate climate trees and shrubs and is criss-crossed by carefully kept pathways. The emperor was fond of Brazil's flora which are still richly exhibited in the royal gardens.

The rose-colored palace, fronting Avenida 7 de Setembro, is modest for a royal dwelling. Everything seems antique. On the topaz esplanade in front of the mansion stands an old-fashioned newsstand. An aged, colorfully uniformed functionary dwells within. He is selling…What else?…antique news in the form of historical society bulletins with learned articles and quaint photos relating to the royal family.

Imperial museum: The palace was converted into a museum in 1943. (Hours are noon to 5:00 p.m. Tuesday through Sunday). Visitors are asked to don felt slippers and must pad gingerly over the gleaming *jacarandá* and brazilwood floors. The museum's modest

furnishings attest to the bourgeois character of its builder, Pedro II, who ordered construction to begin in 1845 (work was completed 10 years later), while its second floor collection of kingly personal artifacts, including telescope and telephone, is a reminder of his scientific dabbling.

The palace's wood-panelled chambers are inviting, the furnishings rich but not extravagant. Among items of interest are the **crown jewels**—a glistening frame of 77 pearls and 639 diamonds—and the colorful skirts and cloaks of the emperor's ceremonial wardrobe, including a cape of bright Amazon toucan feathers. Royal photographs on the second floor, however, show that Brazil's second king felt more at home in conservative suits than in flowing robes.

The second floor exhibits also contain a reconstructed throne room. Its uncomfortable royal couch, more like a fixture from a luxurious bathroom than a chair fit for man or beast, is overbear-

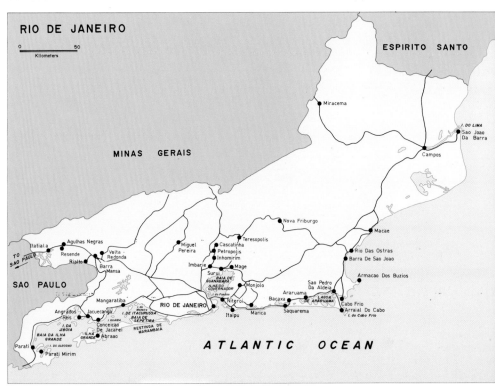

ing. Pedro II preferred the small, intimately furnished office at the rear of the room. Its desk, chairs and gleaming telephone could be the furnishings of a 19th-century telegraph office. It was from this room that Pedro II ruled Brazil six months of the year.

Residence of Dom Pedro's heirs: Across the square from the palace is the former royal guesthouse, now the residence of Dom Pedro's heirs. And the king's in. At least, most of the time. Dom Pedro de Orleans e Bragança, Pedro II's great grandson, is the home's owner and chief symbol of monarchism in Brazil. Although the house is closed to the public, Dom Pedro himself can sometimes be seen walking in the square chatting with local residents and, occasionally, tourists.

A few blocks up Avenida 7 de Setembro is the French Gothic-style **Catedral de São Pedro de Alcântara**. Begun in 1884, the imposing structure was only finished 55 years later. The bodies of Pedro II, his wife Tereza, his daughter

Isabel and her husband the Count of Eu, were interred in the partially completed cathedral in 1925. The four were principals in Brazil's late 19th-century royal drama. The emperor and his family were expelled from Brazil in 1889 after a military coup. They died in European exile. His daughter and son-in-law survived until the early 1920s but never returned to Brazil. Finally, in 1925, the Brazilian government permitted descendants to bring the bodies back to Petrópolis for burial in the magnificent cathedral which had been built for precisely that purpose.

From the cathedral, a web of tree-shaded, cobbled streets spreads into residential Petrópolis. The city is delightful for its rose-colored homes, including many which were once the dwellings of members of the royal family, its numerous overgrown private gardens and public parks and the simple beauty of its streets, which once brought a royal flush of pride to the city's earnest creator.

Dedo de Deus (Finger of God) mountain as seen from Teresópolis.

A few blocks beyond the cathedral, on **Rua Alfredo Pachá**, is the 1879 **Crystal Palace**, a glass-and-iron frame still used for gardening and art exhibits. The palace was built almost entirely of panels shipped from France. Its style is similar to that of other overly decorated Victorian pavilions once popular in Europe and is a marvel of solar heating, rainbow colors and acoustics. A pair of fountains in the adjacent garden send spray more than 20 feet (6 meters) into the air.

A few blocks from the Crystal Palace, on the **Catholic University** campus, is the unusual, slightly spooky **Santos Dumont House**.

Santos Dumont: Alberto Santos Dumont, credited by Brazilians and many Europeans as inventor of the airplane, lived in the strange abode, which he himself designed, from 1918 until his death at age 59 in 1932. Scion of wealthy Franco-Brazilian land-owners, Santos Dumont spent two decades in Paris around the turn-of-the-century.

There, in 1906, he made the first fully documented flight in a heavier-than-air machine. (The Wright Brothers had made a previous flight—at Kitty Hawk, North Carolina in 1903—but only produced documentation for it in 1908.)

Santos Dumont's home, now a museum, is a reminder of his eccentricity. The house has only one room. Santos Dumont used no tables, only shelves designed for various purposes, no staircases, no bed (he slept on top of a chest of drawers) and no kitchen. His meals were delivered by a local hotel. The house employs built-in, wide-step ladders, one of which leads to a loft where his unique bed is located. But the steps on the ladder entering the house are cut so that one side of each is missing. In this way the ladder obliges users "to always start off on the right hand side," which Santos Dumont regarded as a sign of good luck.

The inventor committed suicide at São Paulo's Santos beach resort after telling friends he was despondent over

The Imperial Museum, former residence of the king.

the use of the airplane in warfare.

Other attractions: Other Petrópolis attractions include the sprawling Normandy-style **Hotel Quitandinha**. Completed in 1945, the luxuriously appointed structure was designed to serve as Brazil's leading hotel-gambling complex. A few months after its inauguration, however, gambling was outlawed in Brazil by the Administration of President Eurico Dutra. Quitandinha never fully recovered. Today, the still striking complex, located on the Rio-Petrópolis Highway five miles (eight km) from the main Petrópolis shopping area, is an expensive condominium-cum-social club. (Managers normally set aside a few rooms for hotel guests.) Quitandinha's lobby, night club and ballrooms are vast, gleaming expanses that look like sets from Hollywood musicals of the 1930s. Like most things in Petrópolis, Quitandinha is a journey through time.

More up-to-date Petrópolis attractions include the **Imperial Ski Lift** and **Artificial Ski Run** at the end of **Rua Silva Jardim** three miles (five km) from downtown. The trip up the ski lift—which affords an awesome view of Petrópolis from the 2980-feet (910-meters) summit—is worth the trouble even if a spin down the artificial ski ramp is not.

Five miles (eight km) from downtown, on **Ruo Maestro Octávio Maul**, is the delightful **Florália nursery**. Pleasantly landscaped rose beds and a quaint tearoom help foster a refreshing away-from-it-all atmosphere. The nursery hosts an annual exposition of rare orchids.

Shopping: In downtown Petrópolis, on long, winding **Rua Tereza**, shoppers will find factory outlets for many of Petrópolis' more than 500 textile mills. Bargain hunters delight in excellent buys for everything from jeans and sweaters to children's clothing.

Other shopping highlights include decoration and hardwood furniture outlets on Avenida 15 de Novembro.

Emperor's tomb in the cathedral of Petrópolis.

Petrópolis is also an antique-hunter's paradise with a dozen bric-á-brac-cluttered curiosity shops scattered around downtown. The most noted, **Solar Imperial** at **Rua Coronel Veiga 1080**, could easily double as a museum.

A string of brightly-painted Italian cantinas, with names like Don Corleone and Falconi's, along the main shopping corridor, are intimate and inexpensive. A soda fountain in a five-and-dime store across the plaza from the Imperial Museum looks like small town U.S.A. circa 1940.

Teresópolis: The 33 mile (53 km) jaunt to Teresópolis along steep mountain roads can be made in about one hour. The small towns and valleys of the Serra preserve a sleepy, 19th-century pace (as does the highway maintenance). Antique shops and furniture stores dot the road.

Teresópolis, named after Pedro II's wife the Empress Tereza Cristina, was planned in the 1880s but only incorporated in 1891, two years after the royal couple was exiled.

The picturesque town, 57 miles (92 km) from Rio on the broad Rio-**Teresópolis Highway**, clings to the edge of the *Serra Fluminese* at a bracing 2,960-foot (902 meter) elevation. Population is about 115,000.

Scenic views: Chief attractions are an encompassing, though distant view of Rio's **Guanabara Bay**, complete with the mountainous profile of Rio, and the city's proximity to spectacular **Serra dos Orgãos National Park**. The park, lovingly landscaped with broad lawns and old-fashioned masonry fountains and patios, is dominated by a ridge of sharp peaks. The highest, **Pedra do Sino**, is 7410 feet (2,260 meters) above sea level. But the most striking summit, just below Pedra do Sino, is a rocky spike called **O Dedo de Deus** (The Finger of God). On clear days, the chiseled profile of the Serra dos Orgãos can be seen from many points in Rio itself.

Shopping, restaurant, hotel: Downtown Teresópolis, which occupies a

Banana trees blending in with the scenic rugged mountain of Petrópolis.

narrow valley in the shadow of the *Serra*, offers interesting shopping opportunities in elegant home furnishings, rugs and wall decorations. On Saturdays and Sundays, a handicraft fair is held downtown at the Praça Hygino da Silveina.

For residents of Rio, Teresópolis is a favorite stop for a long, hearty Brazilian lunch in the middle of a day-long drive through the mountains. The city's most famed restaurant is the **Taverna Alpina** at **Rua Duque de Caxias 131.** The Alpina is a convivial wood-panelled, Alpine-style beer hall serving sausages, sauerkraut and other German specialities, all washed down with cold beer.

Other popular eateries are: the **Maison Louis** down the street from the Alpina, famed for its fondues and steaks; the **Cantina Riviera Italiana** at **Praça Baltazar da Silveira 112** for traditional pastas and pizza; and the **Dom Vito**, at **Rua 1 de Agosto 40,** another Italian restaurant but with a more exotic menu.

Teresópolis and environs are also home to several excellent resort hotels. The most traditional is the **Pinheiros Hotel**, a romantic, secluded honeymoon hotel. Located at the end of a bumpy country road four miles (six km) from downtown, the Pinheiros is noted for its near complete isolation. The grounds blend in with the surrounding forest and the hotel buildings—small, pink-pastel bungalows and mansion houses—are typical of imperial-era Brazilian architecture. The overall impression is one of tranquility and remoteness, as if visitors had stumbled *Through the Looking Glass*—an appropriate metaphor for Teresópolis itself.

Nova Friburgo: Continuing east from Teresópolis is the city of **Nova Friburgo** (population 100,000), a Swiss outpost in the heart of the tropics. The city was founded in 1818 when Portuguese King Dom João VI, then living in exile in Brazil, authorized the immigration of 400 Swiss families from the canton of Freibourg. Upon arrival, the immigrants settled in the mountains and dubbed their new home Nova Friburgo or New Freibourg

Today the city remembers its founders in the rich green of its flowering parks and the alpine architecture of many of its homes. Walks through the quiet city streets, long hikes through the forest and visits to nearby peaks and rock formations are the favorite pastimes of visitors to Friburgo.

Along the highway between Teresópolis and Nova Friburgo are many of the best hotels of the region. Several are known as *fazenda* hotels, literally farm hotels, a Brazilian phrase used to describe a mountain-style resort hotel with large gardens, trees and ample recreational facilities. The most sophisticated is the **Hotel-Fazenda Rosa dos Ventos**, a European-style hotel with tennis courts, horseback riding, saunas, a private forest reserve and international cuisine, the type of retreat that Pedro II could well have appreciated.

A long way to go—a salesman with his wares on the highway.

BUZIOS AND THE SUN COAST

According to history books, Buzios was discovered by the Portuguese at the start of the 16th century. Locals, however, know better. Buzios was actually discovered in 1964 by Brigitte Bardot. Convinced by an Argentine friend to visit this tropical paradise, Brigitte spent two well-documented stays in Buzios, parading her famed bikini-clad torso along its unmatched beaches and in the process spreading the fame of Buzios across the globe. The town hasn't been the same since.

Buzios, or more correctly Armação dos Buzios, once was a tranquil fishing village fronting the lapping waters of a bay. After Bardot, however, it became a synonym for all that splendor in the tropics is supposed to be—unspoiled beaches, crystalline water, palm trees and coconuts, beautiful half-naked women and a relaxing, intoxicating lifestyle of careless ease beneath a caressing, tropical sun.

What is amazing about Buzios is that all of this is true. It is one of a handful of over-hyped travel destinations that does not delude or disappoint. It is not as good as the posters. It is better.

The Sun Coast: Located 115 miles (190 km) from Rio, along what is known as the Sun Coast (*Costa do Sol*), Buzios has been compared to the fabled island of Ibiza in Spain. It is a sophisticated, international resort that for most of the year manages to retain the air of a quiet fishing village. The exception is the high summer season just before, during and right after carnival when tranquil Buzios is overrun by tourists its population of 10,000 swelling to 50,000.

For the remaining nine months of the year, Buzios is the type of beach town that most travelers feel exists only in their dreams. Unlike many popular resorts in Brazil, including Rio de Janeiro itself, Buzios has not lost control of its growth. The favorite retreat of Rio's social column set, Buzios has undergone a major real estate boom since the 1970s but fortunately, the city fathers have kept a firm hand on developers. Strict zoning laws limit building heights with the result that Buzios has escaped the highrise invasion that has scarred many Brazilian beaches. The fashionable homes that dot the Buzios beachscape for the most part blend in with the picturesque fishing village. Many new arrivals have purchased homes of the fishermen, remodeling them completely on the inside while retaining the outer shell.

The city has also, so far, been spared an onslaught of hotels. Most of the accommodations in Buzios are *pousadas* or inns, quaint and small with no more than a dozen rooms. The largest hotel occupies an island off the coast, the **Ilha das Rocas**, with 70 rooms and an idyllic resort setting. This in turn has helped preserve the relaxed atmosphere of the town and provides visitors with an intimate setting to enjoy the sun and beach.

The beaches: Altogether, there are 23 beaches in the Buzios area, some fronting quiet coves and inlets and others, the open sea. The main distinction, though, is accessibility. Beaches close to the town such as **Ossos, Geriba** and **Ferradura** are easily reached by foot or car. As could be expected, the "best" beaches are those that require the most effort to reach; in the case of Buzios, either long hikes, sometimes over rocky ground, or a drive along a dirt, pot-holed road. At the end of such efforts are treasures like **Tartaruga, Azeda** and **Azedinha, Brava and Forno**, famed for their beautiful calm waters and equally beautiful topless bathers. As a general rule of thumb in Buzios, the greater a beach's isolation, the greater the nudity— a form of motivation for beach explorers.

Visiting all of the beaches by land, is not only tiring but unnecessary. The fishermen of Buzios have become part-

Preceding page: Fisherman casts his net at end of day. Below, Chez Michou, popular Buzios night spot.

time tour operators and tourists can rent boats by the hour or for the day for cruises along the beaches. Sailboats as well as cars and dune buggies, bicycles, motorcycles and horses may be rented. Diving enthusiasts can also find equipment for rent.

A typical Buzios day begins late (no one wakes up before 11a.m.) with a hearty breakfast at a *pousada*, one of the treats of Buzios' inns. Afterwards, the day centers on the beach, in bathing, in long leisurely walks, in exploration of the distant beaches, to be interrupted only by occasional breaks for fried shrimp or fresh oysters washed down with cold beer or *caipirinhas*, which is Brazil's national drink composed of lime slices, ice and sugar cane liqueur. For shopping, there are fashionable boutiques along cobblestoned **Rua José Bento Ribeiro Dantas** better known as **Rua das Pedras** or street of the stones, and also on **Rua Manuel Turibe de Farias**.

History: When Brazil was first discovered, Buzios and most of the coastline of the state of Rio was inhabited by the Tamoio Indians. The Indians later became allies of French settlers who attempted to establish a colony in what is now the city of Rio de Janeiro. After having been driven out, they fell back along the coast. With the help of their Indian allies, the French attacked ships from Rio on their way to Portugal with goods from the colony. Finally, in 1617, the Portuguese were able to expel the French, eventually turning the area surrounding Buzios into a cattle raising region. From then until the second French incursion, the one led by Bardot, Buzios lived in splendid isolation. With the passage of years, the cattle ranches were replaced by banana plantations whose products were shipped from Buzio's fishing port to London in the 1930s. It was not until after World War II that a road between Rio and Buzios was completed and the *cariocas* were able to discover the beauty of the Buzios coastline.

Paddling in the sheltered waters of Buzios.

At night, the bohemian spirit of Buzios takes charge. Though small in size, the city is considered the third best in Brazil for dining out. There are over 20 quality restaurants, some of which are rated among the country's finest. Gourmets have a wide choice including Brazilian, Italian, French and Portuguese cuisine as well as seafood and a local favorite—crepes. **Le Streghe Buzios** (Italian), **Au Cheval Blanc** (French) and **Adamastor** (seafood) are considered to be the best of Buzio's excellent restaurants. Other small restaurants are constantly popping up, many of them are superb. Among the better ones are **Satiricon**, **La Nuance**, **Casa Velha** and **Oasis**. Visitors should also try out the dining options presented by the *pousadas*, in particular the restaurant of the Auberge l'Hermitage. A word of caution: the bargain prices of Rio's restaurants are not to be found in Buzios.

After an inspiring meal, the in-crowd of Buzios gravitates to the city's bars, many with live entertainment. Bars, like restaurants in Buzios, are as famed for their owners as for what they offer. The town's numerous charms have waylaid dozens of foreign visitors since Bardot's first promenade. Brigitte left, but many others have stayed to open inns, restaurants and bars, providing Buzios with an international air. The Brazilian residents of Buzios have been joined by French, Swiss, Scandinavian and American expatriates, all vowing that they will never leave.

Amiable eccentrics: Among Buzios' amiable eccentrics and engaging dropouts is Madame Michou, owner of **Chez Michou**, Buzio's chic *creperie* where the young crowd gathers at night. Others are Francois Le Mouellic and Vivianne Debon, owners of **La Nuance**, a popular meeting point with live music and where Francois performs puppet shows and opens champagne bottles with a sword; Bruce Henry, an American jazz musician, who owns the **Estalagem**, an inn with a popular res-

A schooner in the placid waters off Azeda Beach in Buzios.

taurant and bar (the barman, Morris, is Irish while the cook is Dutch); Michelle Blondin, another French expatriate whose cave-like restaurant, **Maruelle**, is decorated with Michelle's wood carvings; Pierre Bloch, a member of the French resistance during World War II and now a contented Buzios fisherman; and Matthew, a New Zealand mural painter who lives in a beachside cave. As can be seen, there is no lack of subjects for after dinner conversation in Buzios.

If Buzios has a drawback, it is its distance from Rio and the poor upkeep of the highway linking the two. Also, there are no direct buses between Rio and Buzios. Unless you hire a car and/or driver or your hotel or tour operator has arranged transportation, the journey will be long and complicated. There is bus service to the city of Cabo Frio from where you can take a cab for the remaining 30-minute drive to Buzios. If it is by car, it is suggested that all driving be done during daylight

hours because of the poor condition of the highway. It takes two-and-a-half hours to drive from Buzios to Rio but on summer weekends or during the holiday season, it can take four hours or more in either direction.

There is, however, hope on the horizon for Buzios' transportation woes. In 1988, the city's small airport was enlarged and weekly service began between Buzious and Rio and São Paulo. The planes, with capacity for 20 passengers, make the trip twice a week with extra flights on holidays and during peak season. While still not ideal, the new air link is a giant step in the right direction. The Buzious flights are run by Costair which can be reached at 253-0001 for reservations.

The individual behind the airport expansion is a Rio businessman who is currently investing in the construction of an ambitious, multi-million dollar marina resort complex for Buzios. The project features man-made canals, a golf course and hotel plus vacation

Praia do Forte Beach in Cabo Frio.

homes. When it's completed, the marina will be Buzio's first large-scale international resort

The lake region: Between Rio and Buzios are several beautiful beach areas starting with what is known as the lake region, a series of lagoons separated from the sea by lengthy sand bars. The sea along this unbroken coastline east of Rio is marked by strong currents and large waves, making it a favorite area for surfers. Major surf competitions are held in **Saquarema**, one of the four beach resorts in the lake region. On the other side of the highway, on state road 106, the lagoons are popular spots for wind surfing. Near **Marica**, the first of these cities, is **Ponta Negra** beach, a spectacular, nearly deserted stretch of white sand and wild blue water. After Saquarema, are **Araruama** and **São Pedro d'Aldeia**, all of them are popular among *cariocas* during vacation periods, and especially during carnival, when the lake region's hotels and numerous campgrounds are filled till

overflowing. Salt flats are also visible off the side of the road along this stretch, culminating in a large area of flats at Cabo Frio, which is officially the end of the lake region and beginning of the Sun Coast.

Located 15 miles (25 km) from Buzios, Cabo Frio is famed for the white, powdery sand found on its beaches and its dunes. During vacation season, its population of 40,000 swells with *cariocas* on holiday. Unlike Buzios, Cabo Frio is a historical city with ruins from the 17th century, including the 1616 **São Mateus Fort**, the 1666 **Nossa Senhora da Asunção church** and the 1696 **Nossa Senhora dos Anjos convent**.

Arraial do Cabo: Only eight miles (14 km) from Cabo Frio is Arraial **do Cabo**, the most beautiful attraction of the Sun Coast next to Buzios. Arraial has yet to be discovered by the tourist trade and has only a handful of small and unimpressive hotels. Thus far, tourists have preferred to stay in Buzios and Cabo Frio, making day trips to Arraial. What it does have, is the clearest water in southern Brazil, making it the preferred site of scuba divers and excellent for spear fishing. The city is located at the tip of a cape with a variety of beaches, some of them with quiet waters and a stunning lush green mountain backdrop while others, the surfer beaches, are swept by strong winds, driving the waves against the sand. Off the coast is **Ilha do Farol**, site of a lighthouse but more famed for **Gruta Azul**, an underwater grotto with bright blue waters. The island, reached by boat, also offers excellent views of the mainland.

Like Buzios, Arraial began as a fishing village and is known still for the quality of fresh catches brought in each day. The fishermen of Arraial climb to the top of sand dunes from where they look into the water below in search of schools of fish, a testimony to the unspoiled crystal clear waters of Arraial do Cabo.

Left, one of Buzios' idyllic *pousada* inns. Right, a proud local fisherman with his boat.

THE GREEN COAST

If you wish to get into the *carioca* way of making friends and turning a day at the beach into a festive function, stay in Copacabana and Ipanema. But if it's clean beaches with privacy that you're seeking, head south to the yet unspoiled **Costa Verde** (Green Coast).

Named after the dense vegetation that dominates the coastline and descends right down to the sea, Costa Verde is nature at its best; a unique tropical mix of mountains, rain forest, beaches and islands. The green—in every imaginable shade—is everywhere, invading even the sea with a soft turquoise hue.

Coastal highway: Visiting the area is a must, and is both easy and enjoyable on coastal **Highway BR 101**, known locally as the **Rio-Santos**, after the two port cities it connects. The scenic drive is comparable with that of Spain's Costa Brava or California's State Road 1. At times, it appears as if you are going to take off, as the road rises high up a mountainside for a wide, unobstructed view, then drops and, winds steeply back down to the shoreline. The road passes fascinating and contrasting extremes: a national park, the country's only nuclear power plant, tourist resorts, fishing settlements, ocean vessels, tanking stations, cattle ranches, a shipyard, and **Paraty**, a quaint, colonial village.

The most popular attractions are naturally, the beaches. Some are small, encased by rocky cliffs and shelter clear, tranquil lagoons. Others stretch uninterrupted for miles and are pounded by the rough surf. The whole area is a haven for sports enthusiasts, offering everything from tennis, golf and boating to surfing, deep-sea fishing and diving.

So wrapped up are *cariocas* in their own city and **Buzios**, that it has only been in the last 10 years that they have begun to discover Costa Verde. Now that word of the paradise is out, the area is undergoing rapid transformation. In most cases, too rapid. Costa Verde is one of the last reserves of the Brazilian Atlantic rain forest, of which only three percent of the original forest remains. Already, complete hills have been shaven clean, save the thick bush of the fertile valleys on the sides. In the next decade if this exploitation of national resources and reckless construction continue unchecked, the Green Coast may become the Bare Coast. But for the time being, the area is still a jewel, a finely polished emerald in the midst of other sparkling treasures located in and around Rio.

Costa Verde stretches from Rio southwest 160 miles (260 km) to the São Paulo state border. It is possible to visit the area and return the same day, but to really see the sights, explore the coast and enjoy the beauty, plan on a few days. The area houses some fine hotels and restaurants, even on some of the islands. A word of caution: if you're renting a car, don't drive at night. Not only do you miss the scenery, but in the dark, the highway—with its sharp curves, unmarked shoulders and frequent and poorly lit construction sites—becomes extremely dangerous.

Schooner trips: After leaving Rio on **Avenida das Americas** through **Barra** and **Recreio**, the highway turns inland past **Santa Cruz** and returns to the coast some 40 miles (65 km) later at **Itacuruça** (pop. 2,000), where the Costa Verde really begins. From the town's harbor, schooners which hold up to 40 people leave every morning around 10 o'clock on one-day excursions to the nearby tropical islands (36 of them) in the surrounding **Sepetiba Bay**. The trips cost between US$20 and US$40 and include a seafood lunch on one of the islands. Reservations can be made in advance through a local tourist agency.

The schooners stop at several islands such as **Martins**, **Itacuruca** and

Preceding pages: a vactioneer framed in a colonial window; one of hundreds of secluded coves in Angra dos Reis.

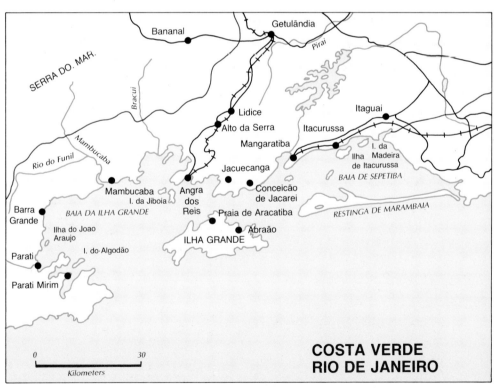

COSTA VERDE
RIO DE JANEIRO

The Santa
Rita Church.
A classic
example of
Brazilian
baroque
arhitecture.

Jaguanum to allow passengers to swim and snorkel. Some of the smaller islands (**Pombeba** and **Sororoca** are recommended) can be visited by hiring a boat and guide (usually a local fisherman) at the harbor. If you wish to stay on the islands, there are several good hotels, including the **Hotel Ilha de Jaguanum** (235-2893) and the **Hotel do Pierre** (788-1560).

The highway continues past **Muriqui** to **Mangaratiba**, site of a new $40 million 350-room **Club Mediterranee** (297-5337). The scenery improves with each mile as you pass several fishing villages before coming to Verolme, a large shipyard. Here the sea is dotted with tankers waiting for repairs or to load up on oil and minerals from nearby storage plants.

Angra dos Reis: Around the bend from Verolme lies **Angra dos Reis** (King's Cove), Costa Verde's largest city (pop. 80,000). The city was discovered only five days after Rio in 1502 by the Portuguese explorer Andre Goncalves. But it was only in 1556 that the first white settlers arrived to plant sugar cane. There is nothing beautiful or noteworthy about Angra other than perhaps, its churches, of which the most interesting is the convent of **São Bernardino de Sena** on the **Santo Antonio** hillside. Its original clock, whose numerals were replaced with the 12 letters of the city, still works.

People don't come to Angra just to tour the city or its churches. The city lies sprawled over several hills at the beginning of a 60-mile (100-km) long gulf. The Angra Gulf contains over 370 islands, 2,000 beaches, seven bays and countless coves. The water is warm, clear and calm, a perfect sanctuary for marine life. Spearfishing along the rocky shores is a popular activity, as is fishing in deeper waters. The tourist information center across the bus station near the harbor can provide you with maps and information on hotels and boat tours.

The best hotels in the area are run by

the Frade Hotels Group and include the **Frade Portogalo Hotel** and **Hotel do Frade** (267-7375). The hotels have their own bus service from Rio and a 90-foot (30-meter) schooner to visit the nearby islands. The Hotel do Frade also has a scenic 18-hole golf course where international tournaments are held every June and November.

Ilha Grande: One-and-a-half hours by boat from Angra is the paradisiacal island of **Ilha Grande** (Large Island), a 115 sq mile (300 sq km) nature reserve blessed with spectacular fauna and flora and some of the country's most beautiful tropical beaches. The cheapest way to get to the island is via ferry from Angra or Mangaratiba to **Abraão**, the island's only city. In Abraão you can rent small boats to visit the more distant beaches such as **Lopez Mendes, Paranaoiaca, das Palmas** and **Saco do Ceu**. There are several campsites on the island, but only two main hotels with limited number of rooms, **Pousada Mar de Tranquilidade** in Abraao (288-4162) and **Paraiso do Sol** in Praia das Palmas (2630-6126).

25 miles (40 km) past Angra and a few bends after the Hotel do Frade, lies the country's only nuclear power plant, **Angra I**, a source more of controversy than energy. Once a symbol of pride for the former military government that built it, it now stands as a great embarrassment, having cost six times more than the original $300 million estimate. Of the three planned reactors at Angra, only one has been completed but it never seems to work. Brazilians have dubbed Angra I, *vagalume* (lightning bug) since it has been turned on and off so often for repairs.

Shortly beyond the plant is one of the coast's most picturesque fishing villages, **Mambucaba**. The homes are built right on the beach and a large white church in the town center faces the sea.

As you approach the other end of the Angra Gulf, the mountains recede and are replaced with grassy fields filled with grazing cattle and locals playing *futebol* (soccer).

Paraty: Some 60 miles (100 km) past Angra and a three and a half hours' drive from Rio, is **Paraty**, (pop. 9,000), a charming town of historical importance which in 1966, was named an international monument by UNESCO. Hardly known outside Brazil, this living colonial museum is, however, one of the country's most unique tourist attractions.

Paraty, sometimes spelled Parati, was founded in 1660 and acquired great importance in the 18th century as the port where gold, diamonds and precious stones from the state of Minas Gerais were shipped back to Portugal. Geographically, it served as the link between São Paulo and Rio where all roads between the country's two largest cities crossed. For over a century Paraty flourished and prospered into a city of great wealth with large mansions and estates. But after Brazil gained its independence in 1822, exports of gold and

Left, a schooner trip on a tropical islands excursion. Right, colonial houses line the narrow streets of Paraty.

diamonds to the fatherland stopped and a new road was eventually built connecting Rio to São Paulo directly. Paraty lost its strategic position was forgotten and its colonial heritage was consequently, preserved.

It is this traditional flavor combined with the locals' friendliness which leads visitors to fall in love with Paraty. The city embraces its visitors, seduces them, and if they're not careful, adopts them as well. Tourists come for a few hours and stay a weekend, others come for a short holiday and stay a month, a year, or a lifetime, becoming part of the city as it becomes a part of them. Unlike Buzios, whose character as a jet-set resort is well defined, Paraty is still looking and hopefully, always will be, for an identity. If today it's a fishing town, historical monument, tourist attraction, artist's gallery or hippie hangout, tomorrow it may be something totally different. But it will always be Paraty.

Even in its early days, Paraty was inhabited by diverse groups, as evidenced by the town's many churches, each built for a different race: mulattos, blacks and whites. The first church to be completed, **Santa Rita de Cassia** (1722), is a classic example of Brazilian baroque architecture and also houses the **Museum of Sacred Art**. Next to it, in what was once the town's prison, is the tourist information office.

Colonial area: The best way to get a feel of Paraty is to walk around the colonial area. You don't have to watch out for cars as they are prohibited in this part, but be careful not to twist an ankle on the large uneven stones that make up the narrow roads. To test your balance even more, the roads slope in towards the center to drain off heavy rains.

Another reason for taking your time is so that you can browse through the many galleries and handicraft stores, and to politely peek through the doorways of the *pousadas* (inns) and homes. From the outside, they look like typical white-washed Mediterranean houses

Historical charm of Paraty— cobblestone streets and colonial buildings.

with heavy wooden doors and shutters painted in bright colored trim. On the inside, however, they open up to delicately landscaped courtyards with ferns, orchids, rosebushes, violets, bromeliads, and begonias. Two of the most beautiful gardens are in **Pousada do Ouro** (both in the main hotel and across the street) and **Coxixo**. Across from the latter is a pleasant open-air bar and restaurant, which also triples as an antique shop. The Frade Hotels Group runs a friendly *pousada* next to the **Nossa Senhora dos Remedios Church**.

If you visit Paraty during a full moon, walk down to the port during high tide, but be sure to take your shoes off first as the rising sea floods the area. Locals claim this cleans the streets, but often, the dirt that is washed away is replaced by rotting seaweed.

Sampling the local brew.

Although like Angra, Paraty is not famed for its beaches, schooners such as the 80-foot (24-meter) long Soberano da Costa, make day trips to the surrounding islands. Reservations can be made through your hotel or at port.

The old gold route: A very different type of excursion can be made by car to **Fazenda Banal**, 5 minutes from Paraty, on the old gold-route up the hill to **Cunha**. The 17th-century ranch has something for everybody: a large zoo complete with wild cats, monkeys and rare birds, waterfalls to bathe in, a restaurant specializing in Brazilian country-home cooking, and an ancient but still operating *cachaça* (sugarcane wine) distillery where you can sample and buy the ten potent flavors made with different herbs and fruits.

Due south of Paraty is one of Green Coast's most prized and carefully guarded treasures, the tiny fishing village of **Trinidade**. Far from the high rises of Rio, Trinidade and its three spectacular beaches with clear waters and natural pools are an example of the best that the Green Coast has to offer—isolation, relaxation and unspoiled tropical beauty.

CARNIVAL

Brazil's greatest symbol, appropriately, is not a thing, but an event—Carnival.

Carnival's sweet song penetrates the Brazilian soul at every level—even those who hate it are influenced by it—and it embraces every social class.

Carnival's influence on literature and art: Novelist Jorge Amado gave it the highest honor by making it the title of one of his books—*Pais do Carnaval* (The Country of Carnival).

It has been an important theme in Brazilian literature for as long as it has been an important event in Brazilian life. Machado de Assis, founder of the Brazilian Academy of Letters, wrote about it in the 19th century. All the great poets make of it a metaphor for Brazil itself. Vinicius de Morais placed it at the center of his lyric play *Orfeu Negro, Uma Tragedia Carioca* (Black Orpheus, A Carioca Tragedy), which audiences the world over know as the luminescent 1959 film *Black Orpheus*. The turn-of-the-century poet, Olavo Bilac described the *carnavalesco,* or Carnival fanatic, eloquently: "He is a different person altogether, from another race. Those who merely love Carnival do not deserve the title, "*carnavalesco*". The true fanatic is an individual who was born for Carnival and for Carnival alone. He lives for it; he counts the passing years according to the number of Carnivals he has celebrated; when he is about to die, he has only one regret—he will miss next year's Carnival and all the other Carnivals which will mark the life of Rio de Janeiro until the end of time."

A young Frenchman named Edouard Manet was deeply impressed by the many moods and colors of Carnival when he visited Rio in 1875. According to historian João Ribeiro, the French artist later confessed the images he recalled from Carnival influenced

Preceding pages: Carnival madness provides stamina to dancers of all ages; green and pink, colors of the Mangueira Samba School; costumes cost anything from $100 up; member of percussion section. Left, anything goes!

the development of Impressionism.

But a Brazilian writer, Isis Valeria, probably captured the essence of Carnival best in her short story, *Folião*, in which a suburban worker, who has spent an entire year preparing for Carnival, dies at the moment his name is called winner of a costume competition: "He took his first steps, dragging behind him the weight of his costume, almost in a trance. He was in his glory. The crowd in the hall was at his feet. He fell before reaching the other side of the room. His face changed expression with the pain but his dentures, even in death, kept grinning. He was carried out of the theater.

Carrum Novalis, a kind of festival float used by the Romans. Another says it comes from the Italian Carne Vale, meaning good-bye to meat, since Carnival marks the last days before the awesome abstinence of Lent. Still others say it means simply Festival de Carne.

Some kind of pre-Lenten observance has existed in Brazil for as long as the Portuguese have been here. But all the way up to the early 20th century that age-old tradition tended to emphasize pranksterism rather than celebration.

This particular aspect of Carnival observance was called *entrudo* and came to Brazil directly from Portugal. *Entrudo* featured

Outside, he was surrounded by enthusiasts who unmindfully congratulated him on his victory."

European in origin: Although modern Rio boasts the most famous Carnival celebration in the world, Carnival's roots are European, going back all the way to Roman times. The ancient Romans had more than 100 festivals during their year of which the most famous was the week-long Saturnalia, held at the end of December, a Carnival precursor.

Experts disagree over the origin of the word, Carnival. According to one school of thought, it comes from the Latin expression

stink bombs, water balloons, mud balls and even arson as forms of entertainment—entertainment for some, a public nuisance for most. Interestingly, many of the perpetrators were sons of the rich.

Entrudo got to be so bad that, by the mid-19th century, decent men and women spent the entire time before Lent locked up in their homes. The observance of *entrudo* was outlawed in 1853. But the ban was hard to enforce since the police were often among the most active perpetrators. It wasn't until the early 1900s that a strict enforcement campaign finally put an end to *entrudo*.

Modern Carnival is a class event. As in Roman or Renaissance Carnival, a temporary class inversion takes place. The poor dress up as royalty and strut before the rich, who come to the parades in blue jeans. When class lines blur in Brazil, Carnival will begin to die.

Carnival balls for society's upper crust: Still, middle and upper class Brazilians do have their own special Carnival bailiwick—the fancy dress ball. These colorful events, today as in the 19th century, center around loud music and elaborate costumes.

Carnival balls hit Rio in 1840 with a chic event at the Hotel Italia at the site of what is

The first modern Carnival ball was the High Life, which premiered at a Copacabana hotel in 1908. The extremely formal City Ball was inaugurated in 1932 at the Teatro Municipal.

What Carnival means to the poor and the rich: The Carnival ball's purpose throughout history has been the same. Where the poorer classes seek to forget their poverty during the four days of Carnival, members of the middle and upper classes discard their inhibitions. A secondary purpose—and this one will never die—is to "appear" at the most fashionable balls. There are some socialites who attend so many of these events during

now the São Jose Theater on Praça Tiradentes. Ironically, the São Jose is now the site of an annual transvestite carnival ball. But the Italia ball lost money and it wasn't until 1846 that a second one was held, this time in the upper crust district of São Cristovão. The São Cristovão event included royal guests so the ball's sponsors were able to attract an elite crowd and charge more.

Left, clowns carrying balloons joining in the dazzling parade. Above, bare-breasted women, a popular topping for parade floats.

the course of a single evening that they spend more time in the limousine going from place to place than on the dance floor.

For Rio's poor, music, dance and drink were, and still are, the main Carnival options. Crude musical instruments, simple but frenetic dance routines and popular music are still the basis of Carnival celebration in most parts of Rio.

How Carnival developed: A Portuguese immigrant named José Nogueira Paredes (dubbed Ze Pereira by revelers) is credited with inventing the first Carnival club. One of his innovations was to get everybody in the

club to play the exact same kind of drum, creating a powerful, unified sound, basis for the modern samba school *bateria* or the percussion section.

The white working class clubs were called *blocos* or *ranchos* and played European-origin ballads known as *choros*, many of which are still popular.

The late 19th century also saw the first involvement of blacks in Carnival. This was at least partly due to an 1877 drought in the Northeast which sent many *nordestinos*, including some freed black slaves, to Rio and São Paulo.

The former slaves brought their own brand of musical and dance traditions with them to the city's Carnival celebration. By the 1890s, black groups were marching around different parts of downtown during the four days of Carnival.

The most colorful event: Everyone agrees the most colorful event in Rio's contemporary Carnival is the main Samba School Parade, held on the Sunday and Monday nights of Carnival. Of all the Carnival events, the parade is the most African in its roots, especially when it comes to samba, Brazil's "national music," a composite of European folk influences and African techniques brought by the slaves.

The parade is also Carnival's most obviously class oriented event. The Samba Schools, composed overwhelmingly of working and poor people from the city's sprawling suburbs, compete against one another for the most luxurious presentation. The socialites and businessmen come to watch the parade in their designer jeans, although increasingly they too are taking part in the parade.

While Carnival is hundreds of years old, the parade is a 20th-century innovation. The very first samba school was called *Deixa Falar* (Let 'Em Talk) and was organized by the mainly black residents of Rio's Estacio district in 1928. (In honor of Estacio's contribution to Carnival, the site of the annual parade was moved there in 1978.)

Deixa Falar paraded for the first time in the Carnival of 1929. Paraders followed no fixed route and weren't very well organized. But their very size made them different from ordinary *ranchos* and *blocos*. And, unlike other parading groups, *Deixa Falar* presented colorful costumes and clever dance routines.

Other black neighborhoods set up rival samba organizations almost immediately. During the 1930 Carnival, there were five such groups and so many spectators that police had to clear a special area around Praça Onze on the day of their parade.

Things became even more sophisticated when the *Mundo Esportivo* newspaper offered a prize to the best samba group in 1932. (By then the black-dominated Praça Onze parade groups had acquired the name "school", probably because local public schools let them practice on school grounds on the weekends before Carnival.) The 1932 prize went to Mangueira, one of the schools which first paraded in 1930.

By 1935, the samba parade had blossomed into one of the major Carnival events. In that year the city government paid a small subsidy to the largest schools and took over the

Left, massive parade floats tells part of the theme-story of the samba school. Above, participant for the most elaborate costume contest.

SAMBA SCHOOL

So what does it actually feel like to samba in a carnival parade? "It was so emotional," sigh *cariocas*. Which tells one as much about Brazilian values as it does about samba—the ability to stir emotions as supreme accolade. And nothing stirs like the collective catharsis of the carnival parade.

The anticipation is part of it. It starts almost as soon as one carnival is over, with the first rumours of the samba school's theme for the next. By mid-year the samba

Months earlier, you had provided measurements, that would have impressed a Seville Row tailor—upper arm circumference, upper thigh, calf, ankle, neck, length from top of shoulder to elbow and so on. But inevitably something doesn't fit. You've got someone else's hat. The shoes are two sizes too large.

Before the Parade begins: With just a few hours to go, a veil of surrealism descends upon Rio. Twenty thousand dancers dressed

has been composed; by October, costume designs are off the drawing boards and the booklets of receipts for the monthly installments printed. The simplest costume in a major samba school costs from US$100 upwards.

Preparation: It's one of the golden rules of carnival that everything that can be left to the last moment is. Seamstresses always promise to deliver costumes days in advance, but they never do. You get yours a few hours before the parade. Inevitably, it has gone over budget—you have no choice but to cough up.

in gleaming costumes called *fantasias* literally fantasies, converge on the *concentracão*, the meeting point behind the grand parade avenue. Spangled kings squeeze through subway turnstyles, hoop-skirted elderly women in *Baianas* costumes sway on crowded suburban trains, flustered drivers seek parking spaces, tassels tangling with gears, feathered hats sticking out of hatch-back. And one of the most magic sights—the Cinderellas and princes-for-a-night, picking their way on foot down the stony paths of hillside shantytowns, gilt and sequins glinting ephemerally in the dark.

The veterans come prepared with thermos flasks, piles of sandwiches, and 6-packs. For the other inevitable rule of carnival—that everything runs late—means hours to while away in the darkness. Heady wafts of marijuana blend with smoke from improvised charcoal grills. Dancers help each other with eyeliner and dust strange shoulders and thighs with glitter. The vainest are the posing, pouting transvestites, platform soles raising them a head and shoulders above the

The Parade: Then suddenly you are on. Your samba blasts out. You march forward in formation, turn that right angle out of the darkness of the *concentracão* into the arc lights of the parade, and wham…butterflies disappear and the crowd up there is singing along with you. The school stewards wield their batons, "For God's sake, smile," they yell, "Sing up, keep in close." Just in case you had forgotten, there is a competition to be won.

rest. One *Baiana* tries in vain to get through the door of the portable W.C. She tries squeezing the hoop-skirt in horizontally, then vertically, gives up and floats gracefully off to some discreet corner.

As each *escola* before yours parades, you move up a place in the queue. The wait seems interminable.

Left, samba school "officials" overseeing their school's performance. Above, young participant and, right, a not-so-young *baiana* share the joy of dancing in the parade.

About half-way through the parade, euphoria sets in. Your limbs move automatically, you're bellowing the chorus for the 46th time, as if your life depended upon it, but your voice seems to belong to someone else. You dance past the drummers and feel the rush of air from three hundred pairs of hands beating simultaneously.

In 50 minutes it's all over. You've got blisters on your feet, bits of your costume were shed on the way down the avenue. The municipal water carts are waiting to hose down dancers prostrate with sweat and exhaustion. And, yes, it was "emotional."

parade organization and awarding of prizes. By 1935, there were 25 schools.

Samba: What *Deixa Falar* added to the black celebration of Carnival in 1929 was size, costume and organization. But the samba music which is such an integral part of the annual parade existed long before that. Most experts agree the distinctively black samba tradition dates from the late 19th century, when the crude music of the former slaves met the stylized European sound of Rio. (The word samba is believed to derive from the Angolese *semba* describing a rhythmic dance.)

The most famous early samba is *Pelo Telefone* (By Phone), about Rio's police chief. *Pelo Telefone* is considered the first samba song to have been recorded for record sales. That was in 1917. The author's name was Ernesto dos Santos (nicknamed Donga), who was originally from Bahia.

Since the glory days of the 1930s and 1940s, when legendary composers such as Pixinguinha, Noel Rosa, Ari Barroso and Cartola were working, samba has become a national landmark. But it wasn't always so. Samba is a poor people's and eminently a black people's music. In fact, it wasn't until the 1950s that the samba parade became one of the main attractions of Carnival for foreign tourists. Said Pixinguinha at that time, "Twenty years ago those of us playing samba were getting beaten up by the police. Today, we're the national music."

Today's celebration of Carnival in Rio de Janeiro has three main features: colorful, often frenzied street events, the traditional club balls and finally the world-famous samba parade.

Street Carnival: Street Carnival can be described as "the opposite of everything".

men impersonating women…
children impersonating adults…
adults acting like children.

It starts on the Friday night of Carnival when Rio's mayor, in a hectic ceremony staged on Avenida Rio Branco downtown, delivers an oversized Key to the City to Rei Momo, the rolly-polly "King" who presides over Rio until Ash Wednesday.

But the best Street Carnival is found in Rio's suburbs—the huge working class dis-

tricts which sprawl away from downtown.

Street Carnival in Meier, Madureira, **Bangu**, **Realengo** and other distant neighborhoods draws hundreds of thousands of revelers. Most of these *cariocas* dress, often elaborately, as clowns, transvestites, TV and film personalities or as bats, tigers and other assorted animals.

The most common get-up, however, is men dressing as women. The "Bloco das Piranhas" is an elaborate version of this idea. It usually includes a number of men dressed as high-priced prostitutes.

Another popular presence is the "Bloco dos Sujos". Members smear themselves with cheap but colorful paint and dress up in Indian garb or as vagabonds and parade through the streets.

The "Bloco de Empolgacão", however, is the most common street Carnival phenomenon. These groups stimulate the largest number of people into dancing up to the dizziest possible frenzy. They do it the same way as the big samba schools—with lots of drums and well-known samba tunes.

Although most districts in the northern suburbs have plenty of activity, music and color, the official headquarters of Street Carnival is Avenida Rio Branco.

A number of special events are featured every year. One is the awarding of the annual Street Carnival costume prize. One recent award went to a group of men calling themselves "The Young Widows". They were splendidly dressed as middle-class women and worked out an elaborate dance routine to please the judges.

Another annual affair, the "Bloco dos Intocaveis" (The Untouchables) parade, takes place in Copacabana. This event, like most street Carnival phenomena, is totally disorganized and open to everyone. Says an organizer, "All you need is to be 21 years old so you can drink." And even that rule gets broken most of the time.

An unusual event inaugurated in 1981 is the parade of the "Bloco Scandinavia". The

Right, revelers cut loose at a carnival ball.

bloco is composed entirely of strippers, who titillate by-standers with an open-air display of their craft. They are assisted by a bevy of bouncers from downtown strip bars, who keep oglers at a "decent" distance.

Street Carnival .in Rio's sophisticated Zona Sul is less frenzied than in the working class Zona Norte. However, there are two traditional Zona Sul events marking any year's Carnival Calendar—the famous "Banda de Ipanema", about 15,000 strong, which annually parades through the streets of that famous district, stopping at every bar along the way, and the "Banda de Sa Ferreira", which does the same in Copacabana.

Annual club balls: Carnival nights belong to the club balls. Among the annual events which attract both *cariocas* and tourists are nightly bashes at the **Sirio-Libanes**, **Flamengo**, **Fluminense** and **Monte-Libano** clubs.

Monte Libano boasts the "hottest" of the balls, especially its annual "Night in Baghdad" held on Carnival Tuesday. The "Night" is so popular, real live Middle Eastern sheiks have been known to attend. However, Monte Libano also has a reputation for over-selling. The hall becomes unbearably hot. Long lines form in front of the bar and the bathroom.

Some of the more interesting balls include the annual Sugarloaf event. This all-night affair takes place atop Rio's landmark, Sugarloaf Mountain. Promoter Guilherme Araujo annually attracts a long list of local and international celebrities, puts on a tasteful show and usually has one of the most picturesque and luxuriously decorated of all Carnival balls. The show goes on until sunrise and guests are permitted, indeed encouraged, to cart the cardboard and colored-paper decorations away with them when they leave.

Another big event is the annual City Ball, the official entertainment event of the city government. This one takes place on Saturday night, usually at one of Rio's large night clubs. The music is top quality and all the celebrities show up. A highlight is the parade of the prize-winning Carnival costumes, which sometimes feature outrageously deluxe get-ups depicting everything from

Medieval troubadours to Roman Catholic archbishops.

But the most talked about balls are the ones promoted by Rio's transvestites. They start on Friday with the "Baile dos Enxutos" at the São Jose Theater on bleak Praça Tiradentes and continue at the same locale on Saturday to Tuesday. The most notable thing about the transvestite balls is the surprising success these former men have in assuming secondary female sexual characteristics. They usually parade themselves, open-bloused, in front of the São Jose on each of the transvestite ball nights.

Samba parade: But the samba parade, re-

cently divided into two parts with seven schools parading on Sunday night and seven on Monday, is the undisputed centerpiece of any Rio de Janeiro Carnival—a veritable compendium of *carioca* and Brazilian culture, the whole history of samba and Carnival in two nights.

Just the names of some of Rio's traditional samba schools—**Mangueira**, the oldest, **Salgueiro**, **Imperio Serrano**, **Beija-Flor**—give most *cariocas* goose bumps.

The parade is witnessed by millions of television viewers and 85,000 ticket-holders in the soaring **Sambadrome**, a $27 million stadium designed especially for the parade by noted Brazilian architect, Oscar Niemeyer and inaugurated in 1984.

The parade is an eyeful.

But the interesting thing is that there's more to it than meets the eye. Lavish costumes, soaring floats and the magic of *samba* form the colorful facade. But to understand what lies behind the parade you need a score card. Because, in the first place, the samba parade is a competition.

Presentation of the parade: The 14 samba schools which parade down Avenida Marques de Sapucai are judged by a government appointed jury for every aspect of their

Sometimes that theme is an historical event or personality. Other times it's a story or legend from Brazilian literature.

The theme embraces almost every aspect of the school's effort. The costumes must be in accord with its historical time and place. The samba song must recount or develop it and the huge floats that push ponderously down the avenue must detail it in depth through the media of paper mache figures and paintings.

Finally, the samba parade is a resurrection of classic samba themes of the past. There are certain things which every school must present even though they do not necessarily

presentation. The emotions (and controversies) stimulated by this unique contest are every bit as hot as those which surround the year-end play-offs in most sports.

The samba parade is an artistic presentation, and not only in the sense of design and musical arts. There is also a literary dimension to each performance. Each school's effort must be based around a central theme.

Left, faces of carnival. Above, the party continues.

combine with the specific theme of the school for that year. In fact, these items are often the most carefully judged and they give a certain unity to the parade as a whole.

Key elements present in each school's presentation include the following:

The *Abre-Alas*, literally, "The Opening Wing". The *Abre-Alas*s consists of a group of colorfully costumed *sambistas* (*sambista* is anybody having anything to do with a samba school) marching just in front of or just behind a large float. The float usually depicts something like an open book or an old-fashioned scroll. Written on this figurative page are the letters G.R.E.S. (Gremio Recreativo Escola de Samba—Samba School Recreational Guild). This first float is, in effect, the title page of the school's theme.

Behind the *Abre-Alas* is a line of formally dressed men, the *Comissão de Frente*, literally "The Board of Directors". These men are usually chosen for their dignified air. Sometimes, they are members of the school's actual board of directors, but usually they are simply honored but aging *sambistas*. The real board of directors is working hard along the sidelines to make sure the parade is on time and all its members are

playing their proper roles within the school's complex choreography.

The real event begins when the *Porta Bandeira* (Flag Bearer) and the *Mestre Sala* (Dance Master) appear a few steps behind the *Comissão de Frente*. These two individuals dress in lavish, 18th-century formal wear no matter what the samba school's theme is that year. The *Porta Bandeira* is a woman dancer who holds the school's flag (on one side is the school's emblem, on the other is the symbol of that year's theme) during an elaborate dance with her consort. The pair must develop a devilishly compli-

cated set of steps but without breaking rhythm, and they have to do it while proceeding at the rate of about one mile per hour, down the avenue.

The weighty part of the samba school follows directly behind the *Porta Bandeira* and the *Mestre Sala*. A number of different components are involved, of which the most important is probably the *bateria*. The *bateria* is nothing less than a small army of percussion enthusiasts. In the larger schools they number up to several hundred. Their job is to maintain a constant rhythm, so the other members of the school can keep up with the tempo of the *samba* song, and to provide an exciting, pulsating undercurrent to the overall enterprise. All the members of the *bateria*, sometimes referred to as *ritmistas* (anyone in the school providing musical accompaniment), must wear the same uniform, which is usually designed in accord with the school's theme.

The *bateria* stops about half way down the avenue to perform, with deafening power, before the judges' box while the rest of the school proceeds to the end of the approximately 1,000-yard long (one km) parade route.

Marching both in front of and behind the *bateria* are the major *alas* of the samba school. These groups of scores or even hundreds of people present different aspects of the school's theme through the medium of costume. Thus, if the school's theme is based on an Amazon myth, then one of its main *alas* might present *sambistas* dressed as Indians; another could have its members dressed in costumes suggesting the animals of the Amazon; a third would represent some of the figures of Amazon Indian mythology, and so forth.

However, there are some *alas* which must be part of every samba school parade no matter what the theme. The chief such *ala* is the *Ala das Baianas*. This group consists of dozens and sometimes hundreds of older women, usually blacks, dressed in the flowing white attire of the northeastern state of

Above, pounding out the samba rhythm for an hour. Right, exotic float replete with tropical birds and Amazon "indians".

Bahia, home to Brazil's African traditions. The presentation of this motif honors the earliest history of samba.

To be chosen for the *Ala das Baianas* is considered a high honor. Says Maria de Lourdes Neves, a long-time member of the Imperio Serrano samba school, "To be a *baiana* you have to be a respected *senhora*, preferably of dignified bearing and advanced age…and you have to be ready to do everything a young person can do."

In between the major *alas* are a number of lavishly costumed individuals depicting the main figures of the motifs of the school's theme. These *sambistas* are called *figuras de*

performers.

Just in front of its main parade floats the school places a small, colorfully decorated van with a musical group and a singer on top. The male singer is called the *puxador de samba*. His job is to keep belting out the school's samba song. Everybody in the parade is expected to sing the song all the way to the end of the presentation. Often members of the school distribute copies of the lyrics in the grandstands just before the parade begins.

At the start, the middle but mainly towards the end of the parade, the school brings up its big guns—the giant Carnival floats, called

destaque, literally "prominent figures". They often include local celebrities, with a preference for voluptuous actresses and models.

Also mixed in between the various *alas* and the giant Carnival floats are groups of dancers known as *passistas*. These incredibly agile young men and women stop in the middle of the street to perform complicated dance routines. They often use a tambourine as a prop and perform acrobatic feats as part of their routines. The women *passistas* wear little more than a G-string. The *passistas* are among the most heartily applauded *samba*

alegorias. These immense paper-mache and styrofoam creations present the major figures and motifs of the school's theme. Using the Amazon example again, the floats might present paper mache figures depicting incidents or characters from a mythological Amazon story plus historical characters and lots of appropriate background scenery such as trees and rivers and wild animals. The floats also feature a number of live models, with a strong preference for minimally dressed females.

The whole presentation, of course, is penetrated by the music of the *samba en-*

redo. The *bateria* is thumping out its rhythm on the drums, the *puxador de samba* is belting out its lyrics and every last *sambista* is singing as loud as possible. The *samba enredo* is the musical version of the school's theme. The words of the song are supposed to tell the story verbally while the costumes and floats tell it visually.

Financing the Carnival: Members of the big samba schools spend literally all year preparing for the event. They are mostly poor people. Support for their efforts comes from a small government subsidy, from dues paid by members and from donations made by businesses and individuals in the neighbor-

honored *jogo do bicho*, the illegal numbers game. The numbers chiefs support the parade because it is great public relations. Most of Rio's poor people have three main passions: soccer, samba and the *jogo do bicho*.

Some critics, however, say the parade has become too extravagant with major schools spending up to $300,000 each year on preparations. Responsible for the move toward Las Vegas-style opulence was Joaozinho Trinta, artistic director for one of Rio's largest samba schools, Beija-Flor. Trinta defended his insistence on big-budget productions with the classic remark: "Only the rich enjoy poverty. The poor want luxury."

hoods where the schools have their headquarters. In recent years, in addition, the samba schools have become popular entertainment in the off-season. Most of the big-name schools appear at night clubs or concerts during the year where they earn a percentage of the gate or a flat fee.

In practice, however, most of the money comes from donations and most of the donations come from the bosses of Rio's time-

Left, enthusiastic spectators dance and sing along with samba schools. Above, tired paraders make their way home at dawn.

Because of the emotions involved in the samba parade, the announcement of the winning school on the Thursday after the parade is one of the most dramatic events of the year in Rio. The losing schools are rarely, if ever, satisfied with the results and cries of fraud are common.

For the winner and its fanatic followers, however, there is an instant coronation—the kings of samba—and a celebration that lasts all the way to the following Sunday! Indeed, all the way to the following year, where another Carnival and another samba parade awaits.

For shoppers, Rio is a tropical bargain basement. In addition to the usual souvenir shops, the city offers some of Latin America's most fashionable boutiques, jewelry stores and leather goods shops. It is a world center for summer fashions, the main outlet for Brazil's sophisticated gemstone business and the tee-shirt and bikini capital of the universe.

Since the 1960s when Brazil first began experiencing inflation woes, the country's currency has taken an annual beating in relation to the American dollar and other strong currencies. Coupled with Brazil's cheap manpower, this has meant lower prices for items made in Brazil. The exception to this rule are electronics products. Brazil is *not* a high-tech center. Since Brazil's currency, the *cruzado* is pegged to the American dollar, the recent sharp decline of the dollar has meant that for European and Japanese tourists, the prices of goods in Rio are even cheaper than for Americans.

The shops, boutiques and department stores of Rio are loaded with products which are not only a bargain but are also of excellent quality. In the virtually unbeatable category are summer clothing, especially swimwear, leather goods with the emphasis on shoes, sandals and handbags and the ubiquitous gemstones which appear to adorn store windows in every street of Copacabana and Ipanema.

Shopping centers: Until the start of the 1980s, Rio had no shopping centers, an oversight that was corrected with the opening of the **Rio Sul Shopping Center**. With this, *cariocas* quickly discovered the advantages of shopping in an air-conditioned mall in a city where the summer temperature averages around 90° (35° Celsius). Since then, malls and shopping centers have sprouted at a rapid pace, giving residents and

tourists alike a wide choice of options. Rio's principal shopping centers are:

Rio Sul—located in the neighborhood of Botafogo a short distance from Copacabana, Rio's first shopping center remains the most popular amongst residents of these two neighborhoods and tourists as well. Buses take tourists free of charge from Copacabana's hotels to Rio Sul where they will find over 400 shops and restaurants plus a supermarket. The latter is a rarity for a Rio shopping center. The mall is open from 10 a.m. to 10 p.m., Monday through Saturday.

Barra Shopping—the largest shopping center in Brazil and according to its promoters, Latin America as well, Barra Shopping has the look and feel of an American suburban mall. Contributing to this is its location in the heart of the Barra da Tijuca, Rio's suburbia. Its half-hour distance from the hotel areas in Copacabana and Ipanema initially kept tourists away but as part of an aggressive marketing philosophy, Barra Shopping is now offering free transportation from the hotels and back in air-conditioned

Left, sidewalk vendor sells tee-shirts in Copacabana. Above, an Ipanema shop window displays swimwear, a Rio specialty.

buses. Like the city's other shopping centers, Barra offers top boutiques, department stores, a wide selection of restaurants including a McDonalds, several movie theaters, book stores and jewelry stores. It also has a mini-amusement park for children and Rio's only ice rink and bowling alleys. Open 10 a.m. -10 p.m., Monday through Saturday.

Cassino Atlantico—on Copacabana's beachfront drive, Av. Atlantica at the Rio Palace Hotel, this mall is excellent in terms of location but falls short of Rio Sul and Barra Shopping in the quality and quantity of its shops. It does, however, have some of Rio's best souvenir shops in addition to

its art galleries which are among the best in Rio. It also has several excellent home furnishing stores.

Besides these more traditional shopping malls, Rio also has two other shopping centers devoted exclusively to interior decorating and home furnishing. The **Rio Design Center** is located in Leblon at Av. Ataulfo da Paiva 270 and **Casa Shopping** behind the Barra Shopping Center.

Boutiques: Even with the recent success of the malls, the corner boutique retains a warm place in the hearts of Rio shoppers. The fashionable shops are concentrated on **Av. Nossa Senhora da Copacabana** between

excellent art galleries and antique shops. Open 9 a.m. - 10 p.m., Monday through Friday and 9 a.m. - 8 p.m. on Saturday.

São Conrado Fashion Mall—close to the Sheraton and Inter-Continental hotels and a 5-minute drive from Ipanema, this mall is as its name implies, devoted to fashion—sports and casual wear as well as elegant fashions, for both men and women. Open 10 a.m. - 10 p.m., Monday through Saturday.

Shopping Center da Gavea—a small shopping center a few minutes from Ipanema and Leblon, this mall is famed for

Rua Paula Freitas and Rua Constante Ramos in Copacabana. Souvenir shops run from Av. Princesa Isabel to Paula Freitas, on Rua Visconde de Piraja in Ipanema and to a lesser degree along the pedestrian streets downtown, off Av. Rio Branco.

The trendiest are found in Ipanema, mainly on **Visconde de Piraja** but also on side streets running in both directions **Rua Garcia d'Avila** is the most popular. Visitors will discover that *cariocas*, men and women, dress as casually and expansively as they behave. The accent is on color and verve with excellent lightweight summer clothing—bright, flashy and youthful. Ipanema's shops and boutiques cater to men, women and children, offering leather goods and shoes in addition to clothing and gifts. The recognized bikini king is the **Bum Bum** boutique at Visconde de Piraja 437. Most of Ipanema's top boutiques are also present at the Rio Sul and Barra Shopping malls. Credit cards are nearly always accepted.

Department stores: The accent on small, intimate shops and boutiques has meant that Rio has not been a boom market for department stores although the arrival of the shopping center fad has opened up a new outlet for the big stores. **Sears** has stores in Bo-

looking for something different, Rio's street fairs are the best bet. The most popular is the **Hippie Fair** in Ipanema at **Praça General Osorio**, Sundays 9 a.m. to 6 p.m. A leftover from Ipanema's flower children days of the 1960s, the fair has an excellent choice of wood carvings, paintings, hand-tooled leather goods and other assorted handicrafts, including a wide selection of Rio's multi-colored tee-shirts with their fractured English messages. Despite its origins, there is nothing hippie or amateurish about the fair today. Vendors accept credit cards and dollars and their goods are top quality. Many of them also sell their wares at night along the

tafogo facing the bay and at Barra Shopping. The largest Brazilian department store, **Mesbla**, is present at Rio Sul and Barra Shopping and has a downtown store at Rua do Passeio. Rio's other department store chain, **C&A**, has stores at Rio Sul, Barra Shopping and at Av. Nossa Senhora de Copacabana 749.

Street fairs: For souvenir hunters who are

Left, fresh produce for sale at a street market. Above, an artist paints with his toes at a handicraft fair.

median strip of Copacabana's beach drive, Av. Atlantica. The median of late has become a popular selling point, attracting crowds of tourists from the hotels across the street, thus serving as a meeting place as well as a street fair.

Farther away, in style as well as distance is the **Northeastern Fair** (Feira do Nordeste). The Sunday fair (from 6 a.m. to 1 p.m.) takes place in a large public square in the neighborhood of **São Cristovão**, a half hour by car from Copacabana and Ipanema. This fair is not aimed at tourists but at the thousands of *cariocas* transplanted from their native northeast, Brazil's most glorified region in national folklore. The dozens of wooden stalls sell regional dishes and beverages of the Northeast plus such exotic ingredients as tripe and dried salted meat. Some of the region's handicrafts are sold at the fair but tourists will find little to buy. The attraction of the fair is its northeastern spirit, offering visitors an opportunity to see the northeast of Brazil without leaving Rio de Janeiro.

Antiques: For antique collectors, the *Feira de Antiquidades* (antiques fair) is a Sunday occurrence downtown at **Praça XV** from 8 a.m. - 5 p.m. On sale are antiques from throughout Brazil. The **Cassino Atlantico**

these huge mobile markets arrive at each day's site in the early morning darkness when the stalls are unpacked from trucks and assembled along the streets. Within two hours, a tranquil residential neighborhood is transformed into a maze of wooden stalls offering everything from bananas to eggplant as well as fish, meat and flowers. The vendors bark out their prices as shoppers stroll by with prices falling as the noon hour approaches and the fairs close down.

Jewelry stores: At the other end of the sophistication scale are Rio's jewelry stores, some of which have evolved into veritable gemstone empires. Brazil is the world's

and **Rio Design Center** also contain antique shops. Indian crafts are found at a downtown shop, **Artindia** at Av. Presidente Wilson 164 it is run by the government Indian bureau, Funai.

Fruit and vegetable markets: A typical *carioca* tradition is the street fruit and vegetable market (*feira* in Portuguese). Although such markets should have been relegated to the history books with the advent of supermarkets, the *cariocas* stubbornly hang on to their habits despite the monumental traffic jams they sometimes cause in Copacabana and Ipanema. Filling entire streets for blocks,

largest producer of colored gemstones and the effects of this are obvious as soon as a tourist steps off the plane. Gem dealers are literally everywhere in Rio as are their salesmen. In most cases, the gem sales pitch is low key and cultivated. Salesman and saleswomen tend to be multi lingual, cultured and often fascinating in themselves. They exude confidence in their products. Brazil is not only famous for its variety of stones but also, for prices which are unbeatable given the quality of the gems, settings and design. Costs are kept down because the operation is 100 percent domestic, from the mining of the gems to cutting, crafting and designing of jewelry.

As valuable as it is to be armed with some prior information about gemstones, shoppers should be aware that unless you are an expert, it is always wiser to buy from a reliable jeweler where you can be sure that you are getting exactly what you are paying for. Rio has several reputable and even world-renowned jewelers. Do watch out for souvenir shops offering cut rate gemstones—many are no more than colored glass.

Rio's two leading jewelers are Jules Sauer and Hans Stern, owners of Amsterdam

airports, the main shopping centers and streets and the city's leading hotels. A special treat awaits visitors to Stern's world headquarters, an impressive modern highrise in Ipanema at **Rua Visconde de Piraja 490**. In addition to Rio's poshest souvenir shop on the ground floor, Stern offers free of charge, a tour showing the process by which a raw stone becomes a polished piece of jewelry. Tourists may arrange for the tour at any Stern outlet in Rio.

Obviously, not all tourists are interested in high quality gemstones. For the more common souvenir stones, mainly agates in a variety of settings or polished stone ash-

Sauer and H. Stern jewelers respectively. Both men and their firms are famed throughout the world, with Sauer receiving top marks for craftsmanship and Stern for marketing. Shoppers looking for quality gemstones in which they can place absolute trust cannot go wrong with either of these two.

The shops of **Amsterdam Sauer** and **H. Stern** are located throughout Rio, at the

Left, Jules Sauer of Amsterdam Sauer Jewelers with an example of Brazil's wealth in gemstones. Above, Rio's colorful tee-shirts.

trays, any of Rio's multitude of gift shops will do the trick. Other popular items at these stores are clay figurines and pottery from the Northeast of Brazil, soapstone objects from the state of Minas Gerais (home of the majority of Brazil's gem mines), straw baskets and hats, colorful cotton hammocks and wooden salad bowls and trays. Brazilian primitive paintings are also prized by foreign visitors. The respected **Jean-Jacques Art Gallery** at **Rua Ramon Franco 49** in Urca near Sugarloaf, specializes in primitive works and is worth a visit to see the explosive colors of Brazilian *naif* art.

CARIOCA AS DRIVER

"Driving in Rio is more frightening than racing in a Grand Prix", according to Nelson Piquet, Brazil's three-time Formula One world racing champion.

In theory, foreign tourists can drive in Rio. In theory, so can the natives. Something strange, however, happens to a *carioca* when he sits behind a steering wheel. Normally a complacent, easy going and relaxed fellow, he is suddenly transformed into an aggressive, wild, macho man of the roadways in Rio.

Most visitors to Rio come away slightly dazed by the mayhem of the city's streets, avenues and even sidewalks. Pedestrians beware—Rio's drivers see nothing wrong with climbing onto the sidewalks to beat a traffic jam. To the uninitiated the city's thoroughfares resemble a war zone populated by thousands of crazed kamikaze drivers.

Cariocas are acknowledged masters at lane switching, cutting in, tailgating, running red lights, speeding and turning from all lanes, except the ones you would expect them to turn from. The painted lines marking lanes on the streets are considered an affront to a driver's creativity and are therefore ignored. It is not unusual to discover four lines of traffic moving along smartly on a two-lane street.

The real art of Rio's drivers is their ability to switch lanes without warning at 60 miles (96 km) an hour, cutting off the car in the lane next to them, provoking a din of shrieking brakes and blaring horns, before driving on, casually with a smile and a flip of the hand, to the next near disaster.

Not surprisingly, *cariocas* see nothing odd or unusual in their driving habits. They point out that despite the apparent mass confusion of the city's traffic, it does move. In fact, the secret to surviving this madness is to discover exactly **how** it moves. Foreign tourists who decide to brave the traffic and

take to the streets, quickly find that the rules of safe driving do not apply here.

Red lights: No self-respecting American driver would run every red light he sees and certainly never with a police car beside him. In Rio, however, such an attitude is pure nonsense and actually dangerous. The unflappable *cariocas* will tell you that stopping for red lights at night is not wise— you'd be a sitting duck for robbers. Should you mention that Rio's drivers also ignore

traffic lights during the day, they will answer that it seems foolish to waste your time at an intersection if there are no cars coming. The point is that imported morality and logic carry no weight on the streets of Rio. Those poor souls who stop at red lights soon learn that the cars behind them don't, an often painful experience. As for the police, well, there is no reason to worry as they too run the traffic lights.

There are approximately 1.2 million vehicles in Rio, counting cars, buses, trucks, motorcycles and scooters, all of them hustling about in a space that by any logic, can

Left, a Rio bus driver, one of the demons of the city's streets. Above, tunnels have been Rio's solution to the city's mountain barriers.

only handle one-third their number. The result is the usual chaos of the morning rush hour which often extends well past noon, followed by the chaos of shoppers returning home and mothers picking up school children and ending with the evening rush hour. There is seldom a moment in a normal working day when part of the city is not bogged down in hopeless traffic jams.

The problem is easy to explain—with the ocean on one side and mountains on the other, there is simply no way that six million people and their one million vehicles can fit comfortably in between. The classic example is Copacabana where 300,000 people own, Copacabana qualifies as the world's worst designed parking lot. Most of its apartment buildings were built at a time when lax building codes and a smaller population permitted developers to get by with a minimum of parking spaces in their garages. The result today is that an estimated 60 percent of the neighborhood's automobiles have no place to sleep at night. These homeless cars are stacked up on sidewalks, in public squares, on top of bushes or packed bumper to bumper on the streets in double or even triple rows. If there were a way to park a car in a tree, the residents of Copacabana would have found it.

are squeezed into high rises that fill a mere 109 streets. Each day, the neighborhood is criss-crossed by an estimated 600,000 vehicles or half of all the vehicles in Rio. With only 109 streets to choose from (of which no more than six can be called thoroughfares), as soon as the traffic backs up on one street, it immediately overflows onto dozens of others.

Parking: For those weary residents of Copacabana who manage to fight their way home on a hot summer evening, the struggle has only just begun. They must now find a place to park. With over 250,000 cars of its

This problem is not confined to the night. Tourists and pedestrians may think that the exotic mosaics of Copacabana's wide beachfront sidewalks were designed for them but car owners, think otherwise. The daylight hours see a repetition of the unending war for parking spaces. The referees of this combat are a singular band of entrepreneurs who appear mysteriously at the right moment, pointing out empty spaces and mediating between rival motorists who saw the same space at the same moment—all for a price, of course.

Acutely aware of this problem, city officials routinely launch massive campaigns aimed at ridding the sidewalks of cars. Horrible punishments are threatened and all *cariocas* are urged to defend their city against selfish *motoristas*. For the next month, the sidewalks are amazingly free of cars. Where the cars actually go no one has yet been able to discover and then everything returns to normal.

Buses and Taxis: Visitors will quickly discover that Rio's bus drivers belong in a special category—Rio's other drivers will tell you they belong in prison. Underpaid and working shifts that often reach 12 hours straight behind the wheel, the bus drivers are

sions you will have no trouble finding one—except, naturally, when its raining—the passengers of Rio's cabbies should be prepared for virtually anything. These demons of the streets have nerves of steel which will turn yours to jelly. The worst mistake you could make is to tell a Rio taxi driver you're in a hurry. The city's cabbies normally exceed the speed limit by a significant margin. Telling them to hurry up only makes it worse. Tourists should also be wary of price gouging, a favorite pasttime of the city's taxi drivers. If you don't know your way around or speak the language, it is best to ask your hotel to call a radio cab. Although their rates

always in a hurry. As a result, they are responsible for a fair share of the city's frequent traffic accidents. The basic rule of Rio's streets is amazingly simple: buses have the right of way, always. It does no good to quarrel over this since the buses have an enormous advantage—they are bigger.

The other scourge of Rio traffic is the city's huge fleet of taxis. While the larger number of taxis ensures that on most occa-

are higher you have the security of knowing that you won't be cheated, plus their drivers tend to be more courteous and slightly more sane.

The Subway: Help, though, is on its way. Rio's subway, which ran out of funds at the start of the 80s, will now be extended to Copacabana. It is a process that will make the neighborhood practically impassable for the construction of vast underground garages. Optimists predict an idyllic Copacabana for the 90s with traffic flowing normally and ample parking spaces, solving once and for all the problem of Rio's cars.

Left, waiting for the bus ride home after a day at the beach. Above, the car has taken over the sidewalks of Rio.

As with almost everything else in Rio, it undoubtedly began on the beach. When it began, however, nobody knows. But somehow, overnight it seems, there it was: Rio de Janeiro, playground of the beautiful people.

Who **are** the beautiful people? At first, they were imports—movie stars, heiresses, princes and princesses, an occasional defrocked king or queen and of course, the tycoons, all of them dripping with notoriety, glamor and cash. Rio was one of their many favorite backdrops, but certainly the most eye-catching and unquestionably the most exotic.

With time, however, the beautiful people discovered other favorite backdrops—the Riviera, Acapulco, Tahiti, Cancun. Rio slipped in popularity, lost its status and finally became a stop-over for only second class beautiful people, not the **real** ones.

New concept: But in the 1960s, two *cariocas* wrote a song that turned Rio's entire concept of beautiful upside down. That popular song was called *The Girl from Ipanema* and not only did it become a pop classic but suddenly, the focus was inverted; the beautiful people were, and still are, the *cariocas* themselves.

As visitors to Rio quickly discover, there is not one girl from Ipanema, but thousands, an eye-popping variety of beautiful, lithe young women whose shapely forms (in particular their rounded bottoms) add a new dimension to the word ecstasy. And while no one has written a song about them, the men of Rio are not bad either.

For both the men and women of Rio, the beach remains the essential ingredient of the *carioca* version of the body cult. It is on the beach that the beautiful people parade their beauty and it is because of the beach that often extraordinary efforts are made to obtain and preserve this beauty. To no one's surprise, Rio is an international center for

Left, the body cult is alive and well in Rio, a paradise for joggers.

gymnastics clubs and plastic surgeons.

Color and shape: As soon as the weather warms up each year, *cariocas* begin to concern themselves with two details—their color and their shape. No one would be caught dead looking like a tourist, pale white with a red topping, especially when a trim form is vital in a city where swim wear is designed to reveal, not to cover.

In previous decades, *cariocas* solved their form problems with crash diets at the start of summer. The health and fitness craze of the 1980s, however, has changed all that. Today, well before the temperature starts to climb a master *carioca* is fit year-round and ready to expose his or her torso on the sands of Copacabana or Ipanema. For this, Rio's health nuts turn primarily to the city's hundreds of health clubs and gymnastics centers. People in the trade claim there are 3,000 of these scattered throughout the city, but concentrated in the affluent south zone.

The gymnastics fad has become an all-consuming passion, creating a minor industry consisting of manufacturers of equipment, designers of exercise "fashions", (a **must** in fashion-conscious Brazil) as well as clubs and centers. A walk down Visconde de Piraja, the commercial center of Ipanema, shows just how extensive this fad has become. In the street's 10 blocks, at latest count there were 22 gymnastics centers and health clubs. In addition, the city is overflowing with dance academies, karate schools and other centers for the teaching of martial arts.

Gym centers: The most popular are the gym centers with their club atmosphere, serving at the same time to firm up silhouettes and bring together attractive, energetic singles. Nearly all of them follow a prescribed formula, heavy on aerobic exercises done to a disco beat—a tropical version of the Jane Fonda formula. Weightlifting has also caught on in Rio following the success of the *Rambo* and *Rocky* films and today, Sylvester Stallone clones strut along the beaches of Ipanema, São Conrado and Grumari. And although most Rio women prefer soft, sensuous curves over hardened muscles, a growing number of them are also pumping iron with the top 20 gathering annually for the title of Miss Rio Muscles.

The majority of the adherents to the exercise clubs are young women, many of whom are looking for what has become a legitimate *carioca* status symbol, the Ipanema *bunda* or behind. The exuberant, well-rounded cheeks of this Rio phenomenon is one of Brazil's most sought after treasures and are amply displayed in *carioca* bikinis, most of which would capture international prizes for truth in packaging. Some exercise class professors are known to have the "secret" for developing this classic *bunda* look (others use more practical sales pitches such as offering to improve a woman's sex life by teaching sex exercises).

In fact, the key to most gym centers is the head professor. Each has his own method, some mixing the metaphysical with the physical, producing sometimes exotic theories on "body analysis", an odd blending of Freud with Arnold Schwarzenegger. Others stick to the basics-sweat followed by more sweat. Brazil's leading actresses and singers, many of whom live in Rio, routinely announce they have discovered the ultimate professor, the man with the cure-all method for gaining the perfect form. Currently, the exercise class professor who has the final word is Rio's João Gaspar Mello, a true artist who only accepts new students if they are recommended by old students and who insists that his followers adhere completely to his program, doing no other physical activity ("How else can I evaluate my work?").

Jogging: For those who eschew the social club atmosphere of the exercise centers, there is always the sidewalk and the beach. Jogging came late to Rio but has become a *carioca* passion. Each day starting at dawn, the beach becomes the city's most densely populated gymnastics center. Regular exercise groups gather to do their sit ups on the sands of Ipanema while along the sidewalks from the bay to the distant Barra da Tijuca, thousands of joggers do their thing. In addition to the wide sidewalks that flank the beach and bay, the most popular jogging trail

is the path that encircles the Rodrigo de Frietas Lagoon, just behind Ipanema. The jogging mania, which encompasses all ages, has also led to more strenuous forms of running with marathons and more recently triathlons becoming fixtures of the *carioca* fitness scene.

The pain, effort and discipline of the jogger and runner is the same in Rio as anywhere else but nowhere else in the world do the men and women who pound feet against pavement have the scenery of Rio de Janeiro to accompany and inspire them. Joggers who have lived in other countries state that without a doubt, it is easier to run in the sun

and beauty of Rio.

Plastic surgery: Obviously, there are those for whom regular exercise is simply not enough to produce the *carioca* form. To compensate, these individuals have become regular customers of Rio's dozens of plastic surgery clinics. The man who popularized cosmetic surgery in Brazil is Dr. Ivo Pitanguy, a legend in his own right. Considered by many as the foremost plastic surgeon in the world for both cosmetic and reconstructive surgery, Pitanguy's sophisticated clinic in the neighborhood of Botafogo is a Rio landmark, frequented not only by Brazilians but by international figures such as Ursula Andress, Gina Lollobriggida and Farah Diba.

Pitanguy, however, is not a name dropper and prefers to keep his patients' names to himself. This is not the case for his patients who proudly announce that they bear a Pitanguy nose or a Pitanguy uplift as one of Rio's premier status symbols. Urbane and communicative, Pitanguy is a friend of stars and celebrities. He has also published hundreds of internationally respected works on plastic surgery. His fame has made him the most sought after plastic surgeon in Rio but since he blazed the trail, the city has attracted

implants to the latest fad, suction lipectomy or simply, liposuction. Brazil's plastic surgeons, led by Pitanguy and his colleagues in Rio, are at the forefront of international research. Breast operations are still the most common procedure performed in Rio, followed by face and nose work.

Hairdressers: Along with the growth of plastic surgery clinics has been the expansion of Rio's weight loss clinics and skin treatment centers. Health spas are just starting to appear but some of the city's hairdressers come close to being mini spas in their opulence and variety of services. Heading the list is the Jambert Haute Coiffure, a

many other excellent surgeons.

Each day, Rio's clinics do battle against wrinkles, blemishes, fatty deposits, cellulite, sagging derrieres, non-aesthetic noses and breasts that need to be compressed or expanded. The struggle to rejuvenate *carioca* matrons or to give the young the perfect body involves all the techniques of the profession, ranging from face lifts and breast

Left, working out in the morning on the sands of Ipanema. Above, *carioca* musclemen on the beach in Copacabana.

beauty salon in Leblon that is a temple to narcissism, serving men as well as women. Run by its founder and owner, Spaniard Miguel Jambert Garcia, the salon is five stories of marble decorated with Persian carpets, oriental statuary and crystal light fixtures. Luxury and the leisure lifestyle ooze from the salon's walls which house veritable artists in hair styling, facials, massages, manicures, etc.

With so much working in their favor, it is easy to understand why the beautiful people have become endemic to Rio. International celebrities eat your hearts out.

Travel Tips

DESTINATION RIO DE JANEIRO

Air: A total of 28 airlines offer international service to and from Brazil with a variety of routes, but most incoming flights head for Rio de Janeiro (see Airlines section for the list of airlines which fly to Brazil). Depending on where you are coming from, there are also direct flights to São Paulo and Brasilia, Salvador and Recife and Manaus on the Amazon River—all of which have air links with Rio. Direct international flights connect Brazil with both the east and west coast of the United States of America, as well as with Florida and Canada, major cities in Europe and South America, Japan and several African cities. Flight to Rio from New York is nine hours, from Miami slightly less, and from Los Angeles 13 hours; flights from Europe average 11-12 hours. Almost all international flights are overnight, so that you arrive conveniently in the early morning.

There are a variety of special low-cost package deals, some of them real bargains. A travel agent will be able to find out what is available and make arrangements at no extra cost to you. See Domestic Air Travel , ON THE MOVE section of the Travel Tips for details on Brazilian air passes, which must be bought outside Brazil.

Upon arrival, Rio's International Airport has facilities for exchanging currency and information posts to help you find transportation into town. (See also ON THE MOVE section).

Sea: Although there is no regular ocean passenger service to Brazil, it is possible to come by boat. Both Oremar and Linea C, which operate cruises up and down the Atlantic coast of South America during the European winter, will take on transatlantic passengers when the ships come over and return. One of Linea C's cruises out of Rio visits Miami. Several round-the-world cruise ships call at Brazilian ports and it is possible to book for just the trip to Rio. Special cruises are also organized to Rio for Carnival. The Blue Star Line, headquartered in London, carries a limited number of passengers on its cargo boats which cross the Atlantic and call at several Brazilian ports, including Rio.

Bus: There are bus services between Rio de Janeiro and major cities in neighboring South American countries, with direct lines to Asuncion (Paraguay), Buenos Aires (Argentina), Montevideo (Uruguay) and Santiago (Chile). While undoubtedly a good way to see the countryside, remember that distances are great and you will be sitting in a bus for several days and nights.

Visas: Until just a few years ago, tourist visas were issued routinely to all visitors upon arrival. Brazil has now adopted a reciprocity policy, requiring an entry visa, which must be obtained before arriving in Brazil, for citizens of those countries which also require Brazilians to apply for visas to visit. U.S. and French citizens are required to arrive with a visa in order to enter the country; Britons and Germans are not. The airline you are flying or your travel agent, should be able to tell you whether you need to apply for a visa before traveling. Alternatively, contact the nearest Brazilian consulate or embassy.

If your passport was issued by one of the countries whose citizens are not required to arrive with an entry visa, it will be stamped with a tourist visa upon entry that will permit you to remain in the country for 90 consecutive days. If you apply for a visa abroad, it will permit entry into Brazil for 90 days following the issue date. Upon entry, you will receive the same tourist visa, valid for 90 days beginning with the entry date stamped in your passport. If you are traveling to several countries and not straight to Brazil, the entry visa needn't be issued in your home country, but it's a good idea to allow for enough time so as to avoid surprises and hassles. The 90-day tourist visa can be renewed once only for another 90 days, so that you can stay a maximum of 180 days as a tourist in Brazil. To obtain such an extension, you must go to the immigration sector of the federal police located at Av. Venezuela, 2 (downtown, near Praça Mauá), tel. 263-3747 *ramal* (extn) 34. Opening hour: Monday-Fridays, 11.00 a.m. to 4.00 p.m. This can be a bit baffling for someone who has not mastered the language. Contact your country's consulate for help and orientation.

Temporary visas are issued to foreigners who will be employed in a specific activity in Brazil, for which they must stay longer than a tourist visa would allow or who will be working or doing business in the country. This is usually the case of a student, journalist or researcher, or someone in the employment of a multinational company. If this is your case, contact a Brazilian consulate or embassy well before you plan to travel, as it is usually difficult or even impossible to change the status of your visa once you are in the country. If you come with a tourist visa, you will probably have to leave the country to obtain and return on another type of visa.

Permanent visas which allow foreigners to reside and work in Brazil without giving up their own nationality are more difficult to obtain. Once again, it's best to contact a Brazilian consulate or embassy for more specific information applying to your particular situation.

Health: Brazil does not normally require any health or inoculation certificates for entry, nor will you be required to have one to enter another country from Brazil. However, if you plan to travel from Rio into areas outside of cities in the Amazon region or in the Pantanal in Mato Grosso, it is recommended that, for your own comfort and safety, you have a yellow fever shot (protects you for 10 years, but is only effective after 10 days, so plan ahead). It is also a good idea to protect yourself against malaria in these jungle areas and although there is no vaccine against malaria, there are drugs that will provide immunity while you are taking them. Consult your local public health service and be sure to get a certificate for any vaccination. You can get a yellow fever shot in Rio at the Health Ministry vaccination post located at Praça Marechal Ancora (near the ferry boat station), tel: 240-8628.

Customs: You will be given a declaration form to fill in the airplane before arrival. Once at the airport, customs officials spot check 50 percent of incoming "nothing to declare" travelers. If you are coming as a tourist and bringing articles obviously for your personal use, you will have no problem. As in most countries, food products of animal origin, plants, fruit, and seeds may be confiscated.

You can bring in $300 worth of anything bought at the airport duty-free shop— with no restriction as to quantity, type of goods or age—and $300 worth of anything brought from abroad, except liqor—limited to one bottle (each) of wine and spirits.

If you are coming on business, it's best to check with the consulate as to what limitations or obligations you are subject to. Brazil has very strict regulations limiting the entrance of computers into the country. If you must bring some type of specialized equipment, especially computers, into the country, apply for written authorization through a Brazilian consulate before traveling and then register with customs for temporary entrance—you must take it out of the country with you.

Electronic devices worth no more than $300 can be brought in on a tourist visa and need not leave the country with you. Although you are obviously not meant to sell such items while visiting as a tourist, they can be left in the country as gifts. Professional samples may be brought in, if the quantity does not lead customs inspectors to suspect that they are, in fact, for sale.

Items that may be allowed into the country, although they won't be confiscated, may be detained by the customs service and returned to you as you leave the country. Once again, if in doubt, consult the nearest consulate and bring their written reply with you.

Baggage of outgoing travelers is usually never checked, except for a security check on hand luggage. If you have purchased what could be considered a reasonable amount for a tourist of any item—including semi-precious stones—you have nothing to worry about. Be wary of wild animal skins, including alligator, as hunting of these species is strictly prohibited. It's a good idea to find out first what you can bring back into your own country.

Departure: Remember to have at least a few hundred *cruzados* left at the end of your stay to pay the airport tax as you check in for your outbound flight. It is about US$8, but can only be paid in *cruzados*.

INSIDE RIO DE JANEIRO

GETTING ACQUAINTED

· **Government:** Rio de Janeiro is the capital city of the state of Rio de Janeiro, one of 27 states which make up the Federal Republic of Brazil, each with its own state legislature. Since the federal government exercises enormous control over the economy, the political autonomy of the states is restricted. The overwhelming majority of government tax receipts are collected by the federal government and then distributed to the states and cities.

The head of government is the president who has large powers and, in fact, exercises more control over the nation than the American president does over the United States. The legislative branch of the federal government is composed of a Congress divided into a lower house, the Chamber of Deputies, and an upper house, the Senate. In February, 1987, however, the federal Congress was sworn in as a National Constitutional Assembly to draft a new federal constitution for Brazil. By the end of 1987, the work on this constitution was still incomplete. The possibility existed, however, that Brazil would undergo a major transformation, turning to a mixed parliamentary system of government with an accompanying weakening of the presidency. The new constitution was also expected to contain several major reforms, including increased powers for the Congress and for the states and cities.

Brazil's main problem throughout this century has been political instability. The next constitution will be the country's fifth since 1930. During this period, Brazil has suffered frequent intervention by the military, leading to a situation where brief attempts at democratic, civilian rule have been substituted by either increased military influence or a direct military takeover. The last military regime began with a coup in 1964 and extended until 1985 when a civilian president, chosen by an electoral college, took office.

Economy: Despite its political problems, Brazil has enjoyed excellent economic growth rates for most of the past 30 years. Today, the country is the recognized economic leader among Third World nations. Through loans and direct investments by multinational companies, Brazil in the 1960s and 1970s underwent a rapid phase of industrialization, emerging as the tenth largest economy in the world in terms of gross national product. Brazil is also the leading exporting nation in Latin America: today, 70 percent of its exports comprise manufactured goods.

Climate: Rio, located just north of the Tropic of Capricorn at a latitude of 22.5° south, is at the southern extreme of the tropic zone. The climate, because of its location on the Atlantic coast, is humid tropical. The average mean temperature in Rio is 73°F (23°C). Temperatures in summer (December-March) are hot, from 84° to 95°F (29°-35°C) on average but can climb up to a sweltering 104°F (40°C). Winter weather (June-August) is a comfortable 68°-70°F (20°-21°C), occasionally dipping down to 65°F (18°C).

Summer and winter are marked by rainfall, with more frequent and heavier rain falling in the hot summer months. Summer rains can be terrific cloudbursts, and because the city is nearby at sea-level and surrounded by mountains down which the rain water streams, streets often become rivers within minutes.

The mountain cities above Rio (such as Nova Friburgo, Petrópolis, Teresópolis) have a high altitude tropical climate, slightly cooler than the low-lying coast. The rainy and dry seasons are more pronounced and temperatures average between 64°-73°F (18°-23°C). In winter, although there is no danger of frost, the mountain air is nippy.

Clothing: As the lifestyle in Rio is casual, so is dressing. But *cariocas* are fashion-conscious and love to dress up. Summer fashions are cool to beat the heat but are also designed to show off as much suntan as possible.

What you bring to wear in Rio depends on what activities you will be engaged in. Generally speaking, for the vacationeer, comfortable, summery, casual clothes will be your best bet in Rio.

Although some restaurants in the downtown business district require a tie at lunch, other restaurants have no such regulations—although obviously, in a swanky establishment, it is expected that you are appropriately dressed, and you yourself will feel better if you blend in.

If you come on business, a suit and tie for men, and suits, skirts or dresses for women, are the office standard. Still, a suit and tie are rarely called for when you go out. Bring a summer-weight suit; for office calls—linen is cool. If you like to dress up, there are plenty of places

to go to in the evening. Try not to be ostentatious and avoid using jewelry that cry out for more attention than you want. There are many desperately poor people in Brazil and unwitting foreign tourists make attractive targets for pick-pockets and purse-snatchers.

Clothing made of synthetic fibers are handy for travelers, easy to wash, and don't need ironing. However, in the tropics these fabrics do not breathe and absorb perspiration as well as natural fibers and will make you feel twice as hot. There is nothing better for the heat than cotton and since Brazil produces linen and exports cotton, you might want to pack the bare essentials and acquire a new wardrobe. Shoes make great bargains, too.

Shorts are acceptable for both men and women in most areas, especially near the beach or in nearby resort towns, but not usually worn downtown. Loose bermudas are comfortable for the hot weather. Most churches and some museums do not admit visitors dressed in shorts. The traditional *gafieira* dance halls will also bar entrance, to those dressed in shorts, especially men. Jeans are acceptable dress for men and women and are worn a great deal in Brazil—but they can be hot.

Don't forget to pack your swimsuit! Or buy a tiny version of the string bikini, called a *tanga*, for yourself or someone back home—there are stores that sell nothing but beachwear. New styles emerge each year, in

different fabrics and colors, exposing this part or that. They seem to get smaller every year, but somehow never disappear completely. Although there have been a few timid—or rather, brave—attempts at topless sunbathing on Rio beaches, it has never really caught on. Women exposing their breasts on the beach have often been hassled and sometimes even attacked, which is ironic becuase the skimpy bikinis that Brazilians wear are actually much more provocative than if everyone were quite naturally naked.

Another contradiction is that, while everyone can walk around with practically nothing on at the beach—indeed the bikini bottoms are small—decently dressed women will get ogled and while Brazilian men don't go for catcalls, they draw their breath in sharply between clenched teeth and murmur comments as the women pass by...just as well you don't understand what they're saying. Brazilian women certainly don't let this cramp their style.

Unless you're worried about sticking out, nothing is too trendy or exotic for Rio. You may get some looks, but *cariocas* are usually concerned about not appearing provincial. Somehow, no matter how foreign tourists are dressed, Brazilians seem able to spot most of them a mile away. Although the locals in the smaller towns you may visit near Rio, may dress more conservatively, they are used to outsiders, including tourists from Rio and other Brazilian cities.

If you come during Carnival, remember that the weather will be very hot and that you will probably be in a crowd, dancing nonstop. Anything colorful is appropriate. If you plan to go to any of the balls, you will find plenty of costumes in the shops—you might want to buy just a feathered hair ornament, flowered lei or sequined accessory to complete your outfit. Many women wear no more than a bikini and makeup and at times, even less. Most men wear shorts—with or without a shirt—or sometimes a sarong. There are also fancy dress balls and most have a theme such as "Hawaii" or "Arabian Nights."

It can be cool in the winter months of June to August. Something about the weight of a sweatshirt is usually warm enough for Rio. However, you'll want a warmer sweater if you visit the nearby mountain towns at that time of year. At other times of the year, you may need a light sweater, jacket or sweatshirt in Rio, if not for cooler evenings, then for the air conditioning in hotels, restaurants and offices!

Rain gear is always handy to have along—Brazilians tend to use umbrellas more than raincoats. Something that folds up small and can be slipped into your bag is best. Sunglasses are also a good idea, especially for the beach. Seaside hotels will provide you with sun umbrellas and beach towels.

Common sense dictates a pair of comfortable walking shoes—there is no better way to get out and explore than on foot. Sandals are comfortable in the heat and even if you don't plan to wear them for walking around the streets, sandals or beach thongs are very convenient for getting across the hot sand from your hotel to the water's edge. If there's one thing that gives Brazilians the giggles, it's the sight of a "gringo" going to the beach in shoes and socks. Brazilians often wear high-heeled shoes and show special agility on the sidewalks which can be veritable obstacle courses—with holes, puddles, beggars, vendors, garbage cans and cobblestones—and are frequently completely taken over by parked cars. You may want to buy shoes or sandals while in Brazil—leather goods are a steal.

A sturdy shoulder bag is a practical item—use it to carry your camera discreetly. Toss in a folding umbrella, guidebook and map and you're ready for a day's outing. But don't wear it slung behind you.

Bring washable clothes, or if you have anything that needs special cleaning, have it washed when you return from your trip. While laundry service in the hotels is usually excellent, dry cleaning in Brazil is generally not very reliable.

When buying clothes, remember that although most material are sanforized, some natural fabrics will shrink. *Pequeno* = Small; *Médio* = Medium, and *Grande* = Large (often marked "P," "M" and "G"). *Maior* means larger; *menor* means smaller.

Time Zones: Standard Time in Rio de Janeiro is three hours behind Greenwich Mean Time. Clocks are set ahead an hour in October for the summer months and back to Standard Time in March or April. Most of the rest of Brazil lies within this same time zone, which extends west to the mouth of the Amazon river. Most of Brazil's northern Amazon region and the central western states of Mato Grosso and Mato Grosso do Sul are in a time zone four hours behind GMT. The far western northern state of Acre and the westermost tip of Amazona state are five hours behind GMT.

Rio time compares as follows to standard times in other parts of the world as well as other cities within Brazil:

7.00 a.m.
San Francisco
9.00 a.m.
Mexico City
10.00 a.m.
New York,
Montreal, Bogota
10.30 a.m.
Caracas
11.00 a.m.
Manaus, Santiago
12.00 noon
Rio de Janeiro, São Pau-lo, Brasilia, Salvador, Recife, Belém, Buenos Aires
3.00 p.m.
London
4.00 p.m.
Berlin, Geneva, Paris
5.00 p.m.
Capetown, Helsinki
6.00 p.m.
Moscow

11.00 p.m.
Hong Kong
12.00 p.m.
Tokyo
1.00 a.m.
Melbourne

Business Hours: Business hours for most offices are 9.00 a.m. to 6.00 p.m., Monday through Friday. Lunch "hours" may last literally hours.

Banks open at 10.00 a.m. and close at 4.30 p.m., Monday through Friday. The *casas de cámbio* currency exchanges operate usually from 9.00 a.m. to 5.00 p.m. or 5.30 p.m.

Most **stores** are open from 9.00 a.m. to 6.30 p.m. or 7.00 p.m., but may stay open much later, depending on their location. The shopping centers are open Monday through Saturday from 10.00 a.m. to 10.00 p.m., although not all the shops inside keep necessarily the same hours. Large department stores are usually open from 9.00 a.m. to 10.00 p.m., Monday through Friday and from 9.00 a.m. to 6.30 p.m. on Saturdays. Most supermarkets are open from 8.00 a.m. to 8.00 p.m., although some stay open later.

Service station hours vary, but they have the option of staying open 24 hours a day, seven days a week.

Post offices are open to the public from 8.00 a.m. to 6.00 p.m., weekdays and from 8.00 a.m. to noon on Saturdays. Some branches are open until later and the post office in the International Airport is open 24 hours a day.

Many **pharmacies** stay open until 10.00 p.m. and there are 24-hour drugstores in several parts of town.

Hours of the day are numbered from "zero hour" to 24, but can also be referred to as being in the morning (*da manha*), in the afternoon (*da tarde*) or at night (*da noite*), so that 8.00 p.m. could either be referred to as *vinte horas* (literally 20 hours, written 20.00) or as *oito* (eight) *horas da noite*.

Money: Brazil's currency was changed in 1986 from the *cruzeiro* to the *cruzado* (abbreviated Cz$). Both currencies are still in circulation, and can be confusing for the foreign visitor. The older *cruzeiro* bills are supposed to bear a stamp with their new value, but not all bills have been stamped. Since the new *cruzado* is worth 1,000 *cruzeiros*, it is easy to convert: simply lop off three zeros or move the decimal point over three places. A *centavo* or "cent" is worth one hundredth of a *cruzado*, i.e. 100 *centavos* = 1 *cruzado*. You may still find 1,000, 5,000, 10,000, 50,000, 100,000 and 500,000 *cruzeiro* bills in circulation, now worth one, five, 10, 50, 100 and 500 *cruzados*, respectively. Although the older *cruzeiro* coins are being removed from circulation, you will still run into them. The newer coins have the arms of the republic on the reverse side and come in units of 10, 20 and 50 *centovos* and one, five and 10 *cruzados*, all worth face value. You will find the older *cruzeiro* coins in denominations of 500

cruzeiros, now worth 50 *centavos*, or one thousandth of their face value.

The use of commas and decimal points in Portuguese is the opposite of what you are probably used to, so that one thousand *cruzados* is written Cz$1.000,00.

Unfortunately, the exchange rate fluctuates so often that even an idea of what it might be, cannot be given here. Leading newspapers list the U.S. dollar—*cruzado* exchange values daily, with a higher rate for "buying" (*compra*) than for "selling" (*venda*) dollars. Right alongside the official is the so-called "pareller" (*paralelo*) rate for buying and selling dollars. Although it is also referred to as the "black market" exchange (*cambio negro*), it is by no means illegal. The amount of *cruzados* that Brazilian citizens and firms can officially exchange into dollars is limited, but they can purchase dollars at the higher parallel rate. The margin between the two rates varies, shrinking at peak tourist seasons when more dollars are coming into the country.

The hotels will exchange your foreign currency into *cruzados* at the offical (fewer *cruzados* per dollar) rate, but do not usually exchange traveler's checks and cannot change any leftover *cruzados* back into your currency at the end of your stay. Money changers at special shops (*casa de cambia*) or at tourist agencies will give you the parallel exchange rate for both buying and selling currency. Some accept traveler's checks and which exchange rate they use for them is optional.

Banks, of course, deal only with the official rate. Many banks (but not all branches) have an exchange (*cambio*) department that can exchange cash or traveler's checks into *cruzados*, but again, will not exchange them back into foreign currency. The only exception is the Banco do Brasil branches located at international airports which, as you are departing, will convert at the official rate, 30 percent of the amount of the currency that you exchanged at a similar airport bank branch, on your way into Brazil (you must show the receipt of the initial exchange). You can't get your traveler's checks cashed into dollars anywhere.

Unless you don't have the time, it's best obviously to exchange money at the parallel rate. Ask your hotel where the nearest money exchange is located. Try to plan so as not to have too many *cruzados* left at the end of your stay or you will be "buying" your foreign currency back at the highest rate (higher than you exchanged them for).

Many Brazilians put what savings they can into dollars, as a hedge against inflation as the *cruzado* devalues. If you have friends or business associates in Brazil, you might offer to exchange money with them at a mutually acceptable exchange rate. If you choose to exchange money with hotel employees, taxi drivers, etc, who are eager to trade their *cruzados* for dollars, keep

informed as to what a good rate is.

Most hotels will accept payment in traveler's checks or with almost any major credit card. Many restaurants and shops also take credit cards and will usually display those which they accept at the entrance. Most frequently displayed are Diners Club, American Express and Visa, all of which have offices in Brazil. Back home, your bill will be calculated using the official exchange rate. You will probably have trouble paying with a credit card if you go to less expensive restaurants away from tourist areas, but meals in these places will seem so inexpensive that you'll hardly feel the need to charge your meal.

Of course, you can also pay with dollars. In this case, hotels, restaurants, stores, taxis, etc. will usually give you an exchange rate between the offical and the parallel rates. If you are going to pay in dollars, do check the exchange rates so you will know what is fair.

Holidays: National holidays in Brazil are moved to the nearest Monday, with the exception of New Year's Day, Christmas, Easter and Carnival.

—January 1
New Year's Day (national holiday)
—January 20
Saint Sebastian Day, Rio's patron saint (holiday in Rio only)
—Feb/March (moveable)
Carnival, celebrated all over Brazil on the four

days leading up to Ash Wednesday
— M a r c h / A p r i l (moveable)
Easter (Good Friday is a holiday)
—April 21
Tiradentes Day honors martyred hero of Brazil's independence (holiday)
—May 1
Labor Day (national holiday)
—May/June (moveable)
Corpus Christi (national holiday)
—June/July
Festas Juninas, a series of street festivals, take place in June and early July in honor of Saints John, Peter and Anthony and feature music and dancing, bonfires, mock marriages and special food and drink
—September 7
Independence Day (national holiday)
—October 12
Nossa Senhora (Our Lady) de Aparecida, Brazil's patron saint (national holiday)
—November 2
All souls Day (national holiday)
—November 15
Proclamation of the Republic (national holiday); also election day in Brazil
—December 25
Christmas Day (national holiday)
—December 31
On New Year's Eve gifts are offered to Iemanjá, the Afro-Brazilian goddess of the sea, on Rio's beaches.

Worship: Catholicism is the official and dominant religion in Brazil, but many people are followers of religions of African origin. Of these, *Candomblé* is the purer form, with dieties (the *orixás*), rituals, music, dance and even the language very similar to what is practised in the parts of Africa from which it was brought. *Umbanda* involves a syncretism with Catholicism, in which each *orixá* has a corresponding Catholic saint.

Spiritualism is also widely practised in Brazil, combining both African and European influences. Many Brazilians who are nominally Catholic attend both Afro-Brazilian or spiritual and Christian rites.

Candomblé is practised mostly in Bahia, and while there are followers in Rio de Janeiro, they keep quite a low profile. *Umbanda* and spiritism, however, have a large following in Rio and your hotel can assist in arrangements to see a ceremony—visitors are welcome so long as they show respect for other's beliefs. Ask permission before taking any photographs.

If you wish to attend a church service of your faith while in Rio, besides the numerous Catholic churches, there are several Protestant sects and synagogues. Both Our Lady of Mercy (Catholic) at Rua Visconde de Caravelas, 48, Botafogo (tel: 246-5664) and Christchurch (Anglican) at Rua Real Grandeza, 99, Botafogo (tel: 226-2978) have English-language church services. For information about other denominations and services in other foreign languages, enquire at your hotel or call a consulate.

Etiquette: Generally speaking, social customs are not vastly different from what you will find in other "western" countries. Brazilians can be both awkwardly formal and disarmingly informal—*cariocas* are the most informal and uninhabited of Brazilians.

Surnames are little used. Though people start out on a first name basis, titles or respect—*senhor* for men and most frequently *donna* for women—are used to be polite to strangers and to show respect to someone of a different age group or social class. In some families, children address their parents as *o senhor* and *a senhora* instead of what would be the equivalent of "you."

While handshaking is a common practice when people are introduced, it is customary to greet not only friends and relatives but also complete strangers to whom you are being introduced with hugs and kisses. The "social" form of kissing consists usually of a kiss on each cheek. While men and women greet each other with kisses, as do women among themselves, in most circles, men do not kiss each other; rather, they shake hands while giving a pat on the shoulder with the other hand. Or if they are more intimate, men will embrace, thumping each other on the back. Although this is the general custom, there are subleties about who kisses whom, governed by social position.

Besides the more formal forms of hugging and kissing, visitors from more con-servative cultures remark that Brazilians are quite unabashed about expressing affection in public.

Brazilians are generous hosts, seeing to it that guests' glasses, plates or coffee cups are never empty. Besides the genuine pleasure of being a gracious host, there is the question of honor involved. The "pot luck" of "bring-your-own-bottle" party is not very popular in Brazil—people like to *give* a party, even in the *favela*.

Although definitely a machist society, "machismo" in Brazil takes a milder and more subtle form than is generally found in neighboring Hispanic America.

While at all other times, a polite, decent people, something happens when Brazilians get behind the steering wheel. *Cariocas* are particularly erratic drivers. Be cautious when driving or crossing streets and be prepared to make a dash. Drivers expect pedestrians to watch out for themselves and get out of their way.

Unless you're in Rio on business, expect schedules to be more flexible than what you may be used to. It's not considered rude to show up half an hour late for a social engagement.

Tipping: Most restaurants usually add a 10 percent service charge on to your bill. If you are in doubt as to whether it has been included, it's best to ask (*O service está incluido?*). Give the waiter a bigger tip if you feel the service was special. Many waiters will make a sour face if you don't tip above the 10 percent included in the bill, but you have no obligation to do so. Tipping at a lunch counter is optional, but people often leave the small change from their bill. It is always appreciated—even if it's as little as US 10 cents.

Hotels will add a 10 percent service charge to your bill, but this doesn't necessarily go to the individuals who were helpful to you. Don't be afraid that you are overtipping—if you tip as much as you would at home, it will be considered very generous indeed; if you tip too little, however, it could be insulting and it would have been better to give no tip at all.

Tipping taxi drivers is optional. Most Brazilians don't. Again, if your driver has been especially helpful or waited for you, reward him appropriately. Drivers should be tipped if they help with the luggage—some will charge from US 35 to 50 cents per bag. Tip the airport porter about this same rate (or he may tell you how much it is)—tip the last porter to help you, as what you pay goes into a pool.

A 10-20 percent tip is expected in barber shops and beauty salons; shoeshine boys, gas station attendants, etc. should be paid about a third to half of what you would expect to tip at home. Boys offering to watch your car on the street expect to get about US 45 to 50 cents when you return to collect your car. If they try to charge you as much as US$1 or US$1.50 in advance outside a busy nightclub or theater, it's best to pay or you may find the car scratched when you return.

If you are a house guest, it is good form to leave a tip for any household help (who cooked while you were there or laundered your clothing). Ask your host how much would be appropriate.

You can always tip in dollars, if you want to. This is especially appreciated.

Electrical Current: In Rio de Janeiro it is **127 volts**. If you are traveling to other parts of Brazil, be aware that the voltage is not standardized throughout the country. São Paulo, Belém, Belo Horizonte, Corumbá, Cuiabá, Curitiba, Foz do Iguaçu, Porto Alegre and Salvador also have a 127-volt current. In Brasilia, Florianopolis, Fortaleza, Recife and São Luis it is 220 volts. Manaus has 110-volt elecricity.

If you use an appliance on a lower current, it will function poorly, but if you plug it into a much higher voltage than it was made for, it will overheat and probably short-circuit. To be sure, enquire as you check into your hotel—most hotels have adaptors and many have more than one voltage available. Also many electric shavers, hair dryers, etc. have a switch so that they can be used on either a 110 or 220-volt current (100-volt appliances work normally on a 127-volt current).

Telephones: Pay phones in Brazil take tokens which are sold at newsstands, bars or shops, usually located near the phones. Ask for *fichas de telefone* (the "i" is pronounced like a long "e" and the "ch" has an "sh" sound). Each *ficha* is good for three minutes, after which your call will be cut off. To avoid being cut off, insert several tokens into the slot—any unused tokens will be returned when you hang up.

The sidewalk *telefone público* is also called an *orelhão* (big ear) because of the protective shell which takes the place of a booth— yellow for local or collect calls, blue for direct-dial, long-distance calls within Brazil, requiring a special, more expensive token. You can also call from a *posto telefônico*, a telephone company station, where you can either buy tokens, use a phone and pay the cashier afterward, or make a credit card or collect call.

The *posto telefonico* at the International Airport, main Novo Rio bus terminal and at Av. N.S. de Copacabana 462 (upstairs) operate 24 hours a day. The one at the domestic Santos Dumont airport operates from 6.00 a.m. to 11.00 p.m. and the Ipanema office, located at Rua Visconde de Pirajá 111/*loja* (or shop) 5 is open from 6.30 a.m. until midnight.

International Calls: Almost any country can be reached by telephone from Brazil. Country codes are listed at the front of the telephone directory.

Direct dialing—00 + country code + area code + phone number;
000333—information regarding long distance calls (area codes, direc-

tory assistance, complaints, etc.);

000111—international operator. Go through operator to place person-to-person, collect and credit card calls. Operators and interpreters who speak several languages are available;

107—collect or telecard calls from a pay phone (no token needed);

000334—information regarding rates—international rates go down 20 percent between 8.00 p.m. and 5.00 a.m. (Brasilia time), Monday-Saturday and all day Sunday.

Long distance Domestic Calls: Area codes within Brazil are also listed at the front of the directory.

Direct dialing (IDD)—dial **0** + area code + phone number;

Direct-dial collect call—**9** + area code + phone number. A recorded message will tell you to identify yourself and the city from which you are calling after the beep. If the party you are calling does not accept your call, they simply hang up;

107—operator-assisted collect call from pay phone (no token needed). Domestic long-distance rates go down 75 percent every day between 11.00 p.m. and 6.00 a.m. and 11.00 p.m. on Sundays and holidays.

Other service telephone numbers:

100—local operator
101—domestic long-distance operator
102—local directory assistance

area code + 102—directory assistance in that area
108—information regarding rates
135—telegrams (local, national and international)
134—wake-up service
130—correct time

Postal Services: Post offices are generally open from 8.00 a.m. to 6.00 p.m., Mondays-Fridays, 8.00 a.m. to noon on Saturdays and are closed on Sundays and holidays. Some branch offices stay open until much later. The post office in the Rio de Janeiro International Airport is open 24 hours a day. Post offices are usually designated with a yellow sign reading *correiros* or sometimes "ECT" (for Empresa de Correios e Telégrafos translated, Postal and Telegraph Company).

An airmail letter to or from U.S.A. takes about a week. Domestic post is usually delivered a day or two after it is mailed. National and international rapid mail service is available, as well as registered post and parcel service (the post office has parcel boxes available). Stamps for collectors can be purchased at the post office.

Have mail sent to you at your hotel. Some consulates will hold mail for citizens of the country they represent, but tend to discourage this practice. If you are a client of American Express, you can have your mail directed to: Kontik Franstur, Avenida Atlantica 2316 A, Rio de Janeiro-RJ 22041, Brazil, tel: 235-1396.

Telegrams: Telegrams

can be sent from any post office. You can send a telegram by telephone by dialing 135. Your hotel can arrange this. If you are a house guest, the operator can tell you how much will be charged on your host's phone bill.

Telex: These can be sent from certain post offices—the branch at Av. N.S. de Copacabana 540-A is closest to most tourist hotels. The post office at the International Airport has telex facilities and most hotels are equipped with this service for their guests.

Facsimile: Some of the top hotels have this service. Call the Rio Palace, Caesar Park, Inter-Continental or Meridien hotels (see section on IN TRANSIT). You needn't be a guest to use it.

Newspapers and Magazines: A daily English-language newspaper, the *Latin America Daily Post*, circulates in Rio de Janeiro and São Paulo, carrying international news from wire services, including sports, financial and domestic Brazilian news. The *Miami Herald*, the Latin American edition of the *International Herald Tribune* and the *Wall Street Journal* are available on many newsstands in the big cities, as are news magazines such as *Newsweek* and *Time*. At larger newsstands and airport bookshops, you can find other foreign newspapers and a good range of international publications, including German, French and English magazines.

You may want to buy a local paper to find out what's on in town (besides the musical shows, there are many U.S. movies showing in the original language with Portuguese sub-titles) or to check the exchange rate. You don't need to be proficient in Portuguese to read the entertainment listings under the headings *cinema, show, dance, músic, teatro, televisão, exposições. Crianças* means "children," and the exchange rates for foreign currencies are listed under *cambia*.

If you know some Portuguese and want to read the Rio newspapers, the most authoritative and respected are the *Jornal do Brasil* and *O Globa*. There is no nationwide paper, but these large dailies circulate throughout a good part of the country.

Television and Radio: Brazilian **television** is very sophisticated; Brazil exports programs, not just to Third World nations, but to Europe too. There are five national and three regional networks, which along with independent stations, bring television service to practically all parts of Brazil. Only one network, the educational television, is government-controlled. Brazil's giant T.V., *Globo*, is the fourth largest commercial network in the world with over 40 stations, and has great influence over the information people have access to, in a country with a high illiteracy rate. Viewers in Rio have a choice of six channels.

The Brazilian soap opera or *telenovela* is a unique feature. Shown on prime time, just about everybody watches, getting so caught up in the continuing drama that they schedule social and even professional activities so as not to coincide with any crucial chapters. The extremely well-made soaps both reflect customs and set trends in fashion, speech and social habits. You might find it interesting to watch a few as they are considered a true mirror of Brazilian urban middle-class society.

Only about a third of all television programs are imports—mostly from U.S.A. Foreign series, specials, sports coverage and movies are dubbed in Portuguese, except for some of the late-night movies and musical shows. Some of the top hotels have satellite dish antennas and receive the English-language Armed Forces Radio and Television Service with a selection of news, sports and entertainment from American networks.

There are close to 2,000 **radio stations** in Brazil—over 100 in the state of Rio de Janeiro—which play international and Brazilian pop hits, as well as a variety of Brazil's rich musical offerings, reflecting regional tastes. A lot of American music, as well as classical music, is played, including Sunday afternoon operas in some areas. The Culture Ministry station often has some very interesting musical programs. All broadcasts are in Portuguese. If you have a radio that picks up short-wave transmissions, the *Voice of America* and *BBC World Service* broadcast English-language programs to Brazil.

Photography: Both Kodakcolor and Fujicolor film for color prints, as well as Ektachrome slide film, can be bought and developed in Brazil. Kodakchrome is not available nor is it developed in Brazil. Hotel shops will have film and specialty shops, easily spotted by signs out front advertising the brands of film they sell, carry equipment and accessories and will take your film for processing.

Developing is quick and of good quality, but quite expensive. There is 24-hour finishing and even one-hour service at the Rio-Sul shopping center. Reliable labs include Kodak, Fuji, Multicolor and Curt. Find out from your hotel where you can take your film to be developed. (*Revelar* = to develop; *revelação* = developing; film is *filme*).

Although it is often easier to have your pictures developed when you return from your trip, if you are going to be traveling around a great deal, remember that exposure to heat and multiple X-ray security checks at airports could ruin them.

For tourists entering with photographic equipment that is obviously for vacation picture-taking, there are no customs restrictions. If you are bringing in a lot of professional equipment, it must be registered with customs for temporary entrance and then leave the country with you. In this case, it would be wise to contact a Brazilian consulate before traveling.

Depending on what you bring, you may need written authorization from a diplomatic mission outside Brazil. It's best to check.

Try to avoid taking pictures during the middle of the day when the sun is strongest and tends to wash out colors. Light in the tropics is very white and bright and you may want to bring an appropriate filter along. Mornings from sunrise to 10.00 a.m. and anytime time between 3.00 p.m. and sunset, are best for photography.

Don't walk around with your camera hanging around your neck or over your shoulder—there's nothing more conspicious than a foreign tourist with a camera, an easy target for a snatcher. Carry it discreetly in a bag slung in front of you. Never leave a camera unattended at the beach. If you have expensive equipment, it's a good idea to have it insured.

Weights & Measures:
The metric system is used throughout Brazil and temperature is measured on the centigrade or Celsius scale. Other, older measuring units are sometimes used in rural areas, but people are generally familiar with the metric. If you are not, here's how to convert to and from the English system:

Temperature:
degrees Celcius x 9/5 + 32 = degrees Fahrenheit
degrees Fahrenheit - 32 x 5/9 = degrees Celcius (degree =*grau*)

Capacity/Liquids:
liter x 1.06 = quart
liter x .26 = gallon
liter x 2.11 = pint

quart x .95 = liter
gallon x 3.79 = liter
pint x .47 = liter
(liter = *litra*)

Weight:
gram x .04 = ounce
kilogram x 2.20 = pound
metric ton x .98 = ton
ounce x 28.35 = gram
pound x .45 = kilogram
ton x 1.11 = metric ton
(gram = *grama*, kilogram = *quilograma* or more often *quilo* or *kilo* and ton = *tonelada*)

Length:
millimeters x .039 = inch
meter x 3.28 = foot
meter x 1.09 = yard
kilometer x .62 = mile
inch x 25.40 = millimeter
foot x .30 = meter
yard x .91 = meter
mile x 1.61 = kilometer (in Portuguese millimeter =*milimetro*, centimeter= *centimetro*, meter= *metro,* kilometer=*quiló-metro*).

Area:
hectare x 2.47 = acre
acre x 0.40 = hectare

Health Precautions and Services

Drinking Water: Don't drink tap water in Brazil. Although water in the cities is treated and is sometimes quite heavily chlorinated, people filter water in their homes. Any hotel or restaurant will have inexpensive bottled mineral water, both carbonated (*com gas* or "with gas") and uncarbonated (*sem gas* or "without gas"). If you are out in the hot sun, make an effort to drink extra fluids.

At the Drug Store: Prescription drugs are available in abundance—frequently without a prescription—and you may find old favorites that have been banned for years in your home country. Bring a supply of prescription drugs that you take regularly, but simple things like aspirin, antacids, bandaids, sunscreen, etc. are easily available.

Drugstores offer a variety of cosmetics, including many familiar brands. Sanitary napkins can be found in any drugstore or supermarket, but tampons are not always available. The Farmácia Piaui (Av. Ataulfo de Paiva 1283-A in Leblon, tel: 274-8448; and Rua Barata Ribeiro 646-B in Copacabana, tel: 255-7445), the Drogaria Cru-zeiro (Av. N.S. de Copacabana 1212 in Copacabana, tel: 287-3636) and the Farmácia do Leme (Av. Prado Junior 237-A in Copacabana, tel: 275-3847) never close.

Sunburn Preventives:
Don't underestimate the tropical sun! Often, there is a pleasant breeze as you loll on the beach and you are not aware of how the sun is baking you, until it's too late; You should be especially if you're coming from a cold, northern winter, when your skin has not been exposed to the sun for months.

Use an appropriate sunscreen or *filtro solar* (there are several excellent brands on sale in Brazil), start out with short sessions and avoid the hottest part of the day. It's silly to be too eager and end up with a painful sunburn that will cause peeling. Take care of your skin after the beach by using a moisture cream. Remember to drink enough—coconut water, fruit juice or mineral water are excellent.

Medical Care: Should you need a doctor while in Rio, the hotel you are staying at will be able to recommend reliable professionals who often speak several languages. Many of the better hotels have a doctor on duty. Your consulate will also be able to supply you with a list of physicians who speak your language. The English-speaking Rio Health Collective runs a 24-hour referral service (call (021) 325-9300 ramal, or extension, 44) for the Rio area only.

Check with your health insurance company or travel agent before traveling—some insurance plans cover any medical service that you may require while abroad.

Emergency hospitals:
Miguel Couto - Rua Mario Ribeiro 117, Gavea, tel: 274-2121
Rocha Maia - Rua General Severiano 91, Botafogo, tel: 295-2095

Sousa Aguiar - Praça da República 111, Centro, tel: 296-4114/242-4539
Information medical emergencies: dial 191
Ambulance: dial 193.

Tourist Information

In Brazil: Besides the national tourism board, **Embratur**, each state has its own tourism board—Rio's is called **Flumitur**. Rio has a city tourism board as well—**Riotur**.
In Rio: Tourist facilities at the Rio de Janeiro international airport are available to orientate the visitor and help you find transportation and accommodation (if you don't have reservations).

Riotur
Rua da Assembleia 10
8°/9° *andares* (8th/9th floors)
Centro (downtown)
Telephone: 242-8000
Monday—Friday
9.00 a.m.-6.00 p.m.

Flumitur
Rua da Assembléia 10
7°/8° *andares* (7th/8th floors)

Centro (downtown)
Tel: 252-4512
Monday—Friday
9.00 a.m.-6.00 p.m.

More handy are Riotur's stands found around town:
The cablecar station at Pão de Açucar (Sugarloaf)
Av. Pasteur 520, Urca
Daily, 8.00 a.m.-8.00 p.m.

The Marina da Gloria
Aterro do Flamengo
Gloria
Tel: 205-6447
Daily, 8.00 a.m.-5.00 p.m.

The main bus station Rodoviaria Novo Rio
Av. Francisco Bicalho 1
São Cristovão
Telephone: 291-5151
Daily, 6.00 a.m.-midnight
Flumitur runs the information counters at the arrival section of the international airport, from 5.00 a.m.-11.00 p.m., tel: 398-4073/4077.

Hotels are always an excellent source of information and can indicate local happenings and tourist offerings such as sightseeing and excursions, entertainment and transportation.

ON THE MOVE

TRANSPORT

Transportation to and from Airport: Until you get your bearings, you are better off taking a special airport taxi for which you pay in advance at the airport at a fixed rate, set according to your destination. There will

be less of a communication problem, no misunderstanding about the fare and even if the driver takes you around by the "scenic route," you won't be charged extra for it.

If you should decide to take a regular taxi, check out the fares posted for the official taxis so that you'll have an idea of the normal rate.

Special airport bus service provides transportation from Rio's International Airport, passing through the downtown business district (*Centro*) and then on to the domestic Santos Dumont airport or looping by the major beach hotels in Copacabana, Ipanema, Leblon, São Conrado and out to Barra da

Tijuca. Enquire at the airport information desk as to whether your hotel is on the route. Another option is to take the special bus to the in-town Santos Dumont airport and take a taxi from there. If you're really adventurous, you can rent a car at either one of the airports.

Some of the top class hotels will send a driver to pick you up at the airport—it's best to make arrangements beforehand when you make your room reservations.

Taxis: Taxis are probably the best way for visitors to get around in Rio. Of course, it's easy to get "taken for a ride" in a strange city. Whenever possible, take a taxi from your hotel where someone can help you tell the driver where you want to go. **Radio taxis** that you order by phone are slightly more expensive, but safer and more comfortable. Although the drivers of the **yellow cabs** you flag down on the street won't actually rob you, some occasionally try to overcharge or take you the long way around. Try to find out about how much you should expect to pay for a given destination—most trips will be just a few dollars. **Airport taxis** charge exorbitant rates by Brazilian terms—US$10 to US$20, depending on the distance—but you will probably find fares relatively low compared to North America or Europe.

Because of inflation and, consequently, frequent fuel price increases, it is impossible to keep all meters regulated at the latest authorized fare. Drivers are required to post a chart on the inside of the left rear window so that passengers can find out how much is owed, based on what the meter reads. Radio taxis charge a percentage (usually about 30 percent) above the meter rate. **Special taxis** charge a pre-established amount depending on your destination. If you hail a taxi at the curbside, be sure the driver raises the no. 1 tag when he resets the meter for your run. The black no. 2 tag indicates that the meter is set at a 20 percent higher rate, which is charged from 10.00 p.m. until 6.00 a.m. and on Sundays and holidays or when going beyond certain specified city bounds or up into steep areas. Cab drivers can also use the no. 2 rate during December to earn the "13th month salary" that Brazilian workers receive as a sort of Christmas bonus.

You can book a regular taxi (no extra fee) from Cooper-Transpa, tel: 593-2598. For a radio taxi (percentage above meter) call Coopertramo, tel: 260-2022. For a special taxi (pre-set rate) call Cootramo, tel: 270-1442; or Transcoopass, tel: 270-4888.

The Metró: Rio de Janeiro has an excellent, though not extensive, subway service with bright, clean, air-conditioned cars. The *metró* is one of the easiest way for a tourist to get around without getting lost. Maps in the stations and in each car help you find your way without having to communicate in Portuguese. Lines run out from the city center and service is further extended by bus links, with train-bus combination tickets. Buses which are an extension of subway lines are marked *integração*.

Rio's two lines reach out from downtown only as far south as Botafogo and as far as the northern suburb of Irajá, with stops near the Sambadrome and Maracanã soccer stadium. Bus link-ups extend service on both ends. The Rio subway is closed on Sundays and runs from 6.00 a.m. to 11.00 p.m., Monday-Saturday.

There is just one price for a single (*unitério*) ticket, even if you transfer from one line to another. There are round-trip (*ida e volta*) and multi-fare tickets as well as different combination tickets with buses (*metró-óni-bus*). Tickets are sold in the stations and on the *integração* buses and prices are clearly posted. (*Entrada* = entrance; *saida* = exit).

Buses

City Buses: Only a small percentage of Brazilians can afford cars, so public transportation is used a great deal.

Special air-conditioned buses (known as a *frescão*) connect residential areas to the downtown business district. One line links Rio's two commercial airports and another runs from the international airport out to Barra da Tijuca, passing by the beach hotels in Copacabana, Ipanema, Leblon and São Conrado. The *frescões* stop at regular bus stops. As you get on, you will be handed a ticket. Take a seat and an attendant will come around to collect your fare—US$0.15 to just over US$1, depending on the route. Your hotel can help provide information about bus routes, but most hotels discourage tourists from riding anything but the special buses. The *Guia Quatro Rodas* guide to Rio, on sale at newsstands, lists all the bus routes (in Portuguese).

Another special bus line, the *jardineira*, follows the beaches from Leme to São Conrado (through Copacabana, Ipanema and Leblon). White posts mark where the *jardineiras* stop along the way. The open sides (giving the buses the appearance of an old-fashioned street car) and slower pace allow you to take in the sights.

The regular buses cost around US 15 cents. Get on through the back door (often quite a high step up) and after paying the *trocador,* who will give you change, move through the turnstile. It's a good idea to have your fare ready—several people may board at your stop and all have to get through the turnstile before they can sit down. This is a favorite bottleneck for pickpockets who can jump out the back door as the bus takes off. If you travel standing, be sure to hold on tight. Although many Rio bus drivers are friendly and helpful, some are particularly inconsiderate of passengers, jamming on the brakes suddenly, careening around corners. Signal when you want to get off by pulling the cord (some buses have buttons) and exit through the front door.

Robberies do occur, even on crowded buses, in broad daylight. If you ride the regular city buses, try to avoid the rush hour when passengers on certain lines are packed in tighter than the proverbial sardines in the can. Don't carry valuables, keep your camera inside a bag and shoulderbags in front of you, avoid calling attention to yourself by speaking loudly in a foreign language. In short, be discreet.

Out of Town Buses: Comfortable, on-schedule bus service is available to all parts of Brazil and to several other South American countries from Rio. Remember that distances are long and bus rides can take days. You might prefer to break a long journey with a stop along the way. For the foreigner, bus service is inexpensive: the six-hour ride between Rio de Janeiro and São Paulo, for example, costs around U.S.$4 for the regular bus, with upholstered, reclining seats, comparable to what you would expect in the U.S.A. and around U.S.$8 for the *leito* sleeper, with wider and fully reclining seats with foot rests, as well as coffee and soft drinks abroad. At busy times like holidays, buses on the Rio—São Paulo line depart at the rate of one per minute. On other routes, there may be one bus per day (such as the Rio—Belém route which costs around US$30 for the 52-hour trip) or just one or two per week. You can buy your ticket in advance through a travel agent or at the bus station.

If you're on a flexible holiday schedule, try to avoid the weekend exodus when *cariocas* escape to the resort cities up and down the coast and in the mountains. Traffic bogs down and the bus depot becomes impossibly crowded, especially during the school holidays (January-March and July).

Car Rental: Cars are easily rented in Rio. Both Avis and Hertz operate in Brazil while the two largest Brazilian national chains are Localiza and Nobre. There are also other good local companies. Rates will vary from around $30 up to $85-$90 a day (including insurance and taxes), depending on the type of the car. Some companies charge a flat daily rate, while others charge for mileage. Payment can be charged on major international credit cards. Some companies will charge extra if you rent a car in one city and hand it back in another. If you plan to drive one way only between cities, it's best to rent from one of the two largest chains which have more branches.

Arrangements can be made at the airport as you arrive, through your hotel or at the agencies. An international driver's license facilitates matters, but you can rent a car with your driver's license from home. For another US$20 or so, you can hire a driver along with the car for an eight-hour shift plus about US$4 for each extra hour.

Driving in Brazil may be chaotic compared to what you are used to. Rio drivers are notorious for their erratic lane changing, in-town speeding and disregard for pedestrians and other drivers on the road. Be on the defensive and expect the unexpected. Parking can be difficult downtown. A good solution is to park your car at the Botafogo subway station and take the underground into town. It seems wherever you park, within seconds a freelance car "guard" will appear, either offering to keep an eye on your car in the hopes of receiving a tip or actually demanding that you pay him in advance for his (dubious) vigilance. The equivalent of US 40 to 50 cents is sufficient. It's best to pay or risk finding some slight damage to the car upon your return.

The highways, especially the interstates, are quite good, but are crowded with many trucks which slow down traffic on winding, climbing stretches in the mountains. If you plan to travel much by road in Brazil, buy the Q*uatro Rodas* (Four Wheels) Brazil road guide, complete with road maps and itineraries, available at most newsstands.

Boats: There are regular ferryboat services across the bay to Niteroi and to the bay islands of Paquetá and Governador from the Praça Quinze (XV) station downtown. Both services use huge double-decker ferries and hydrofoils (*aerobarcos*).

A visit to Paquetá makes a nice outing—the regular boat takes an hour and a half while the hydrofoil makes the trip in 15 minutes. The ferries run all day until 11.30

p.m. The hydrofoils run from 10.00 a.m. to 4.00 p.m., Monday-Friday and 8.00 a.m. to 5.00 p.m. on Saturdays, Sundays and holidays.

A half or full day outing can be booked on the **Bateau Mouche**, Tuesday-Sunday and on holidays. The morning cruise sails out of the bay to visit the islands that you see from the beach in Ipanema and Leblon. The afternoon cruise tours the bay, including a stop at Paquetá. The full day cruise offers both routes with lunch included. The boat leaves from the Sol e Mar restaurant located at Av. Nestor Moreira, 11 in Botafogo (tel: 295-1997).

Sailboats, yachts, schooner-like *saveiros* and speed boats can be rented at Marina da Gloria, Aterro do Flamengo (tel: 265-0797/285-2247).

Ocean cruises are organized out of Rio to Buenos Aires and the Caribbean, with stops along Brazil's coast, by Linea C and Oremar. These must be booked well in advance.

Domestic Air Travel:
For travel within Brazil, the major arilines are Transbrasil, Varig/Cruzeiro and Vasp. There are also several regional carriers with service to smaller cities. The three larger airlines fly extensive routes throughout the country and have ticket counters at the airport and ticket offices in most cities. Tickets can also be purchased at travel agencies at hotels, and reservations can be made by phone or telex. Unless you want to play

things by ear, it is easier to make reservations from home through your travel agent, before traveling.

Different lines have similar prices for the same routes. Some sample fares (at mid-1987 dollar equivalent) from Rio de Janeiro to...

Belém	US$167
Brasília	US$ 67
For do Iguaçu	US$ 87
Manaus	US$194
Recife	US$126
Salvador	US$ 86
São Paulo	US$ 34

There is a 20 percent discount for night flights (*vóo económica* or *vóo noturno*) with departures between midnight and 6.00 a.m. Most routes will have a night flight by one or another of the major airlines.

Transbrasil and Varig also offer **air passes** which must be bought outside Brazil. There are two types: one costing US$250 (mid-1987 price) is valid for 14 days and allows you to visit four cities; the other costs US$330, is valid for 21 days, and permits unlimited travel. Ask your travel agent about these —good deals if you plan to travel within Brazil.

The large airlines also cooperate in a shuttle service between Rio and São Paulo (with flights every half hour), Rio and Brasília (flights every hour) and Rio and Belo Horizonte (usually about 10 flights per day). You can just get on the next flight with no reservation, but this can entail a long wait. For information on flight times and reservations call 220-7728 (Rio—SP only) or 398-3665 (for all three shuttle routes).

On domestic flights, there is a 20 kg (44 lb) weight limit for checked baggage and the international standards apply for hand luggage.

Air taxi service is also available to fly anywhere in the world. Enquire at the airport or make arrangements through a travel agent or your hotel.

Be sure to verify the airport from which your flight leaves. Your hotel will be able to assist and provide transportation to the airport.

Trains: Except for overcrowded urban commuter railways, trains are not a major form of transportation in Brazil and rail links are not extensive. If you have the time, the night train is one of the nicest ways to travel between Rio and São Paulo. Reserve in advance (tel: 233-3390). The train leaves at 11.30 p.m. and arrives at 8.00 a.m. You can enjoy dinner in the diner car or in your sleeper compartment— a double is $17, single $11.

IN TRANSIT

WHERE TO STAY

There is no shortage of good hotels in Rio de Janeiro. High quality international standard hotels have multi-lingual staff prepared to help you find what you want and need. Many hotels have their own travel agencies. We list here only a selection of the best hotels in town, in which all rooms have private baths with hot showers, air conditioning, telephone, television and refrigerator-bar. Rates include breakfast and a 10 percent service charge is added on to the bill. But there are less expensive hotels .

You can rent a furnished apartment from just a few days up to several months. Look in the classified advertisements section of the *Jornal do Brasil* or *O Globo* under *Imóveis* (real estate)— *Aluguel* (rental)—*Temporada* (short-term). There are also several decent apartment-hotels in Rio.

It is always best to make reservations well in advance, especially during Carnival or on a major holiday, when hotels are full of Brazilian tourists as well as visiting foreigners. Travelers often come to get away from the Northern Hemisphere winter and Brazilians also travel more during the summer school holidays in January and February, as well as in July. Even if you are traveling to an area that you think is off the usual international tourist route, beware, local facilities there may be saturated with Brazilian vacationers.

If you are venturing away from the usual places visited by tourists, for which no hotels are listed here, you will find the *Quatro Rodas Guia Brasil* road guide useful. Available on newsstands, it has road maps and listings including hotels, restaurants and local attractions for 715 Brazilian cities. Although available only in Portuguese, it uses a system of symbols with explanations in English and Spanish.

In smaller towns with fewer options, some of the hotels indicated here offer more modest accommodations. Cheaper hotels cost as little as $15-$20 for a couple.

They are usually clean with polite service, but you will most likely have to communicate in Portuguese. It's always a good idea to ask to see the room before deciding to take it.

If traveling by car, you should be aware that motels in Brazil are not what you're used to at home: rooms, usually garishly decorated and outfitted with mirrors, private pools and round beds, are rented out by the hour for amorous trysts.

If you are interested in camping, contact the Camping Clube do Brasil at their national headquarters in Rio de Janeiro at Rua Senador Dantas 75, 29th floor (tel: 262-7172). There are several campgrounds on the outskirts of Rio. The Casa do Estudante do Brasil, located at Praça Ana Amelia 9, 8th floor, Castelo, in downtown Rio (tel: 220-7223) has a list of hostels in 10 Brazilain states, including several in Rio, which are registered with the International Youth Hostel Federation and charge just a few dollars. Despite the name, there is no age restriction.

Hotels in Rio de Janeiro

The Very Best: Room rates for these hotels start at about $115 for a couple at the official exchange rate. All have swimming pools and saunas, some of the city's top restaurants, beauty parlors, jewelers, shops, travel agencies, medical personnel, satellite dish antennas (to receive television programs from the U.S.A.), secretarial services, telex and facsimile and ample facilities for conventions and banquets.

Caesar Park
Av. Vieira Souto 460
Ipanema
Tel: 287-3122
Reservations toll-free:
(021)-800-0789
Telex: (21) 21204
On the beach in Ipanema. Beautiful view from the sundeck, poolside bar on the roof. Tea room, baby-sitters. Petronius restaurant specializes in sea-food and has a *sushi* bar.

Inter-Continental Rio
Av. Pref. Mendes de Morais 222, São Conrado
Tel: 322-2200
Telex: (21) 21790
Besides being on the beach, has fabulous view of surrounding green mountains. Three tennis courts, gymnasium and discotheque nightclub. Barber shop, baby-sitters, car rentals. Restaurants include gourmet Monseigneur and branch of Alfredo's of Rome.

Meridien
Av. Atlântica 1020
Leme
Tel: 275-9922
Reservations: 295-0299
Telex: (21) 23183)
On the Leme end of Copacabana beach. Has its own cinema and nightclub. Also a barber shop, car rental. Its rooftop Saint-Honoré restaurant is one of Rio's finest.

Rio Palace
Av. Atlântica 4240
Copacabana
Tel: 521-3232
Reservations: 262-017
Toll free: (021)-800-6158
Telex: (21) 21803
At Ipanema end of Copacabana beach. Nightclub, English-style bar with live music. Baby-sitters, tea room, car rental. The Cassino Atlântico shopping mall is on the ground and basement levels. Le Pré Catalan restaurant is one of the best in Rio.

Other Five-star Hotels: These hotels, which have also earned the Brazilian tourism board, Embratur's maximum five-star rating, are well-served in terms of bars and restaurants, have boutiques and jewelers, beauty parlors and saunas. Rates also start at about $115 for a couple at the official exchange rate.

Copacabana Palace
Av. Atlântica 1702
Copacabana
Tel: 255-7070
Reservations: 237-3271
Toll free: (021)-800-1533
Elegant old building on the beach in Copacabana, a relic of the casino days. Pleasant poolside restaurant, art gallery and theater, medical service, barber shop, baby-sitters, secretarial service and telex.

Everest Rio
Rua Prudente de Morias 1117, Ipanema
Tel: 287-8282
Telex: (21) 22254
One block off the beach in Ipanema, in Rio's most fashionable restaurant and shopping area. Barber shop. Rooftop pool with view.

Marina Palace
Rua Delfim Moreira 630, Leblon
Tel: 259-5212
Telex: (21) 30224
On the beach in Leblon. Satellite dish antenna.

Rio Othon Palace
Av. Atlântica 3264
Copacabana
Tel: 255-8813
Telex: (21) 22655
On Copacabana beach, has a pool, barber shop, babysitting, secretarial and telex services. Rooftop Skylab bar has a great view; chic basement. Also the Studio C nightclub.

Rio Sheraton
Av. Niemeyer 121
Vidigal
Tel: 274-1122
Reservations toll-free:
(021)-800-0722
Telex: (21) 21206
On its own little beach halfway between Leblon and São Conrado. Barbecue house, tennis courts and three swimming pools on seaside grounds. Satellite dish antenna, car rental, travel agency, medical staff, baby-sitters, secretarial and

telex services. Beach service. Large banquet and conference facilities.

Luxury Hotels:
Rates range around $60 to over $115 for a couple at the official exchange rate. All these hotels have their own restaurants and bars.

Leme Palace
Av. Atlântica 656, Leme
Tel: 275-8080
Telex: (21) 23265
On the beach. Beauty parlor, meeting rooms.

Luxor Copacabana
Av. Atlântica 2554
Copacabana
Tel: 257-1940
Reservations toll-free:
(021)-800-1537
Telex: (21) 23971
On the beach. Jewelers.

Marina Rio
Av. Delfim Moreira
696, Leblon
Tel: 239-8844
Telex: (21) 30224
On the beach. Meeting rooms for small groups.

Hotel Nacional Rio
Av. Niemeyer 769
São Conrado
Tel: 322-1000
Telex: (21) 23615
On the beach in São Conrado. Two pools, sauna, tennis courts. Auditorium, large convention facilities. Art gallery, boutique, jewelers, nightclub. Hair-dressers, travel agency, medical staff. Secretarial, telex and babysitting services. Satellite dish anetenna. Heliport.

Praia Ipanema
Av. Vieira Souto 706
Ipanema
Tel: 239-9932
Telex: (21) 31280
On Ipanema beach. Rooftop pool, beauty parlor, meeting rooms.

Sol Ipanema
Av. Vieira Souto 320
Ipanema
Tel: 227-0060
Telex: (21) 21979
Small rooftop pool, beauty parlor and satellite dish antenna.

Also Excellent:
Rates vary from around $45 to $115 for a couple at the official exchange rate. All have bars and restaurants.

California
Av. Atlântica 2616
Copacabana
Tel: 257-1900
Telex: (21) 22655
Good beachfront location. Beauty parlor.

Gloria
Rua do Russel 632
Gloria 222
Tel: 205-7272
Telex: (21) 23623
Located near downtown and close to the Marina da Gloria. Pool, sauna, beauty parlor, tea room, theater, convention facilities, handicraft shop.

Luxor Continental
Rua Gustavo Sampaio
320, Leme
Tel: 275-5252
Telex: (21) 21469
One block from beach in Leme. Boutique, jewelers, small meeting room.

Luxor Regente
Av. Atlântica 3716
Copacabana
Tel: 287-4212
Reservations toll-free:
(021)-800-1537
On Copacabana beach. Convention facilities, jeweler, sauna. Excellent Forno e Fagão restaurant.

Miramar Palace
Av. Atlântica 3668
Copacabana
Tel: 247-6070
Telex: (21) 21505
On Copacabana beach. Tea room, convention facilities, jeweler.

Ouro Verde
Av. Atlântica 1456
Copancabana
Tel: 542-1887
Telex: (21) 23848
Small hotel on the beach in Copacabana. Traditional, high quality Ouro Verde restaurant.

Trocadero
Av. Atlântica 2064
Copancabana
Tel: 257-1834
Telex: (21) 22655
On Copacabana beach. Moenda restaurant specializes in Brazilian food.

Accommodations outside Rio

The following is a list of hotels in other cities in the state of Rio de Janeiro.

Angra dos Reis

Hotel do Frade/ Portogalo
161, Copacabana
Tel: (021) 267-7375

Telex: (021) 31034
Reservations for both ho-
tels can be made at Rua Joaquim Nabuco.

Búzios

Pousada Casas Brancas
Morro Humaitá, 712
Tel: (0246) 23-1458

Pousada La Chimere
Praça Eugênio Honold
36, Praia dos Ossos
Tel: (0246) 23-1460;
Reservations in Rio
Tel: (021) 220-2129

Pousasa nas Rocas
Ilha Rasa
Marina Porto Buzios
Tel: (0246) 23-1303
Telex: (021) 31356;
Reservations in Rio
Tel: (021) 253-0001

Auberge de l'Hermitage
Baia Formosa
Tel: (0246) 23-1103;
Reservations in Rio
Tel: (021) 224-6757

Cabo Frio

Ponta de Areia
Av. Espadarte, 184
Caminho Verde, Ogiva
Tel: (0246) 43-2053

Pousada Porto Pero
Av. dos Pescadores
2002
Tel: (0246) 43-1395
Telex: (021) 34343

Pousada Portoveleiro
Av. dos Espardartes
129, Caminho Verde
Ogiva
Tel: (0246) 43-3081

Itacuruçá

A'guas Lindas
Itacuruçá Island
Reservations in Rio
Tel: (021) 220-0007

Hotel do Pierre
Itacuruçá Island
Tel: (021) 788-1016

Jaguanum
Jaguanum Island
Reservations in Rio
Tel: (021) 237-5119

Itatiaia

Cabanas de Itatiaia
Parque Nacional 6 km
Tel: (0243) 52-1328

Hotel do Ypê
Parque Nacional 13 km
Tel: (0243) 52-1453

Simon
Parque Nacional 13 km
Tel: (0243) 52-1122

Nova Friburgo

Bucsky
Estrada Niteroi-Nova
Friburgo, km. 76.5, Mury
Tel: (0245) 22-5052
Telex: (021) 32243

Fazenda Garlip
Estrada Niteroi-Nova
Friburgo, km. 70.5, Mury
Tel: (0245) 42-1330

Mury Garden
Estrada Niteroi-Nova
Friburgo, km. 70, Mury
Tel: (0245) 42-1176

Park Hotel
A1. Princesa Isabel

Parque São Clemente
Tel: (0245) 22-0825

Sans Souci
Rua Itajai, Sans Souci
Tel: (0245) 22-7752
Telex: (0245) 34348

Parati

Pousada do Ouro
Rua Dr. Pereira, 145
Tel: (0243) 71-1311;
Reservations in Rio
Tel: (021) 221-2022

Petrópolis

Casa do Sol
Estr. Rio-Petrópolis, km.
115
Quitandinha
Tel: (0242) 43-5062

Riverside Paraque
Rua Hermogêneo
Silva, 522, Retiro
Tel: (0242) 42-3704

Resende

Espigão Palace
Rua Sebastião José
Rodrigues, 255
Tel: (0243) 54-1855

Teresópolis

Alpina
Estr. Teresópolis
Nova Friburgo, km. 22.6
Tel: (021) 742-8833
Telex: (021) 34958

São Moritz
Estr. Teresópolis
Nova Friburgo, 36 km
Tel: 742-4360

FOOD DIGEST

There are restaurants to suit every taste and budget in Rio where you can get a meal at practically any time of the night. A big meal early in the morning, however, may be more difficult to find. Breakfast usually consists of *café com leite* (hot coffee with milk), bread and sometimes fruit. Lunch is the heaviest meal of the day and you might find it very heavy indeed in the hot climate. Supper can be quite late.

Traditional Brazilian cuisine is tastily seasoned, usually not peppery. In a country as large and diverse as Brazil, there are naturally, regional specialities, some of which can be sampled in Rio restaurants. Rio itself does not have a special cuisine, but borrows recipes from other regions and around the world. The staple diet for working class *cariocas* is rice and (usually black) beans, supplemented by some kind of meat and vegetables. A typical lunch in a modest restaurant is rice, beans, French fries and a thin slice of beef steak (*bife*).

If there is one dish that is truly *carioca*, it would be black bean *feijoada*. Although *feijoada* is popular in Brazil, in Rio is it somewhat of an institution for a Saturday lunch. Many consider the best *feijoada* in town to be served at the **Domus Aurea** and **Tiberius** restaurants in the Caesar Park hotel in Ipanema. Other good places to try this local favorite (only served on Saturday) are **Moenda, Dinho's Place, Sal e Pimenta, Atlantis, Monte Carlo** and **Chalé**.

Although travel books will encourage you to get out of your hotel and sample the local fare, in Rio, it just so happens that many of the top restaurants are located in hotels! And that includes not only the excellent French and "international" restaurants but also excellent Brazilian meals offered by some of these hotels.

The most unusual variety of Brazilian food is the style of cooking from the northeastern state of Bahia, which has a strong African influence. Bahian cuisine uses a lot of seafood, prepared with coconut milk and *dendê* palm oil. Bahian food can be very hot, although restaurants usually serve the *pimenta* sauce separately. If you do like it hot, ask for hot *malagueta* pepper sauce which many restaurants prepare themselves, often jealously guarding the recipe. Favorite dishes from Bahia include: *vatapá* (fresh and dried shrimp, fish, ground raw peanuts, coconut milk, *dendé* oil seasonings thickened with bread into a creamy mush); *moqueca* (can be made of fish, shrimp, crab meat or a mixture of seafood in a *dendé* and coconut milk sauce); *xinxim de galimba* (a chicken fricassee with *dendé* oil, dried shrimp and ground raw peanuts); *caruru* (a shrimp-okra gumbo with *dendé* oil); *babá de camarão* (cooked and mashed manioc root with shrimp, *dendé* oil and coconut milk); and *acarajé* (a patty made of ground beans fried in *dendé* oil and filled with *vatapá*, dried shrimp and *pimenta*).

In Rio, restaurants serving Bahian specialities include: **Chalé, Moenda, Sal e Pimenta** and **Netas de Maria de São Pedro**. A stand at the handicraft fair on Praça General Osório in Ipanema on Sundays, also sells Bahian food. Also, most seafood restaurants include at least one or two Bahian dishes, most often a *moqueca*.

Other exotic Brazilian regional cuisine can be sampled at **Arataca**, which specializes in food from the Amazon region: Amazon River fish, *pato no tucupi* (duck with *tucupi*, made of numbing manioc leaves) and *tacacá* broth, also prepared with *tucupi*. A modest restaurant in Santa Teresa, **Bar do Arnaudo**, serves food from the northeast. The speciality is dried, salted beef (*carne seca* or *carne do sol*).

Cuisine from the mountainous state of Minas Gerais goes heavy on pork and beans. Some of the restaurants specializing in Brazilian cuisine have such offerings as: *tutu* (mashed black beans thickened with manioc meal) or *fei-jão tropeiro* (*fradinho* beans, bacon and manioc meal). Minas Gerais also produces delicious pork sausage and *queijo minas*, a fresh, white, bland cheese) traditionally served with fruit paste for dessert.

While barbecued meats are not unique to Brazil, the way in which they are served, is. Originating in Brazil's south where the *gaucho* cowboys roasted meat over an open campfire, *churrasco* is popular all over the country and foreign visitors are usually delighted with the *churrascaria* barbecue restaurants.

Those that specialize in the *roizio* system, offer all the meat you can eat for a set price. But it's not just one type or cut of meat. Waiters come round to your table with skewers of chicken, pork, sausage and several cuts of beef. Choose what looks best to you and it is sliced right onto your plate. They keep coming back, so don't worry that you'll miss anything. Meanwhile, your table is loaded with a variety of side dishes.

As you would expect in a seaport city, there is plenty of seafood. Most "international" restaurants have many fish, shrimp and other seafood offerings on their menus. The Portuguese restaurants also serve a great deal of seafood (although the *bacalhau,* dried salted codfish, is imported from colder seas). One of the tastiest local varieties of fish is the *badeja* sea bass, with firm, white meat. *Peixe a Brasileira,* which many restaurants include in the menu, is a fish stew served with *pirão* (manioc root meal cooked with broth from the stew to the consistency of porridge).

Rio's very best restaurants are French. French chefs at such elegant establishments

as the **Le Saint Honoré, Claude Troisgros** and **Clube Gourmet** include tropical ingredients in their imaginative nouvelle cuisine creations.

Fast food is available at almost every corner in Rio. You will see the familiar golden arches of **Mac-Donald's** which have sprouted up in several neighborhoods. The biggest chain of fast food stores is **Bob's**. **Gordon's** (with a branch in Copacabana and one in Leblon) has good sandwiches.

There is a Brazilian alternative, which is worth trying: the *salgadinho*. These are little pastries filled with beef, chicken, cheese, shrimp, *palmita*, etc. can be tiny, usually served as hors d'oeuvres at a reception or to go with a drink at a bar, or of the size filling enough for a light lunch.

There are little lunch counters with a variety of these snacks and some of the best can be bought at the bakeries, which you can either take home or eat standing up at the counter, along with a fruit juice or soft drink.

Also at the bakery, try *pão de queijo*, a cheesy quick bread. *Pastelarias* which specialize in *pasteis* (two thinly-rolled layers of pasta-like dough with a filling sealed between, deep-fried), almost always offer *caldo de cana* or sugar cane juice as well. Instead of French fries, try *aipim frito*, deep-fried manioc root, to go with beer.

Pizza parlors are to be found all over town. The **Mister Pizza** chain probably has the largest number of stores. Many of the sidewalk

restaurants along the beach will serve a cheesy and often quite doughy pizza.

Many Brazilian **desserts** are made out of fruit, coconut, eggs and milk. Compotes and thick jams, often served with mild cheese, are made out of many fruits and even squash and sweet potatoes. Avocado is also used as a dessert, mashed or whipped up in the blender with sugar and lemon juice. There are wonderful tropical fruit sherbets and ice creams. Coconut appears in many types of desserts and candies—sidewalk vendors sell molasses—colored and white *cocadas*. Portuguese-style egg yolk desserts are delicious, especially *quindim* (a rich, sweet egg yolk and coconut custard). *Dace de leite* is a Brazilian version of caramel, made by boiling milk with sugar, often served with cheese. *Pudim de leite* is a very common dessert, a pudding made with sweetened condensed milk and caramel syrup. Manioc is also used as a dessert in the form of *bolo de aipim*, a stiff pudding made out of the grated root and coconut. Special sweet shops sell a variety of *docinhos*, or candies and cakes, pies, etc. One of the most special desserts, (and after a large meal on a hot day, perhaps the most appropriate) is the wonderful tropical fruit—there's always something exotic and delicious in season.

The restaurants listed below are just a selection of some of the very best.

Beverages: Brazilians are great social drinkers and

love to sit for hours talking and often singing with friends. During the hottest months, this will usually be in open air restaurants where most of the people will be ordering *chope*, cold draft beer, perfect for the hot weather. Brazilian beers are really very good. There may be some confusion when ordering—although *cerveja* means beer, it is usually used to refer to bottled beer only.

Brazil's own unique brew is *cachaca*, a strong liquor distilled from sugar cane, a type of rum, if you will, but with its own distinct flavor. Usually colorless, it can also be amber. Each region boasts of its locally produced *cachaca*, also called *pinga, cana* or *aguardente*, but traditional producers are the states of Minas Gerais, Rio de Janeiro, São Paulo and the northeastern states where sugar cane has long been a cash crop.

Out of *cachaca*, some of the most delightful drinks are concocted. The most popular is *caipirinha* which can be considered the national drink: lime, crushed in glass, peel, and all, sugar, ice and *cachaca*: perfect in its simplicity. Variations of this drink are made using vodka or rum, but you should try the real thing. Some bars and restaurants mix their *caipirinhas* sweeter than you may want—order yours *com pouco acucar* (with a small amount of sugar) or even *sem acucar* (without sugar).

Batidas, as the name suggests, are beaten in the blender or shaken and come in as many varieties as there are types of fruit in the trop-ics. Basically fruit juice with *cachaca*, some are also prepared with sweetened condensed milk. Favorites are *batida de maracuja* (passion fruit) and *batida de coco* (coconut milk)—exotic flavors for visitors from cooler climates. When imbibing *batidas*, don't forget that the *cachaca* makes them a potent drink, even though they taste just like fruit juice.

Straight *cachaca* or beer is what the working class Brazilian will drink in the neighborhood *botequim*, little bars where you drink standing up at the counter. Some of these will serve *cachaca* steeped with herbs—the resulting infusion is considered to be "good for what ails you." The *botequims* are quite often filled with men, and while women are not barred and won't usually be hassled, they may not feel comfortable about being the only female in this male stronghold. And a single female foreigner will be more than obvious.

Try the **Brazilian wines**. Produced in the cooler southern states, they are quite good. Restaurants offer a selection of the best— ask the maitre d' for help in ordering what you like. *Tinto* is red, *branco* is white and *rose* is the same; *seco* is dry and *suave*, which actually means soft, refers to the sweetness of the wine. Excellent wines imported from Argentina and Chile are not expensive in Brazil, so you may want to take advantage of this.

The usual variety of spirits are available, both *impor-tado* (imported) and *nacional* (domestic). There are really no good Brazilian whiskeys and imports are very expensive. Some of the brands you may be familiar with are produced locally— you will know by the price.

Among the non-alcoholic beverages, fresh fruit juices are a real treat. Any hotel or restaurant will have three or four types but the snack bars specializing in *suco de fruita* have an amazing variety. The fruits on display—guavas, mangoes, pineapples, passion fruit, persimmons, tamarind, fruits that even if their names were translatable you would never have heard of, as well as the more familiar apples, melons, bananas and strawberries—are as tasty as they are colorful.

They will also whip up a glass of lemonade for you or squeeze a plain orange. All juices are made fresh for each order. Delicious fruit milkshakes called *vitaminas* make a nutritious snack. Most common are the *mista* or mixed fruit—usually papaya and banana with a touch of beet root to give it a pretty color; banana *com aveia*, which is banana and raw oatmeal; and *abacate* which is made of avocado. These make great breakfast accompaniments.

If you've never sipped coconut water—the water from the green fruit—you can stop at a street vendor, often a trailer near the beach. Restaurants or bars that serve *agua de coco* will usually hang the *cocos* near the door (pronounced like cocoa—if you want hot chocolate *quente*, otherwise you'll probably get a coconut). The top is lopped off and you drink the clear, colorless juice with a straw. After drinking the water, you can ask to have the *coco* split open so that you can eat the soft, gelatin-like flesh inside the shell.

Another tropical treat is the juice of sugarcane, which is squeezed and served at snack bars that advertise *caldo de cana*. Street vendors use a little crank wringer. This juice, as is to be expected, is sweet and filling, and has a pleasant, subtle flavor.

Among soft drinks, you will find the familiar Coco-Cola and Pepsi products as well as domestic brands. A uniquely Brazilian soft drink is *quarana*, flavored with a small Amazon fruit. Quite sweet, but good, it is a favorite with children.

Bottled mineral water is available everywhere, both carbonated (*com gas*) and plain (*sem gas*), and it's best for visitors to stick to it. Although water in the cities is treated, people further filter it in their homes and if you are a houseguest, you will no doubt be served *agua filtrada*. Not drinking unfiltered tap water is a question of common sense.

If you are traditional and can't do without your morning tea, never fear. Tea is grown in Brazil and many of the fancier hotels and restaurants can offer you an English brand. Try the indigenous South American *mate* (pronounced "maw-tchee") tea. The black tea is usually drunk as a refreshing iced tea; the green tea, called

chimarrao, is sipped with a silver straw and a strainer at the lower end; in Brazil's far south it's a gaucho tradition.

Last but certainly not least, is the coffee for which Brazil is justly famous. *Cafe* is roasted dark, ground fine, prepared strong and taken with plenty of sugar. Coffee mixed with hot milk (*cafe com leite*) is the traditional breakfast beverage throughout Brazil. Other than at breakfast, it is served black in tiny demitasse cups and never with a meal.

The *cafezinhos* or "little coffees" will be offered the visitor to any home of office. They are served piping hot at any *botequim* (little stand-up bars that serve only *cafezinho*), and are the traditional and, you will agree, perfect ending to every meal.

Decaffeinated coffee is, of course, unheard of, a heresy even. If you should want to take ground coffee back, you can buy it at the airport, vacuum-packed to last longer, or pick it up at any supermarket or bakery.

Restaurants

Brazilian

Arataca
Rua Figueiredo de Magalhães
28, Copacabana
Tel: 255-7448;
Rua Dias Ferreira
135A, Leblon
Tel: 274-1444
Credit cards: Major ones.
Specialities from Amazon state of Pará and the Northeast. Amazon river fish and some unusual seasoning. Amazon fruit served as

juice, ices, compotes. The Copacabana branch is more comfortable. Both restaurants open every day 11.00 a.m.-2.00 a.m. A meal will cost around $10.

Bar do Armaudo
Rua Almirante Alexandrino
316, Santa Teresa
Tel: 252-7246
Tuesday-Sunday
11.30 a.m.-11 p.m.
Under $10
Credit cards: American Express
Specialities of the Northeast in the quaint Santa Teresa hillside district. A favorite order is dried salted beef (*carne de sol*) and manioc root. There can be a long wait on weekends, but reservations are not accepted.

Chalé
Rua da Matriz 54
Botafogo
Tel: 286-0897
12-4 p.m., 7 p.m.-1 a.m.
$10-$20
Credit cards: Major ones.
Brazilian, especially Bahian, cuisine. *Feijoada*. Colonial decor with antiques, waiters/waitresses in costume. Also international cuisine. It's a good idea to make reservations on weekends.

Escondidinho
Beco dos Barbeiros
12, A & B, Centro
Tel: 242-2234
11 a.m.-6 p.m.
Closed Saturday and Sunday
About $10
No credit cards.
Full menu of Brazilian food plus each day's special: *muqueca, feijoada, cozido,*

sarapatel, chicken in blood sauce, specialities from Minas Gerais.

Maria Thereza Weiss
Rua Visconde Silva 152, Largo do IBAM
Botafogo
Tel: 286-3098
Noon-1 a.m.
Closed Monday
$10-$20
Credit cards: Major ones.
Maria Thereza Weiss is well known in Brazil for her books on Brazilian cooking. Restaurant in big old house serves selection of Brazilian dishes and traditional international fare as well as an array of traditional Brazilian desserts. A shop outside also sells pastries, sweet snacks and cakes to go.

Moenda
Av. Atlântica 2064
(Hotel Trocadero)
Copacabana
Tel: 257-1834
Daily, noon-midnight
$10-$20
Credit cards: Major ones.
Brazilain dishes and Bahian specialities. Waitresses in Bahian garb will explain the ingredients. Good *feijoada*. View of Copacabana beach.

Netas de Maria de São Pedro
Rue Miguel Lemos 56-B, Copacabana
Tel: 257-9689
Monday-Saturday
11 a.m.-1 a.m.
Sunday, 11 a.m.-6 p.m.
About $10
No credit cards accepted.
Two granddaughters carry on the tradition of the original Maria whose restaurant

in the Mercado Modelo in Salvador is one of the Bahian city's best eateries. *Xinxim, muqueca, sarapatel* and Bahian receipes seasoned with *dendê* palm oil and coconut milk.

Sal & Pimenta
Rua Barão da Torre 368, Ipanema
Tel: 521-1460
Monday-Friday
Noon-4 p.m. and 8 p.m.-2 a.m.
Saturday and Sunday
Noon-2 a.m.
Over $15
Credit cards: Major ones.
Pleasant, glassed-in balcony overlooks square. Attracts fashionable set, good idea to reserve. Fish and shrimp *muquecas, bobó de camarão, xinxim de galinha*, Saturday *feijoada*. Also Italian food. Sunday brunch. Upstairs from chic Alô-Alô piano bar (5 p.m. - 5 a.m.).

Villa Riso
Estrada da Gávea 729, São Conrado
Tel: 274-1708/322-0899
Tuesday-Sunday
12.30-4 p.m.
Brazlian specialities served on the veranda of an 18th-century plantation house—only for groups as part of Villa Riso's colonial tour. Call to make your own arrangements or go through your hotel.

Chinese and Japanese

Centro China
Ave. Epitácio Pessoa 1164, Lagoa
Tel: 287-3947
Tuesday-Friday
7 p.m.-2 a.m.

Saturday and Sunday
Noon-4 p.m. and 7 p.m.-midnight;
Rua Alice 88, Laranjeiras
Tel: 225-5398
Tuesday-Friday
12-3 p.m. and 7-11 p.m.
Saturday and Sunday
Noon-4 p.m. and 7 p.m.-midnight
Up to $10
Credit cards: Only some are accepted.
Good Chinese food. Owner, Ming, is from Shanghai. Shark's fin soup, *tofu*, sweet and sour pork. View of the lagoon. Original restaurant at Rua Alice serves lunch during the week as well.

Edo Garden
Av. das Americas 2578, Barra da Tijuca
Tel: 325-3319
7 p.m.-1 a.m.
Sunday, noon-10 p.m
$10-$20
Credit cards accepted.
Japanese-style house set in a garden with fish pond. Private dining rooms and *sushi* bar. *Sukiyaki, teppanyaki, kushi, sushi, sashimi, yoenabe.*

Grande Muralha
Rua São Clemente 409, Botafogo
Tel: 266-4402
Monday-Saturday
Noon-3 p.m. and
7 p.m.-11.30 p.m.
Sunday, noon-10.30 p.m.
Up to $10
No credit cards.
Peking and Cantonese cuisine at moderate prices.

Mariko
Av. Vieira Souto 460
(Caesar Park Hotel)

Ipanema
Tel: 287-3122
Monday-Saturday
6 p.m.-1 a.m.
$10-$15
Credit cards accepted.
Excellent *sushi* bar in the Japanese-owned and managed Caesar Park Hotel. Although *sushi* is the house speciality, it also serves other Japanese delicacies—*sashimi*, *tempura*, shrimp or salmon *tekamaki*. Ginger or tea-flavored ice creams.

Miako
Rua do Ouvidor
45, upstairs, Centro
Tel: 222-2397
Monday-Saturday
11.30 a.m.-3 p.m. and 6 p.m.-10 p.m.
Closed Sunday
Up to $10
Credit cards: American Express.
One of Rio's best Japanese restaurants. *Sushi*, *sashimi*, *teppan-yaki*, *tanuki-udon*, *tempura*. Downtown location.

Mr. Zee
Av. General San Martin
1219, Leblon
Tel: 294-0591
7.30 p.m.-2 a.m.
Lunch on Sunday
Closed Monday
$10-$20
Credit cards accepted.
Rio's most elegant Chinese restaurant. Refined cuisine. Reservations only.

Oriento
Rua Bolivar 64, upstairs
Copacabana.
Tel: 275-7798.
Noon-2.30 p.m. and 6 p.m.-midnight
Closed Monday

Up to $10
Credit cards accepted.
All parts of China represented in the extensive menu. Chinese government delegates have used this restaurant for official dinners.

Churrascarias (Barbecue)

Carreta
116, Barra da Tijuca
Tel: 399-4055
11 a.m.-1 a.m.
$10-$20
Credit cards: Diners.
Good barbecued meats, attentive, friendly service. Praça São Perpétua.

Carretão
Rua Siqueira Campos
23, Copancabana
Tel: 236-3435
11 a.m.-12 midnight
All you can eat for under $10
Rodizio-style barbecue, top quality meats and side dishes.

O Casarão
Avenida Niemeyer 121
(Rio Sheraton Hotel)
Vidigal
Tel: 274-1122
Noon-4 p.m. and 7 p.m.-midnight
$10-$20
Credit cards: Major ones.
For a fixed price, help yourself at the barbecue pit and salad bar in a small restaurant in the hotel grounds. Lovely sea breezes.

Copacabana
Av. N.S. de Copacabana
1144, Copacabana
Tel: 267-1497
11 a.m.-2 a.m.
$10-$15

Credit cards: Major ones.
Rodizio or á la carte barbecue plus international menu. Dancing, 8 p.m.-4.30 a.m. at the Vinicius nightclub.

Dinho's Place
Rua Dias Ferreira
57, Leblon
Tel: 294-2297
11 a.m.-3 a.m.
$10-$20
Credit cards: Major ones.
Good cuts of meat, salad bar, Saturday *feijoada*.

Jardim
Rua República do Peru
225, Copacabana
Tel: 235-3263
11 a.m.-1.30 a.m.
$10-$15
Credit cards: Major ones.
Traditional barbecue restaurant. Indoor and garden dining areas.

Majorica
Rua Senador Vergueira
11/15, Flamengo
Tel: 245-8947
Noon-midnight
Up to $10
Credit cards: American Express.
Good quality barbecued meats—choose the cut you want from the pit if you like. Pleasant, cozy decor.

Mariu's
Av. Atlântica 290B
Leme
Tel: 542-2393
11 a.m.-2 a.m.
$10-$15
Credit cards: Major ones.
Rodizio-style barbecue. Fine meats, large variety of excellent side dishes, efficient service, used to dealing with foreigners. On the beach in Leme.

Palace
Rua Rodolfo Dantas
16, Copacabana
Tel: 541-5898
11 a.m.-2 a.m.
Up to $10
Credit cards: Only some
are accepted.
Good barbecued meats
served *rodizio*-style at a fast
pace. Next to the Copaca-
bana Palace.

Pampa
Av. das Américas 5150
Barra da Tijuca
(Carrefour supermarket)
Tel: 325-0861/399-0861
11.30 a.m.-11.30 p.m.
Up to $10
Credit cards: Visa, Diners
Rodizio service with qual-
ity cuts of meat.

Plataforma
Rua Adalberto Ferreira
32, Leblon
Tel: 274-4022
11 a.m.-3 a.m.
$10-$20
Credit cards: Major ones.
Large barbecue house
with international menu as
well. Upstairs, the Plat-
aforma I samba show.

Porcão
Rua Barão da Torre
218, Ipanema
Tel: 521-0999
11 a.m.-2 a.m.;
Av. Armando Lombardi
591, Barra da Tijuca
Tel: 399-3355
10.30 a.m.-1 a.m.
$10-$15
Credit cards: Major ones.
Traditional *rodizio*-style
barbecue restaurants, one in
Ipanema and one in Barra da
Tijuca. Large groups are not
a problem here.

Rodeio
Av. Alvorada 2150 B1
G, Loja A (Casa Shop-
ping)
Barra da Tijuca
Tel: 325-6166
Monday-Saturday
Noon-5 p.m. and
7 p.m.-1.30 a.m.
Sunday, noon-1.30 a.m.
$10-$15
Credit cards: Major ones.
Some of the choicest bar-
becued meats in town, mari-
nated for extra tenderness,
ordered á la carte. Local car-
nivores generally rate
Rodeio as Rio's leading
churrascaria.

T-Bone
Rua Laura Müller 116
(Shopping Rio Sul)
Botafogo.
Tel: 275-7895
11 a.m.-11 p.m.
$10-$15
Most major credit cards
are accepted.
Take a break from shop-
ping—good barbecue steak
house right in the mall.

French

Le Bec Fin
Av. N.S. de Copacabana
178A, Copacabana
Tel: 542-4097
7 p.m.-3 a.m.
Over $15
All major credit cards
accepted.
Classic French cuisine in
deluxe restaurant with impeccable service. One of
Rio's most traditional. Pleasant piano music.

Café de la Paix
Av. N.S. de Copacabana
178A, Copacabana
Tel: 542-4097
7 p.m.-3 a.m.
Over $15
Credit cards: Major ones.
Charming art nouveau
decor, informal. High quality French food. Afternoon
tea. On Saturday, *feijoada*
and Brazilian buffetare offered. On the beach.

Le Champs Elysées
Av. Presidente Antônio
Carlos 58
12th floor (maison de
France), Centro
Tel: 220-4129
Noon-5 p.m.
Closed Saturday and
Sunday
Over $15
Credit cards: American
Express.
Attractive downtown res-
taurant with French country
cooking, upstairs from the
French consulate. Great
rooftop view of Sugarloaf.

Claude Troisgros
Rua Custódio Serrão
62, Jardim Botânico
Tel: 226-4542/246-7509
Monday-Saturday
7.30 p.m.-3 a.m.
Over $20
Credit cards: Major ones.
One of Rio's finest restaurants, in pretty house on
quiet street. Chef Trosgros
introduce native fruits and
vegetables into his imaginative nouvelle cuisine receipes. Order á la carte or be
daring and try the surprise
menu confiance. Reservations necessary.

Clube Gourmet
Rua General Polidoro
186, Botafogo
Tel: 295-3494
Noon-3 p.m. and

8.30 p.m.-1 a.m.
No lunch on Saturday
Over $15
No credit cards.
Unusual Brazilian ingredients also turn up in the French recipes here. In-formal atmosphere despite its elegance. Choose one dish from each of four-course from the full gourmet menu at dinner for a set price.

Laurent
Rua Dona Mariana
209, Botafogo
Tel: 266-3131
Noon-3 p.m. and 8 p.m.-12.30 p.m.
Dinner only on Saturday
Closed Sunday
Over $15
Credit cards: Major ones.
Old-world elegance. Light French cuisine with Brazilian influence. *Prix fixe* menu at lunch. Reservations recommended.

Monseigneur
Av. Pref. Mendes de Moraes 222
(Hotel Inter-Continental)
São Conrado
Tel: 322-2200
7 p.m.-11 p.m.
Friday and Saturday until 1 a.m.
Over $20
Credit cards: Major ones.
French cuisine somewhere between classic and nouvelle with Brazilian touches. Elegant, luxurious. One of Rio's best eateries.

Ouro Verde
Av. Atlântica 1456
(Hotel Ouro Verde)
Copacabana
Tel: 542-1887
12.30 p.m.-past midnight
$15 and up

Credit cards: Major ones.
Classic French food. Discreetly elegant. Long-standing tradition. Also international menu. On the beach.

Le Pre Catelan
Av. Atlântica 4240
(Rio Palace Hotel)
Copacabana
Tel: 521-3232
Monday-Friday
Noon-3 p.m.
Daily, 7.30 p.m.-midnight
(until 1 a.m. on Friday and Saturday)
Over $20
Credit cards: Major ones.
Lovely belle époque dining room. French nouvelle cuisine with surprises, impeccable service. Branch of the Paris original, supervised by Gaston Lenotre. Reservations are recommended.

Le Saint Honoré
Av. Atlântica 1020
(Hotel Meridien)
37th floor
Leme
Tel: 275-9922
Noon-3 p.m. and 8 p.m.-11.30 p.m.
Dinner only on Saturday
Closed Sunday
Over $20
Credit cards: Major ones.
An outstanding restaurant. Imaginative nouvelle cuisine supervised by chef Paul Bocuse. *Prix fixe* set menu at lunch, á la carte for dinner. Elegant decoration, fabulous view of Copacabana, superb eating.

International

Antonino
Av. Epitácio Pessoa
1244, Lagoa

Tel: 267-6791
Noon-2 a.m.
$15 and up
Credit cards accepted.
View across the Lagoa to the mountains beyond. Classic menu, high quality food. Piano bar on ground floor. Reservations necessary for evenings (try to get a window seat).

Antonio's
Av. Bartolomeu Mitre
297, Leblon
Tel: 294-2699
Noon-3 a.m.
$10-$15
Credit cards accepted.
Varied menu, fish, meats, some Italian food. Outdoor terrace in front. Favorite spot of intellectuals, actors, artists. Reservations are recommended.

Atlantic
Av. Atlântica 4240
(Rio Palace Hotel)
1st floor
Copacabana
Tel: 521-3232
6 a.m.-1 a.m.
$10-$20
Credit cards: Major ones.
Window seats and outdoor tables have beautiful view of Copacabana beach. Seafood buffet Friday, Saturday *feijoada*, New York Sunday brunch. Live music at night.

Bife de Ouro
Av. Atlântica 1702
(Copacabana Palace Hotel)
Copacabana
Tel: 255-7070
11.30 a.m.-3.30 p.m. and 7 p.m.-1 a.m.
$10-$20
Credit cards: Major ones.

Elegant restaurant in historic Copacabana Palace. Fifty years old in 1988. Good meats, good service.

Café do Teatro
Av. Rio Branco
(Teatro Municipal)
Centro
Tel: 262-4164
11 a.m.-4 p.m.
Closed Saturday and
Sunday
$10-$20
Credit cards: Major ones.
Assyrian decor a la Cecil B. deMille. Located on the ground floor of the opera house. Varied menu with daily specials.

Colombo
Rua Gonçalves Dias
32-36, Centro
Tel: 232-2300
11 a.m.-6 p.m.
Saturday tea room only
9 a.m.-1 p.m.
Closed Sunday;
Av. N.S. de Copacabana
890, Copacabana
Tel: 257-8952
Tuesday-Sunday
11 a.m.-11 p.m.
Around $10
No credit cards.
Lovely belle eqóque restaurant dating from 1984. Stained glass skylight, background piano. Downstairs, turn-of-the-century mirrored tearoom. Copacabana beach. Fifty years younger than the original downtown establishment.

English Bar
Travessa do Comércio 11
Centro (near Praça XV)
Tel: 224-2539
Noon-4 p.m.
Closed Saturday and
Sunday

$10-$20
Credit cards accepted.
British atmosphere, excellent service with international menu. Well-stocked bar on ground floor. In preserved historic area of downtown. Reservations recommended.

Florentino
Av. General San Martin
1227, Leblon
Tel: 274-6841
Noon-2 a.m.
$15 and up
Credit cards: Major ones.
Small, intimate dining area upstairs. Downstairs, a cozy bar. Many fish dishes. Elegant, fashionable spot. Reservations necessary.

Guimas
Rua José Roberto Macedo
Soares 5
Gávea
Tel: 259-7996
Noon-4 p.m. and
8 p.m.-2 a.m.
Sunday, lunch only from
12.30-6 p.m.
$10-$15
No credit cards.
Small, charming. Popular with the art set. Always busy but won't take reservations.

Hippopotamus
Rua Barão da Torre
354, Ipanema
Tel: 227-8658
8.00 p.m. until at least
4 a.m.
Over $20
Credit cards accepted.
The "Hippo" is an exclusive private club, for members only and their guests. But five-star hotels can make reservations for their guests. Sophisticated and elegant. Good food, good

service. The chef is French and his speciality is fish. Bar and discotheque. Crowded on weekends.

Monte Carlo
Rua Duvivier 21
Copacabana
Tel: 541-4147
Noon-2 a.m.
$10-$20
Credit cards accepted.
Traditional menu also includes Brazilian favorites. Saturday *feijoada*; *cozido* on Sundays. Comfortable bar. Reservations recommended on the weekend.

Nino
Rua Visconde de Inhaúma
95, Centro
Tel: 253-2176
Noon-10 p.m.
Closed weekends;
Rua Domingos Ferreira
242A, Copacabana
Tel: 255-0785
Noon-2 a.m.;
Praia de Botafogo
228, Botafogo
Tel: 551-8597
Noon-2 a.m.
Tel: 399-0018
Noon-2 a.m.
$10-$20
Credit cards accepted at all branches.
Food is always good, service efficient. Downtown restaurant popular at lunch. Many Brazilian dishes on the menu. Same high standards at all branches.

Rio's
Parque do Flamengo
Flamengo
Tel: 551-1131
Noon-2 a.m.
$15 and up
Credit cards accepted.
Large windows open to

spectacular view of the bay and Sugarloaf. Complete menu with many fish dishes and a variety of meats. Comfortable, spacious. Outstanding service. Piano bar at night. Outdoor beer garden. Reservations accepted.

Un, Deus, Trios
Rua Bartolomeu Mitre 112, Leblon
Tel: 293-0198
Daily, 7 p.m.-4 a.m.
Saturday and Sunday serves lunch—12-4 p.m.
$10-$20
Credit cards accepted.
Quality restaurant downstairs. Live music for dancing upstairs, where food is also served. Popular spot. Reserve for both restaurant and nightclub.

Italian

Alfredo di Lello
Av. Prefeito Mendes de Moraes 222
(Hotel Inter-Continental)
São Conrado
Tel: 322-2200
Noon-3 p.m. and 7.30 p.m.-11 p.m.
$15 and up
Credit cards: Major ones.
Rio's branch of the famous Alfredo of Rome, one of the only three outside Italy. The house specialty is *Fettuccine al Alfredo*.

Baroni Fasoli
Rua Jangadeiros 14-B
(on Praça General Osório)
Ipanema
Tel: 287-9592
Wednesday-Monday
Noon-1 a.m.
Tuesday, 7 p.m.-1 a.m.
Up to $10
Credit cards: Major ones.

This restaurant's forte is its excellent pasta dishes.

Enotria
Rua Constante Ramos 115, Copacabana
Tel: 237-6705
8 p.m.-past midnight
Closed on Sundays
$15 and up
Credit cards: Major ones.
Many consider Enotria Rio's best Italian restaurant. Owner Danio Braga is certainly one of the city's foremost authorities on wines and the restaurant boasts one of the best-stocked wine cellars in town. Excellent northern cuisine. Reservations necessary for this small, cozy eatery.

Mediterranean
Av. Prudente de Morais 1810, Ipanema
Tel: 259-4121
11.30 a.m.-4 a.m.
$10-$15
Credit cards: Major ones.
Pastas, pizzas, seafood with an Italian flair. Pleasant open balcony.

La Mole
Rua Dias Ferreira 147, Leblon
Tel: 294-0699;
Praia de Botafogo 228, Botafogo
Tel: 551-9499;
Av. N.S. de Copacabana 552, Copacabana
Tel: 257-5593
11 a.m.-1 a.m.
$5-$10
No credit cards.
Familiar pasta dishes, pizzas, steaks, chicken. Nothing fancy, but food is reliable and inexpensive. You may have to wait for a table. Botafogo branch has glass

roof under trees.

Quadrifoglio
Rua Maria Angelica 43
Jardim Botânico
Tel: 226-1799
Noon-3 p.m. and
8 p.m.-1 a.m.
Closed Sunday
$15 and up
No credit cards.
Homey, small restaurant with delicious pastas and other Italian classics. Reservations are a good idea.

Satiricon
Rua Barrão da Torre 192, Ipanema
Tel: 521-0627
7 p.m.-2 a.m
Sundays, noon-2 a.m.
$15 and up
Credit cards: Only some are accepted.
Pasta and Italian recipes featuring seafood.

Le Streghe
Rua Prudente de Morias 129 (on Praça General Osório), Ipanema
Tel: 287-7147
7 p.m. until the last customer leaves.
$15 and up
Credit cards: Major ones.
One of Rio's top restaurants. Local Italians generally consider it Rio's best Italian restaurant. Light *nuova cucina* style meals. Attractive, airy decor and relaxed atmosphere. Calígola club with piano bar and discotheque downstairs.

Valentino's
Av. Niemeyer 121
(Rio Sheraton Hotel)
São Conrado
Tel: 274-1122
7 p.m.-midnight

Over $20
Credit cards: Major ones.
Excellent northern Italian
nuova cucina served with
panache. A la carte or five-
course chef's gourmet
menu-of-the-week. Elegant
atmosphere, excellent service, piano music. Reservations accepted.

North American/British

Neal's
Rua Sorocaba
695, Botafogo
Tel: 266-6577
Tuesday-Friday
11.30 a.m.-4 p.m.
Tuesday-Sunday
7 p.m.-4 a.m.;
Estrada da Barra da Tijuca
1636, Barra da Tijuca
Tel: 399-3922
Daily, noon-4 a.m.
$10-$20
Credit cards: Major ones.
New York-style bar and
restaurant with rock video
clips. House speciality bar-
becued ribs. Barra branch in
Western decor. Reserva-
tions accepted.

The Lord Jim Pub
Rua Paul Redfern
63, Ipanema
Tel: 259-3047
Tuesday-Saturday
4 p.m.-1 a.m.
Sunday, 11 a.m.-1 a.m.
Closed Monday
$15-$20
No credit cards.
The ground floor recreates
a country pub. English home
cooking served on the second and third floors. Also
great complete afternoon tea
service (Reservation needed
for tea).

Portuguese

Adegão Portuguese
Campo de São Cristóvão
212-A, São Cristóvão
Tel: 580-7288
11 a.m.-11.30 p.m.
$10-$15
Credit cards: Major ones.
Authentic Portuguese cui-
sine, modest surroundings.
Cozido, *bacalhau*, octopus,
roast suckling pig, Portuguese desserts. On the
square where the Northeastern Fair is held on Sundays.

Antiquarius
Rua Aristides Espinola
19, Leblon
Tel: 294-1049
Noon-2 a.m.
$10-$20
Credit cards: Major ones.
An attractive restaurant
decorated with antiques.
Alenteja recipes, lighter than
most Portuguese cuisine.
Good *bacalhau* dishes,
many *lusitanian* seafood
dishes, fabulous Portuguese
desserts. Also "interna-
tional" selections. The
Sunday *cozido* is considered
by some to be the best in
town. Reservations recom-
mended for dinner.

Negresco
Rua Barãoda Torre 348
(on Praça N.S. da Paz)
Ipanema
Tel: 287-4842
Noon-2 a.m.
Friday, 5 p.m.-2 a.m.
$10-$20
Credit cards: Most are
accepted.
Portuguese and interna-
tional menu, featuring
bacalhau, squid, rabbit and
seafood stew. Small, stylish

restaurant. Reservations are
a must.

Ponto de Encontro
Rua Barata Ribeiro
750-B, Copacabana
Tel: 255-969
Noon-2 a.m.
$10-$15.
Credit cards: Major ones.
Portuguese and interna-
tional cuisine served in cozy
wood-paneled dining room.
Shop next to entrance sells
pastries, Portuguese sweets
and take-home food.

Penafiel
Rua Senhor dos Passos
121, Centro
Tel: 224-6870
11 a.m.-4 p.m.
Closed Saturday and
Sunday
$10-$15.
No credit cards.
Unsophisticated eatery.
Has been in the same family
since it opened in 1912. Offering plain but good Portuguese cooking, you may
have to wait for a table. On
pedestrian street in the Saara
shopping district downtown.
Desserts are Brazilian (try
the banana-cheese *Mineiro
com Botas*).

Seafood

Albamar
Praça Marechal An-
cora184/186
(near Praça XV,
downtown)
Tel: 240-8378
11.30 a.m.-10.00 p.m.
Closed Sunday
Around $10
Credit cards: American
Express.
Near the port and terminal
for the ferry boats, housed in

the sole remaining tower of what was once a municipal market, has beautiful view of the bay. Fish is the speciality, but also an international menu to choose from. Busy at lunch, but not at night.

Barracuda
Marina da Gloria
(Parque do Flamengo)
Tel: 265-3997
11.30 a.m.-1 a.m.
$10-$20
Credit cards: Major ones.
Picturesque location at the marina. Popular with the business crowd. Seafood and international. Reservations essential for lunch.

Cabaça Grande
Rua do Ouvidor
12, Centro
Tel: 231-2301
Noon-4 p.m.
Closed weekends
$10-$15
Credit cards accepted.
Traditional downtown seafood restaurant, serves some of the tastiest fish in Rio. Try the house speciality: seafood soup.

Cándido's
Rua Barros de Alarcão
352
Pedra de Guaratiba
Tel: 395-2007/395-1603
Monday-Friday
1.30 a.m.-7 p.m.
Saturday
11.30 a.m.-11 p.m.
Sunday, 11.30 a.m.-8 p.m.
$15
Credit cards: Diners.
This outstanding fish and seafood restaurant is actually out of Rio and lunch here could be included in an outing to the fishing village of Pedra de Guaratiba. Sophis-

ticated eating in a relaxed atmosphere. On the weekend, reservations are a must—if possible go on a weekday.

Grottammare
Rua Gomes Carneiro
132, Ipanema
Tel: 287-1596
6p.m.-2 a.m.
Sundays, open at noon
$10-$20
Credit cards: Major ones.
Fresh grilled, poached seafood. Restaurant has its own fishermen and you can choose your fish and have it made to order. Good service, large portions. Also serves meat and pasta dishes. Make reservations.

A Marisqueira
Rua Barata Ribeiro
233, Copacabana
Tel: 237-3920/236-2602
Daily,11 a.m.-1 a.m.;
Rua Gomes Carneiro
Ipanema
Tel :267-9944
Closed Monday
$10-$15
Credit cards: Major ones.
Traditional restaurant specializing in a variety of good seafood. Also serves other meats. Plain and simple.

Petronius
Av. Vieira Souto 460
(in the Hotel Caesar Park)
Ipanema
Tel: 287-3122
7 p.m.-1 a.m.
Saturday, noon-4 p.m.
Over $15
Credit cards: Major ones.
Elegant restaurant, with excellent service, exquisite cuisine. View of Ipanema beach, piano music.

Principe
Avenida Atlântica
974B, Leme
Tel: 275-3996
Noon-1 a.m.
$10-$15
Credit cards: Major ones.
Variety of fish/seafood dishes, good food in simple surroundings, on the beach.

Quatro Sete Meia (476)
Rua Barros de Alarcão
476, Pedra de Guaratiba
Tel: 395-2716
Monday-Thursday
Noon-5 p.m.
Friday and Saturday
1-10 p.m.
Sunday, 1-6 p.m.
Over $15
Cash only; no credit cards.
Also out in Guaratiba. Small, simple restaurant near the sea. Excellent seafood. Reservations absolutely necessary.

Real
Av. Atlântica
514A, Leme
Tel: 275-9048
Noon-2 a.m.
$10-$15
Credit cards: Major ones.
Variety of fish/seafood dishes. Good food, no frills. Facing Leme beach.

Shirley
Rua Gustavo Sampaio
610, Leme
Tel: 275-9013
Noon-1 a.m.
$5-$10
No credit cards.
Tasty Spanish and Portuguese seafood recipes. Small, modest and always busy, there is usually a wait for a table and reservations are not accepted. Have a seafood snack as you wait.

Sol e Mar
Av. Reporter Nestor Moreira 11
Botafogo
Tel: 295-1896
11 a.m.-3 p.m.
Over $15
Credit cards: Major ones.
Bayside seafood restaurant with view across the water of Sugarloaf, sailboats. Very pleasant, also an outdoor cocktail area. Take-off spot for the Bateau Mouche boat tours. Menu also features Spanish dishes.

Tia Palmira
Caminho do Souza 18
Barra de Guaratiba
Tel: 310-1169
11.30 a.m.-6 p.m.
Closed Monday
Up to $10
No credit cards.
Modest restaurant out in Barra de Guaratiba has a set menu offering a sampling of seafood specialities and fruit desserts. Indoor/outdoor dining areas. No reservations accepted.

Vice-key
Av. Monsenhor Ascâncio 535
Praça do O
Barra da Tijuca
Tel: 399-1683
Noon-2 a.m.
$10-$20
No credit cards.
Live lobsters, crayfish, oysters raised in tanks—really fresh. Colonial setting.

Restaurants with a view

Albamar
Downtown, located on the bay near the ferry station and the port. (Address under Seafood).

Antonino
On the Lagoa Rodrigo de Freitas lagoon. (Address under International).

Atlantis
Terrace restaurant in Rio Palace Hotel on the beach in Copacabana. (Address under International).

Céu
Av. Niemeyer 769
27th floor
(Hotel Nacional)
São Conrado
Tel: 322-1000
Opens every day at 7 p.m.
$10-$15
Credit cards accepted.
At the top of Hotel Nacional. Traditional international menu, open for dinner only. View of São Conrado beach and surrounding green mountains. Romantic, candlelight interior.

Le Champs Elysées
Downtown restaurant with view of bay, Sugarloaf. (Address under French).

Cota 200
Av. Pasteur 520, Urca
(at cable car station)
Tel: 541-3737
Tuesday-Sunday
11 a.m.-7 p.m.
Mondays, 11 a.m.-4 p.m.
Dinner at 8 p.m. before the *samba* show
Around $10
Credit cards accepted.
On the top of Morro da Urca, the first station on the cable car trip up to Sugarloaf. View of southern residential areas, downtown, the bay, its bridge and surrounding mountains. International cuisine. Accommodates large groups easily.

Os Esquilos and A Floresta
Both in the Tijuca Forest Park. Look on the map of the park roads located in the parking lot near the Cascatinha waterfall as you enter the park. Traditional home cooking served in old colonial houses with open veranda surrounded by the lush green forest. Fireplace for chilly days. Afternoon tea service. Just as pretty—and even greener—on a rainy or foggy day.

Os Esquilos
Tel: 399-8655
11 a.m.-6.30 p.m.
$5-$10
Some credit cards.

A Floresta
Tel: 399-8947
11 a.m.-9 p.m.
Under $10
No credit cards.

Maenda
In the Hotel Trocadero, Copacabana. (Address under Brazilian).

Petronius
In the Caesar Park, on the beach in Ipanema. (Address under Seafood).

Quatro Sete Meia (476)
Near the water at Pedra de Guaratiba fishing village. (Address under Seafood).

Rio's
Beautiful view of Guanabara Bay—dramatic on stormy days. (Address under International).

Rive Gauche
1484, Lagoa
Tel: 521-2645

8 p.m. until the last customer leaves
$10-$15
Credit cards accepted.

Elegant restaurant with view of the Lagoa Rodrigo de Freitas lagoon, with green mountains beyond. International menu. Live music in the bar Monday-Saturday. Popular Biblos Bar nightclub on ground floor.

Le Saint Honoré
Spectacular view of Copacabana and Leme beaches from the 37th floor of the Meridien Hotel. (Address under French).

Sol e Mar
On the bay near the Yacht Club. (Address listed under Seafood).

Tiberius
Av. Vieira Souto 460
23rd Floor
(Caesar Park Hotel)
Ipanema
Tel: 287-3122
7 a.m.-12.30 a.m.
Under $10 up to $20
Credit cards: Major ones.
View of Ipanema and Leblon beaches and the mountains beyond Leblon from the 23rd floor of the Caesar Park Hotel in Ipanema. Open all day serving breakfast, lunch, afternoon tea and dinner. International menu includes light snacks as well as full meals. Buffet in town. *Feijoada* served on Saturday is one of the best in town. Opens onto rooftop, where you can have a drink and admire the view.

La Tour
Rua Santa Luzia 651
34th floor, Centro
Tel: 240-5795
Noon-midnight
$10-$20
Credit cards accepted.
Roof-top revolving restaurant downtown. View of bay, Flamengo parkway, downtown, mountains, Corcovado. Full rotation: 50 minutes. International cuisine. Reservations accepted.

ACTIVITIES

CULTURAL ACTIVITIES

Music is definitely Brazil's forte. A variety of musical forms has developed in different parts of the country, many with accompanying forms of **dance**. While the Brazilian influence is to be heard around the world (especially in jazz), what little is known of Brazilian music outside the country, is just the tip of the iceberg. Take in a concert by a popular singer (look under "Shows" in the newspaper) or ask your hotel to recommend a nightclub with live Brazilian music: bossa nova, *samba*, *choro* and *seresta* are popular in Rio. If you are visiting at Carnival, you will see and hear plenty of music and dancing in the streets, mostly *samba*, but also *frevo* and *afoxé*. There are also shows all year long, designed to give tourists a taste of Carnival and of Brazilian folk music and dance. If you like what you hear, get some records or tapes to take home with you.

The **classical music** and **dance** season runs after Carnival through December, centered at the **Teatro Municipal** (on Praça da Veiga, downtown, tel: 210-2463). Many concerts are also held at the nearby **Sala Cecilia Meireles** (Largo da Lapa 47, tel: 232-9714) and there are many other auditoriums and small recital halls where performances are held. Rio's symphony is the *Orquestra Sinfonica Brasileira*. The Teatro Municipal's own orchestra accompanies the ballets and operas held there. Besides presentations by local talent, Rio is included in world concert tours by international performers. Look under *"musciá"* in the newspapers; both classic ballet and modern dance presentations are listed under *"dançé"*.

Art galleries showing the work of contemporary Brazilian artists abound in Rio, especially in Ipanema. There is also a concentration of galleries in the Shopping Center da Gavea (Rua Marquês de São Vicente 52, Gavea) and the Shopping Cassino Atlantico (Av. Atlantica 4240, Copacabana). Periodic exhibits are also held at the Museum of Modern Art (Museu de Arte Modernomam), the National Fine Arts Museum (Museu Nacional de Belas Artes), which also has a permanent collection of Brazilian art and the restored Imperial Palace (Paço Imperial). See Museums (below) and look in the newspaper under *"exposições"* for announcements of exhibits.

Some Brazilian **cinema** is very good—Brazil has, in fact, exported films quite successfully to North America and Europe. Without a knowledge of Portuguese, however, you may well wait and see exports back home with sub-titles in your language. But the majority of films shown in Rio are foreign-made, mostly American, all in the original language with Portuguese subtitles. Check out what's playing under the "cinema" heading in the local papers. An international film festival, Fest Rio, is held annually in Rio de Janeiro at the Hotel Nacional Rio.

In order to enjoy most **theater** performances, you really would have to understand the language. Rio de Janeiro has a busy season which runs from after Carnival through November.

Museums

Art
Museu Chácara do Céu
Rua Murtinho Nobre
93, Santa Teresa
Tel: 232-1386/224-8981
Tuesday-Saturday
2-5 p.m.;
Sunday, 1-5 p.m.

Museu Nacional de Belas Artes
(National Museum of Fine Arts)
Av. Rio Branco
199, Centro
Tel: 240-0160/240-0068
Tuesday—Thursday
10 a.m.-6.30 p.m.
Wednesday—Friday
12-6.30 p.m.
Saturday, Sunday
and holidays, 3-6 p.m.

Museu do Açude
Estr. do Açude 764
Alto da Boa Vista
Tel: 238-0368
Tuesday-Saturday
2-5 p.m.
Sunday, 1-5 p.m.

Museu de Arte Moderna
(Modern Art Museum)
Av. Infante D. Henrique 85
Parque do Flamengo
Tel: 210-2188
Closed for restoration. Scheduled to reopen in the second half of 1988.

Ethnology
Museu do Folclore Edison Carneiro
(Folk Museum)
Rua do Catete
181, Catete
Tel: 285-0891
Tuesday-Friday
11 a.m.-6 p.m.
Saturday, Sunday
and holidays, 3-6 p.m.

Museu do Indio
(Indian Museum)
Rua das Palmeiras
55, Botafogo
Tel: 286-8799
Tuesday-Friday
10 a.m.-5 p.m.
Saturday and Sunday
1-5 p.m.

Museu do Negro
(Negro Museum)
Rua Uruguaiana 77
Centro
Tel: 221-3119
Monday-Friday
7 a.m.-5 p.m.
Saturday
8 a.m.-noon.

History **Museu da República**
(Museum of the Republic)
Rua do Catete 179
Flamengo
Tel: 225-4302
Closed for restoration. Scheduled to reopen in November, 1988.

Museu Histórico Nacional
(National Historical Museum)
Praça Marechal Ancora
(near Praça XV) Centro
Tel: 240-7978/220-2628
Tuesday-Friday
10 a.m.-5,30 p.m.
Saturday, Sunday and holidays, 2.30-5.30 p.m.

Museu do Palácio do Itamarati
(Itamarati Palace Museum)
Av. Marechal Floriano 196, Centro
Tel: 291-4411 *ramal* 6.
Closed for restoration.

Museu Casa de Rui Barbosa
(Rui Barbosa House)
Rua São Clemente 134, Botafogo
Tel: 286-1297 ramal 45
Tuesday-Friday
10 a.m.-4.30 p.m.
Saturday, Sunday
and holidays, 2-5 p.m.

Museu da Cidade
(City Museum)
Estr. de Santa Marinha
(inside the Parque da
Cidade), Gávea
Tel: 322-1328
Tuesday-Sunday and holidays, noon-4.30 p.m.

Museu do Primeiro Reinado
(Museum of the First Reign—Marquesa de Santos House)
Av. D. Pedro II 283
São Cristóvão
Tel: 254-0698
Tuesday-Friday
10 a.m.-5 p.m.
Saturday, Sunday
and holidays, 1-5 p.m.

Performing Arts/Music
Museu da Imagem e do Som
(Museum of Image and Sound—Popular Music)
Praça Rui Barbosa 1
(near Praça XV de Novembro)
Centro
Tel: 262-0309/210-2463
Monday-Friday
1-6 p.m.

Museu Villa-Labos
Rua Sorocaba 200
Botafogo
Tel: 266-3845
Monday-Friday
9 a.m.-6 p.m.

Museu Carmem Miranda
Parque do Flamengo
(across from Av. Rui Barbosa no. 560)
Tel: 551-2597
Tuesday-Friday
11 a.m.-5 p.m.
Saturday, Sunday
and holidays, 1-5 p.m.

Science/Technology
Museu Nacional
(National Museum)
Quinta da Boa Vista
São Cristóvão
Tel: 264-8262
Tuesday-Sunday
10 a.m.-4.45 p.m.

Museu do Trem
(Train Museum)
Rua Arquias Cordeiro
1046, Engenho de Dentro
Tel: 269-5545
Tuesday-Friday
10 a.m.-4 p.m.
Saturday and Sunday
1-5 p.m.

Sports

Soccer (*futebol*): This is *the* sport in Brazil, a national passion that unites all ages and classes. During World Cup season, the country comes to a halt as everyone tunes in to watch the Cup matches on T.V. If you're a soccer fan, arrange through your hotel to see a professional game—there are organized tours.

The boisterous fans are often as interesting to watch as the game itself at Rio's giant **Maracanã Stadium** which squeezes in crowds of up to 200,000. There is rarely any violence, but it is recommended that you get a reserved seat (around $5-8) rather than sitting in the packed bleachers (about $1.50). Most weekend afternoons or in the early evening, you can see a "sandlot" match between neighborhood teams on the beaches or in the parks (also the venue for volleyball matches).

Private clubs are big in Brazil and besides the socializing, this is where most upper and middle class Brazilians practise sports. Although you can usually visit as a guest, some of these sports facilities can be found in top class hotels.

As to be expected in a tropical seaside city, a variety of **aquatic sports** can be enjoyed in Rio. Ocean **swimming** is refreshing in the hottest months. The waves that break on Rio's ocean beaches are quite strong and it's difficult to do any actual "swimming"—it's more like playing in the waves. The water in the bay is too polluted for swimming, yet the bay beaches are just as crowded as the sea. Several of the hotels have swimming pools as do almost all of the private clubs, but there are no public swimming pools in Rio.

If you're interested in **sailing, surfing, windsurfing, fishing** or **scuba diving**, go to the **Marina da Gloria**, on the Aterro do Flamengo in Gloria, right in town (tel: 265-0797/285-2247). Sailboats, yachts, speedboats and schooner-like Brazilian *saveiros* can be rented, complete with fishing equipment and crew starting around $100 a day. Resort hotels in small beachtowns near Rio also have boats, surf and windsurf boards, diving equipment and instructors. Popular spots for diving near Rio are off the "Sun Coast," east of Rio (Cabo Frio, Búzios) and off the "Green Coast" to the south and west (Angra dos Reis, Parati) where the water is calm and breathtakingly clear.

The Rio Sheraton, Inter-

Continental Rio and Nacional Rio hotels have **tennis** courts. There a few public courts, as the game is played mostly at clubs.

Golf is not a popular sport in Brazil, but Rio has two beautiful courses at the **Gavea** and **Itanhangá golf clubs**. Although exclusive, you can arrange through your hotel to play as a visitor for about $17 (excluding rental of equipment). The mountain towns of Petrópolis and Teresópolis each have a country club and you can also play at the seaside city of Angra dos Reis.

Horse racing is popular and you can watch and bet at races almost every Monday and Thursday evening and Saturday and Sunday afternoon. The most important race in Brazil, the *Grande Premio do Brasil* sweepstakes, is held at Rio's 35,000-spectator racetrack (Praça Santos Dumont, 31, Joquei, tel: 274-0055) on the first Sunday in August.

Rio is on the world **Grand Prix Formula I** auto racing circuit. The event at the autodrome is scheduled for March or April.

Hang gliding is popular. Gliders leap off the **Pedra Bonita** peak and soar in circles like hawks on the air currents before landing on the beach at São Conrado. Inexperienced flyers can go tandem with an instructor. Contact the **Associação de Vôo Livre** at Av. Rio Branco 156 *sala* (room) 1119, tel: 220-4704. If you prefer to just watch, go to the end of the beach at São Conrado on a Sunday.

Joggers have some beautiful places to keep in shape while in Rio. The wide sidewalks along the beach in Leme, Copacabana, Ipanema and Leblon have the "distance" marked in kilometers. Other favorite spots for *carioca* runners are around the Lagoa Rodrigo de Freitas lagoon, along the parkway in Flamengo and up in the Floresta da Tijuca national park. Rio has its own marathon which attracts international contenders.

If you enjoy **climbing**, you won't need to leave the city. There are many peaks to climb, including Rio's landmarks, Sugarloaf and Corcovado. Excursion clubs arrange outings to areas outside Rio where you can go mountain climbing, **spelunking, white-water canoeing** and **kayaking** and sailing. Rapids shooting and rubber **rafting** excursions can be arranged through the hotels. Contact the **Clube Excursionista Carioca** (Rua Hilário de Gouvéia 71/206, Copacabana, tel: 541-3531) or the **Centro Excursionista do Rio de Janeiro** (Av. Rio Branco, 277/805, Centro, tel: 220-3548).

There are beautiful **hiking** trails in the **Floesta da Tijuca** national park, all unmarked. For more information on hiking and **camping**, contact the **Camping Clube do Brasil**. They rent trailers and organize treks. **Hunting** is forbidden by law throughout Brazil.

Capoeira is an uniquely Brazilian sport. The tradition has been kept alive chiefly in Salvador, Bahia, but there are also academies in Rio de Janeiro. A relic from slavery days, when fighting, especially training for fighting, by the slaves had to be dissimulated, *capoeira* is a stylized fightdance, with its own accompanying rhythms and music, using the feet a great deal to strike out and requiring graceful agility. Presentations are included in folk dance or samba shows— enquire at your hotel. There are occasional performances by street groups.

Tours: A variety of individual and group tours to Rio are available. Some are all-inclusive packages with transportation, food and lodging, excursions and entertainment thrown in; some include only international air transportation and hotel accommodation. Special tours to Rio for Carnival usually include tickets to the big samba parade and club balls. Other special interest tours are also organized. A travel agent will be able to supply you with information about different options being offered.

If you aren't in Rio on a tour which includes "everything" or if you are but would prefer something else to what is scheduled on a given day, arrange through your hotel or a local travel agent to join a variety of local tours. Air-conditioned buses take tour groups to Corcovado, Sugarloaf and other lookout points. On city tours, you visit the Botanical Gardens and Tijuca National Park and there's also a soccer game at Maracanã stadium.

Day tours on the water include visits to Paquetá Island, the Bateau Mouche cruises, one in the bay and one to outlying islands (Av. Nestor Moreira, 11, Botafogo (tel: 295-1997) and the Paradise Island Tour.

Gray Line (tel: 294-1444, 294-1196, 274-7146) offers many tours, the most unusual of which are a helicopter ride over the city (20-30 minutes costs $55) and a thrilling day of river rafting in the mountains.

H. Stern Jewelers offer a tour of their workshops at their headquarters in Ipanema (Rua Visconde de Pirajá, 490, tel: 259-7442).

The **Roteiros Culturais** historic walking tours (in English) of the older parts of the downtown *Centro* district can be arranged for groups (tel: 322-4872).

Evening tours will take you to one of the samba shows, often with dinner included. Or visit Afro-Brazilian spiritualist rites.

Day trips out of Rio by bus can be taken to beach towns in both directions—Buzios, Cabo Frio and other spots up the coast and Angra dos Reis, Paraty and, closer, Pedro de Guaratiba and Itacuruçá down the coast—or to the mountain towns of Petrópolis and Teresópolis.

If you want to venture farther afield, you can take a tour to another part of Brazil from Rio. There are **day trips by plane** to Brasilia or the Iguassu falls, or tours to the Amazon and Pantanal, the south, the northeast or the colonial cities of Minas Gerais. In the peak season there may be a wait, so it would be best to make reservations beforehand.

Ocean cruises out of Rio go south to Buenos Aires and up in the Caribbean, calling at Brazilian ports. Make reservations well in advance.

The camping Clube do Brasil (Rua Senador Dantas 75, 29th floor, tel: 262-7172) organizes **trekking tours** in remote scenic areas.

NIGHTLIFE AND ENTERTAINMENT

There's always plenty to do at night in Rio. Things get going late—dinner is never before 9.00 p.m. and shows are scheduled to begin at 10.00 p.m. or later. Nightclubs don't begin to warm up until midnight and you may be surprised by the sunrise on your way out.

The two big names for live **concerts** by Brazilian and international pop singers are **Canecão** (Av. Wenceslau Brás 215, Botafogo, tel: 295-3044) and **Scala 2** (Av. Afrânio de Melo Franco 296, Leblon, tel: 239-4448). Concerts are also periodically scheduled for **Morro da Urca** (first station half-way up to Sugarloaf, tel: 541-3737) and the **Maracanãzinho** stadium (Rua Prof. Eurico Rabelo, São Cristóvão, tel: 264-9962). International superstars occasionally fill the giant **Maracanã** soccer stadium next door (at the same telephone number).

Many singers give reprise of their show in the **João Caetano** theater on Praça Tiradentes, downtown (tel: 221-0305). Informal concerts (rock, jazz, popular Brazilian music) are held in

the **Parque da Catacumba** on the Lagoa (tel: 287-8293)—be prepared to sit on the grass. And the **Circo Voador** (near the Arches in Lapa) schedules a variety of shows, with room to dance along. Pop concerts are listed in the newspapers under "shows."

Many **bars** around town also have **live music**. the best include: **Alô-Alô** (Rua Barão da Torre 368, Ipanema, tel: 521-1460), **Antonino** (Av. Epitácio Pessoa 1244 on the Lagoa, tel: 267-6791), **Jazzmania** (Av. Rainha Elisabeth 769, Ipanema, tel: 227-2447), **People** (Av. Bartolomeu Mitre 370, Leblon, tel: 294-0547), **Harry's Bar** (Av. Bartolomeu Mitre 450, Leblon, tel: 259-4043), **Mistura Fina** (Rua Garcia d'Avila 15, Ipanema, tel: 259-9394), **Equinox** (Rua Prodente de Morais 729, Ipanema, tel: 247-0580), **Double Dose** (Rua Paul Redfern 44, Ipanema, tel: 294-9791), **Chico's** (Av. Epitácio Pessoa 1560 on the Lagoa, tel: 287-3514), **The Cattleman** (Av. Epitacio Pessoa 846 on the Lagoa, tel: 239-2863), **Mariu's** (Av. Atlântica 290, Leme, tel: 542-2393) and **Rio's** (Parque do Flamengo, tel: 551-1131).

Popular **bars** with **live music for dancing** include: **Sobre as Ondas** (Av. Atlântica 3432, upstairs, Copacabana, tel: 521-1296), **Un, Deux, Trois** (Av. Bartolomeu Mitre 112, upstairs, Leblon, tel: 239-0198, **Vogue** (Rua Cupertino Durão 173, Leblon, tel: 274-8196), **Carinhoso** (Rus Visconde de Pirajá 22, Ipanema, tel: 287-3579), **Ragtime** (Av. Sernambetiba 600, Barra da Tijuca, tel: 389-3385), **Vinicius** (Av. N.S. de Copacabana 1144, upstairs, Copacabana, tel: 267-1497), and **Café Nice** (Av. Rio Branco 277, downstairs, Centro, tel: 240-0490).

If you want something a little livelier, there are many **night clubs** and **discotheques**. The social set hang out at the fashionable private clubs: **Hippopotamus** (Rua Barão da Torre 354, Ipanema, tel: 247-0351), **Palace Club** (Hotel Rio Palace, Av. Atlântica 4240, downstairs, Copacabana, tel: 267-5048) or **Studo C** (hotel Rio Othon Palace, Rua Xavier da Silveira 7, downstairs, Copacabana, tel: 236-0695).

Two of the trendiest nightclubs are **Barão com Joana** (upstairs at the corner of Barão da Torre and Joan Angelica in Ipanema) and the punk hangout, **Crepúsculo de Cubatão** (Rue Barata Ribeiro 543, Copacabana, tel: 235-2045).

Other popular spots include: **Caligola** (Rua Prudente de Morais 129, Ipanema, tel: 287-1369), **Zoom** (Largo de São Conrado 20, São Conrado, tel: 322-4179), **Help** (Av. Atlântica 3432, Copacabana, tel: 521-1269), **La Dolce Vita** (Av. Min. Ivan Lins 80, Barra da Tijuca, tel: 399-0105), **Mistura Fina** (Estr. da Barra da Tijuca 1636, Itanhangá, tel: 399-3460), **Biblos** (Av. Epitácio Pessoa 1484, Lagoa, tel: 521-2645), **Mikonos** (Rua Cupertino Durão 177, Leblon, tel: 294-2298) and

Circus Disco (Rua Gen. Urquiza 102, 2nd floor, Leblon, tel: 274-7895. There is also **Assyrius** (Av. Rio Branco 277, downstairs, Centro, tel: 220-1998).

Gafierias are traditional old-fashioned dance halls with live music. The Asa Branca (Av. Mem de Sá 17, Lapa, tel: 252-0966) is a modern version and often features a popular singer. More authentic *gafieras* are: **Elite** (Rua Frei Ca-neca 4, upstairs, Centro, tel: 232-3217) and **Estudantina** (Praça Tiradentes 79, Centro, tel: 232-1149).

Brazil is the land of samba and if you miss the biggest samba show of all, which is Carnival in Rio, there is plenty of samba to be heard and seen all year long. Every Monday night, members of the *Beija Flor* (hummingbird) samba school perform on **Morro da Urca** (the first stop half-way up to Sugarloaf). Tickets can be purchased at the cablecar station in Urca (tel: 541-3737) or you can join a tour group (enquire at your hotel).

There are other immemsely popular samba shows for tourists: **Scala-Rio** (Av. Afrânio de Melo Fran-co 296, Leblon, tel: 239-4448), **Oba-Oba** (Rua Humaitá 110, Botafogo, tel: 286-9848) and **Plataforma 1** (Rua Adalberto Ferreira 32, Leblon, tel: 274-4022). All have restaurants and dance floors. (Enquire at your hotel for group tours).

You can also visit an actual rehearsal for the big Carnival parade at one of the **samba schools**. Most of the

groups rehearse in the poorer suburbs or near *favelas*, and it is advisable to arrange a visit through your hotel.

Two nightclubs in Barra da Tijuca also have samba music: **Clube do Samba** (Estr. da Barra da Tijuca 65, tel: 399-0892) with top samba singers coming on stage around 1.00 a.m., and **Labaredo** (Estr. da Barra da Tijuca 410, tel: 399-1582).

Rio has many nightclubs with **strip tease** and **sex shows**. In Copacabana they concentrated at the **Leme** end, around **Av. Princesa Isabel**, **Av. Prado Junior** and **Praça do Libo** square, bordered by Av. N.S. de Copacabana and the beach drive Av. Atlântica between Rua Ronald de Carvalho and Rua Belford Roxo. Less classy are the **Praça Mauá** bars near the port and the nightclubs along **Rua Mem de Sá** in Lapa, which feature transvestites.

Something Quiet: If you're not up to a wild night on the town, have a quiet drink at one of the sidewalk restaurants along the beach and enjoy the sea breeze. Many of the top beachfront hotels have quiet rooftop bars with fabulous views where you can enjoy a nightcap. Try the **Skylab** on the 30th floor of the Rio Othon Palace (Av. Atlântica 3264 on Copacabana beach, tel: 255-8812) or the **Ponte de Comando** at the top of the Miramar Palace (Av. Atlântica 3668, Copacabana, tel: 247-6070), both open till 2 a.m.

LANGUAGE

SURVIVAL PORTUGUESE

Portuguese, not Spanish, is the language of Brazil. If you have a knowledge of Spanish, it will come in handy—you will recognize many similar words and most Brazilians understand Spanish. Although many upper-class Brazilians know at least some English or French and are eager to practise on the foreign visitor, don't expect the man on the street to speak your language. A foreigner's effort to learn the local language is always appreciated.

You can get by at large hotels and fancy restaurants with no problems in English. However, if you like to wander around on your own, one of the pocket dictionaries, available in several languages to and from Portuguese, would be helpful. If you are unable to find one at home, they are on sale at the airport, hotel shops and book stores in Brazil.

First names are used a great deal in Brazil. In many situations in which English-speakers would use a title and surname, Brazilians often use a first name with the title of respect. *Senhor* for men (written *Sr.* and usually shortened to *Seu* in spoken Portuguese) and *Senhora* (written *Sra*) or *Dona* (used only with first name) for women. If João Oliveira or Maria da Silva calls you Sr. John, rather than Mr. Jones, then you should correspond-ingly address them as Sr. João and Dona Maria.

There are three second-person pronoun forms in Portuguese. If you stick to *você*, equivalent to "you," you will be all right. *O senhor* (for men) or *a senhora* (for women) is used to show respect for someone of a different age group or social class or to be polite to a stranger. As a foreigner, you won't offend anyone if you use the wrong form of address, but if you are trying to learn when to use the formal or informal style, observe and go by how others address you. In some parts of Brazil, mainly the northeast and the south, *tu* is used a great deal. Originally, in Portugal, *tu* was used similarly to the German "Du," among intimate friends and close relatives, but in Brazil, when this form is used, it is equivalent to *você*.

If you are staying longer and are serious about learning the language, there are Portuguese courses for non-native speakers. Meanwhile, here are some essential words and phrases.

English (Portuguese)

Please/Thank you (very much)
Por favor/(muita) Obrigago

You're welcome
De nada ("its nothing")

Excuse me
Desculpe (to apologise)/

Com licença (to take leave or get past someone who is in your way)

Greetings

Tudo Bem, meaning "all's well," is one of the most common forms of greeting: a person asks, "*Tudo bem ?*" and the other replies, "*Tudo bem.*" This is also used to mean "OK," "all right," "will do," or as a response when someone apologizes, indicating, as it were "That's all right, it doesn't matter."

Good morning/Good afternoon
Bam dia/Boa tarde

Good evening, good night
Boa noite

How are you?
Como val?

Well, thank you
Bem, obrigado

Hello
Aló (used mostly to answer the telephone - *bom dia, boa tarda* etc. are a more common form of greeting)

Hi, hey!
Oi (informal form of greeting also used to get someone's—like the waiter's—attention)

Goodbye
Tchau (very informal, most used), *até logo* (literally "until soon"), adeus similar to "farewell")

My name is .../I am...
Meu nome é.../Eu sou...

What is your name?
Como é seu nome?

It's a pleasure
E'um prazer, or frequently just *prazer* (used in introductions as, "Pleased to meet you")

Good! Great!
Que bom!

(To your) Health! (the most common toast)
Saúde!

Do you speak English?
Você fala inglés?

I don't understand/
I didn't understand
Não entendo/Não entendi

Do you understand?
Você entende?

Please repeat more slowly
Por favor repete, mais devagar

What do you call this (that)?
Como se chama isto (aquilo)?

How do you say...?
Como se diz...?

Nouns/Pronouns

Who?
Quem?

I/We
Eu/ Nós

You
Você (singular)
Vocés (plural)

He/She/They
Ele/Ela/Eles

My, Mine
Meu, Minha (depending on gender of object)

Our, Ours
Nosso, Nossa (depending on gender of object)

Your, Yours
Seu, Sua (depending on gender of object)

His/Her, Hers/
Their/Theirs
Dele/Dela/Deles (also *Seu, Sua* in all three cases)

Where is the...?
Onde é...?

...beach
...a praia

...bathroom
...o banheiro

...bus station
...o rodoviário

...airport
...o aeroporto

...train station
...a estação de trem

...post office
...o correio

...police station
...a delegacia de polícia

...ticket office
...a bilheteria

...marketplace
...o mercado/a feira

...embassy/consulate
...a embaixada/ oconsulado

Where is there a...?
Onde é que tem...?

...currency exchange
...uma casa de cámbio

...bank
...um banco

...pharmacy
...uma farmácia

...(good hotel) restaurant
...um (bom) hotel

...(good) restaurant
...um (bom) restaurante

...bar
...um bar

...snack bar
...um lanchonete

...bus stop
...um ponto de onibus

...taxi stand
...um ponto de taxi

...subway station
...uma estação de metró

...service station
...um posto de gasolina

...newsstand
...um jornaleiro

...public telephone
...um telefone público

...supermarket/
shopping center
...um supermercado/um shopping center

...department store/
boutique
...uma loja de departamentos/um boutique

...jeweler

250

...*um joalheiro*

...hairdresser/barber
...*um cabeleireiro/um barbeiro*

...laundry
...*uma lavanderia*

...hospital
...*um hospital*

Do you have...?
Tem...?

I want...please.
Eu quero...por favor.

I don't want...
Eu não quero...

I want to buy...
Eu quero comprar...

Where can I buy...
Onde posso comprar...?

...cigarettes
...*cigarro*

...film
...*filme*

...a ticket for-
(entertainment)
...*uma entrada para...*

...a reserved seat
...*um lugar marcado*

...another (the same/
different)
...*outro (igual/differente)*

...this/that
...*isto/aquilo*

...something less
expensive
...*aglo mais barato*

...postcards
...*cartões postais*

...paper/envelopes
papel/envelopes

...a pen/a pencil
...*uma caneta/um lápis*

...soap/shampoo
...*sabonete/xampu or shampoo*

...toothpaste/sunscreen
...*pasta de dente/filtro solar*

...aspirin
...*aspirina*

I need...
Eu preciso de...

..a doctor
...*um médico*

...a mechanic
...*um mecánico*

...transportation
...*condução*

...help
...*ajuda*

How much?
Quanto?

How many?
Quantos?

How much does it cost?
Quanto custa? Quanto é?

That's very expensive
E' muito caro

A lot much (also very)/
Many
Muito/Muitos

A little/Few
Um pouco, um pouquinho/Poucos

Numbers

one
um

two
dois

three
trés

four
quatro

five
cinco

six
seis (or often *meia*, meaning "half" for half dozen)

seven
sete

eight
oito

nine
nove

10
dez

11
onze

12
doze

13
treze

14
quatorze

15
quinze

16
dezesseis

17

dezessete

18
dezoito

19
dezenove

20
vinte

21
vinte e um

30
trinta

40
quarenta

50
cinqüenta

60
sessenta

70
setenta

80
oitenta

90
noventa

100
cem

101
cento e um

200
duzentos

300
trezentos

400
quatrocentos

500
quinhentos

600
seiscentos

700
setecentos

800
oitocentos

900
novecentos

1,000
mil

2,000
dois mil

10,000
dez mil

100,000
cem mil

1,000,000
um milhão

Commas and periods in numbers are used in an inverted form in Portuguese, so that one thousand is written 1.000 and one and a half (1.5) is written 1,5.

Opposites

Yes/No
Sim/Não

More/Less
Mais/Menos

Large/Small
Grande/Pequeno

Larger/Smaller
Maior/Menor

Expensive/Inexpensive
Carol/Barato

Warm/Hot/Cool/Cold
Morno/Quente/Fria/
Gelado

With/Without
Com/Sem

First/Last
Primeiro/Ultimo

Good/Well/Better/Best
Bom/Sem/Melhor/
O melhor

Bad/Worse/Worst
Ruim, Mal/Pior/Opior

Far/Near
Lange/Perto

Fast/Slow
Rápido/Devagar

Right/Left
Direita/Esquerda

Here/There
Aqui/Lá

Now/Later
Agora/Depois

Time

When?
Quando?

What time is it?
Que horas são?

Just a moment please
Um Momento, por favor

What is the schedule?
(Bus, tour, show, etc.)
Qual é o horário?

How long does it take?
Leva quanto tempo?

Hour/day/week/month
Hora/dia/semana/mês

At what time?
A que horas?

At 1.00, at 2.00, at 3.00
*A uma hora/as duas ho-
ras/as tres horas*

An hour from now
Daqui a uma hora

Which day?
Que dia?

Yesterday/Today/
Tomorrow
Ontem/Hoje/Amanhã

This week last week/
Next week
*Esta semana/ a semana
passada/ a semena
que vem*

Monday
Segunda-feira,
often written *2a*

Tuesday
Terca-feira,
often written *3a*

Wednesday
Quarta-feira,
often written *4a*

Thursday
Quinta-feira,
often written *5a*

Friday
Sexta-feira,
often written *6a*

Saturday
Sábado

Sunday
Domingo

The weekend
O fim de semana

Transportation

Taxi/Bus/Car
Taxi/Onibus/Carro

Plane/Train/Boat
Avião/Trem/Baroo

A ticket to...
Uma passagem para...

I want to go to...?
Quero ir para...

How can I get to...?
Como posso ir para...?

Please take me to...
Por favor, me leve para...

Please call a taxi for me.
*Por favor, chame um
taxi para mim.*

What is this place called?
*Como se chama
este lugar?*

Where are we?
Onde estamos?

How long will it take to get
there?
*Leva quanto tempo para
chegar lá?*

Please stop here/Stop!
Por favor pare aqui/Pare!

Please wait.
Por favor espere.

I want to rent a car.
Quero alugar um carra.

What time does the bus
(plane, boat) leave?
*A que horas sai o ónibus
(avião, barco)?*

Where does this bus go?
*Este ónibus vai para
onde?*

Does it go by way of...?
Passa em...?

Airport (Bus station) tax
Taxa de embarque

I want to check my lug-
gage (on bus etc.).
*Quero despachar minha
bagagem.*

I want to store my luggage
(at station).
*Quero guardar minha
bagagem.*

At the hotel

I have a reservation.
Tenho uma reserva.

I want to make a reser-
vation.
Quero fazer uma reserva.

...a single room/A double
room
*...um quarto de solteiro/
Um quarto de casal*

...with air conditioning
...com ar condicionado

I want to see the room.
Quero ver o quarto.

Suitcase/Bag, purse
Mala/Bolsa

Room service
Serviço de quarto

Key
Chave

The manager
O gerente

Money

Cash
Dinheiro

Do you accept credit

cards?
Aceita cartão de crédito?

Can you cash a traveler's check?
Pode trocar um traveler's check? (cheque de viagem)

I want to exchange money.
Quero trocar dinheiro.

What is the exchange rate?
Qual é o câmbio?

The bill, please
A conta, por favor.

I want my change, please.
Eu quero meu troco, por favor.

I want a receipt.
Eu quero um recibo.

At the restaurant

Waiter
Garçon

Matre d'
Maitre

I didn't order this.
Eu nao pedi ista.

Is service included?
Está incluido o serviço?

The menu/The wine list
O cardápio/A carte de vinhos

Breakfast/Lunch/Supper
Caré da manhãl/Almaça/ Jantar

The house speciality
A especialidade da casa

Mineral water (carbonated/uncarbonated)
A'gua mineral (com gás/ sem gás)

Coffee/Tea/Beer
Café/Chá/Cerveja

White wine/Red wine
Vinho tinto/Vinho branco

A soft drink/Juice
Um refrigerante/Suco

A drink (alcoholic)/a cocktail
Um drink/Um cocktail

Ice
Gelo

Salt/Pepper/Sugar
Sal/Pimenta/Açucar

An appetizer/A snack
Um tira-gostol/ Um lanche

Beef/Pork/Chicken/Fish/ Shrimp
Carne/Porco/Frango/ Peixe/Camarão

Well done/Medium rare/ Rare
Bem Passado/Ao ponto/ Mal Passado

Vegetables/Salad/Fruit
Verduras/Selada/Fruta

Bread/Butter/Toast/Eggs
Pão/Manteiga/Torrades/ Ovos

Rice/(french-fried) Potatoes/Beans
Arroz/Batatas (Fritas)/ Feijão

Soup/Sandwich/Pizza
Sopa/Sandviche/Pizza

Dessert/Sweets
Sombremesa/Doces

A plate/A glass/A cup
Um prato/Um copo/Uma xícara

A napkin
Um guardanapo

Addresses: To help you understand the addresses in the Travel Tips, here's what the Portuguese words mean: *Alameda* (abbreviated Al.) = lane; *Andar* = floor, storey; *Av.* or *Avenida* = avenue; *Centro* = the central downtown business district, also frequently referred to as a *cidade* or "the city"; *Cj.* or *Conjunto* = a suite of rooms or sometimes a group of buildings; *Estrada* (abbreviated Estr.) = road or highway; *Largo* (*Lgo.*) = square or plaza; *Praça* (*Pça.*) = square of plaza; *Praia* = beach; *Rodovia* (*Rod.*) = highway; *Rua* (abbreviated R.) = street; *Sala* = room; *Sobreloja* = mezzanine.

Ordinary numbers are written with a °sign after the numeral, so that 3° *andar* means 3rd floor.

The federal interstate highways are written with a BR in front of the number, for example, BR-101, which follows the Atlantic coast.

The Rio de Janeiro area code, if you are placing a long-distance call, is 021 (21 on the telex). Area codes for hotels in other cities in the state of Rio de Janeiro are in parentheses in front of the phone number. *Ramal* (pronounced 'ha-maul') = telephone extension.

DIPLOMATIC MISSIONS

EMBASSIES AND CONSULAR SERVICES

Addresses and telephone numbers for consulates in Rio de Janeiro are listed below. It's a good idea to call before visiting—diplomatic missions frequently do not keep normal business hours. If you're coming to Brazil on business, remember that your consulate's commercial sector can be helpful.

Brazilian Embassies Abroad

Australia
Canberra House
40 Marcus Clarke Street
Canberra

Austria
Am Sugeck 1/V/15
1010 Vienna

Belgium
350 Avenue Luise
150 Brussels

Canada
255 Albert St, Suite 990
Ottawa KIP 6A9

Denmark
Ryvangs Alle 24
2100 Copenhagen

East Germany
1971 Berlin
Pankow
D.R. Ebenstrasse

France
34 Cours Albert Ler
75008 Paris

Great Britain
32 Green Street
London W1Y 4AT

Holland
Mauritskade 19
The Hague

Israel
Hei Beyar 14
Kikar Hamedinah
Tel Aviv

Italy
Palazzo Navona
00186 Rome

Japan
11-13 Kita - Aoyama
2 Chome Minato-ku
Tokyo 107

Malaysia
41 Pesiaran Duta
Taman Duta
Kuala Lumpur
50480

Norway
Drammemsvein 82-C
Oslo 2

Singapore
302 Orchard Road
#15-03/04 Tong Building

South Africa
182 Balmoral Ave
Aze Arcadia
Pretoria 0083

Sweden
Sturegalan 12
11456 Stockholm

United States of America
3006 Massachusetts Avenue, N.W.
Washington, D.C. 20008

West Germany
Marienbura Parktrasse 20
West
5000 Köln

Consulates in Rio de Janeiro

Argentina
Praia de Botafogo
228, *sobreloja* (Botafogo)
Tel: 551-5198

Australia
Rua Voluntários da Pátria 45
5° *andar* (Botafogo)
Tel: 286-7922

Austria
Av. Atlântica 3804
(Copacabana)
Tel: 227-0040

Belgium
Av. Visconde de Albuquerque 694
1° *andar* (Lbelon)
Tel: 274-6747

Bolivia
Av. Rui Barbosa 664
apt. 101 (Flamengo)
Tel: 551-2395

Canada
Rua D. Gerardo 35
3° *andar* (Centro)
Tel: 233-9286

Chile
Praia do Flamengo 382
apt. 401 (Flamengo)
Tel: 552-5349

Colombia
Praia do Flamengo 82
apt. 202 (Flamengo)
Tel: 225-7582

Costa Rica
Rua Jardim Botânico 700
sl. 215 (Jardim Botânico)
Tel: 259-1748

Cyprus
Av. Rui Barbosa 16
apt. 1601 (Botafogo)
Tel: 551-5446

Czechoslovakia
Rua Maria Angélica
503 (Jardim Botânico)
Tel: 266-2207

Denmark
Praia do Flamengo 284
apt. 101 (Flamengo)
Tel: 552-6149

Egypt
Rua Muniz Barreto
741 (Botafogo)
Tel: 246-1852

Ecuador
Praia do Flamengo 382
apt. 402 (Flamengo)
Tel: 552-4949

Finland
Rua Paissandu 7
4° *andar* (Flamengo)
Tel: 225-6145

France
Av. Pres. Antonio
Carlos 58
6° *andar* (Centro)
Tel: 220-3729

Greece
Praia do Flamengo 382
apt. 802 (Flamengo)
Tel: 552-6849/552-6749

Guatemala
Rua Garcia d'Avila
113, sl. 802 (Ipanema)
Tel: 294-1849

Honduras
Praia do Flamengo 66

sl. 1309 (Flamengo)
Tel: 205-0397

Iceland
Praia do Flamengo 66
sl. 1015 (FLamengo)
Tel: 285-1795

Ireland
Rua Fonseca Teles
18 (São Cristóvão)
Tel: 254-0960

Israel
Av. N.S. de Copacabana
680
Cobertura (Copacabana)
Tel: 255-5432

Italy
Av. Pres. Antônio Carlos
40
7° *andar* (Centro)
Tel: 262-9090

Ivory Coast
Av. Rui Barbosa 870
Apt. 1101 (Botafogo)
Tel: 551-0094

Japan
Praia do Flamengo 200
10° *andar* (Flamengo)
Tel: 265-5252

Lebanon
Rua Dona Mariana
39 (Botafogo)
Tel: 266-6564

Luxemburg
Rua Alm. Mariath
1 (São Cristóvão)
Tel: 248-2625

Mexico
Praia de Botafogo 28
sl. 301 (Botafogo)
Tel: 551-9696

Netherlands
Rua Sorocaba
570 (Botafogo)

Tel: 246-4050

Nicaragua
Praia de Botafogo 28
sl. 602 (Botafogo)
Tel: 551-1497

Norway
Rua da Glória 122
sl. 102 (Glória)
Tel: 242-9742

Panama
Av. N.S. de Copacabana
1183
sl. 601 (Copacabana)
Tel: 267-7999

Paraguay
Rua do Carmo 20
sl. 1208 (Centro)
Tel: 242-9043

Peru
Av. Rui Barbosa 314
2° *andar* (Flamengo)
Tel: 551-6296

Portugal
Av. Pres. Vargas 62
3°/4° *andares* (Centro)
Tel: 233-7574

Romania
Rua Cosme Velho
526 (Cosme Velho)
Tel: 225-2212

South Africa
Rua Voluntários da Pátria
45
9° *andar* (Botafogo)
Tel: 266-6246

Spain
Rua Duvivier 43
apts. 201/202
(Copacabana)
Tel: 541-2299

Sweden
Praia do Flamengo 344
9°*andar* (Flamengo)

Tel: 552-2422

Switerland
Rua Candido Mendes
157, 11° *andar* (Glória)
Tel: 242-8035

Syria
Rua Emb.Carlos Taylor
150 (G®avea)
Tel: 259-8893

Thailand
Av. Venezuela 110
5° *andar* (Centro)
Tel: 291-5153

Tunisia
Av. N.S. de Copacabana
906, apt. 301
(Copacabana)
Tel: 235-4060

U.K.
Praia do Flamengo
284, 2° *andar* (Flamengo)
Tel: 552-1422

Uruguay
Rua Arthur Bernardes
30 (Catete)
Tel: 225-0089

U.S.A.
Av. Pres. Wilson
147 (Centro)
Tel: 292-7117

U.S.S.R.
Av. Prof. Azevedo
Marques 50 (Leblon)
Tel: 274-0097

Venezuela
Praia de Botafogo 242
5° *andar* (Botafogo)
Tel: 551-5698

West Germany
Rua Pres. Carlos de Campos 417
(Laranjeiras)
Tel: 285-2333

INTERNATIONAL AIRLINES

Aerolineas Argentinas
Reservations
Tel: 221-4255
International Airport
Tel: 398-3520/3737
398-3375

Aeroperu
Reservations
Tel: 240-1622
International Airport
Tel: 398-9585

Air France
Reservations
Tel: 220-3666
International Airport
Tel: 398-3311

Alitalia
Reservations
Tel: 262-5088
International Airport
Tel: 398-3663/3143

Avianca
International Airport
Tel: 398-3775/3778

British Airways
Reservations
Tel: 242-6020/
Toll-free: (021)-800-6926
International Airport
Tel: 398-3888

Canadian Pacific
Reservations
Tel: 398-3168/3370

Iberia
International Airport
Tel: 398-3168/3370

Iraqi Airways
International Airways
Tel: 398-3541/3448

398-3349

Japan Air Lines
Reservations
Tel: 221-9663

KLM
International Airport
Tel: 398-3700

Ladeco
International Airport
Tel: 398-3601

Lan Chile
Reservations
Tel: 242-1423/
Toll-free (021)-800-6110
International Airport
Tel: 398-3799/3797
398-3529

Lineas Aerras Paraguayas
International Airport
Tel: 398-3950
383-7395

Lloyd Aereo Boliviano
Reservations
Tel: 220-9548

Lufthansa
Reservations
Tel: 262-1022/0273/
262-0223
International Aiport
Tel: 398-3620

Pan American
Reservations
Tel: 240-2322/6662

Pluna
International Airport
Tel: 398-3920/3921

Royal Air Maroc
International Airport
Tel: 398-3766

SAA—South African
Reservations

Tel: 262-6252
International Airport
Tel: 398-3767/3365
398-3366

SAS
International Airport
Tel: 398-3708/3809

Swissair
Reservations
Tel: 203-2144
International Airport
Tel: 398-3304/3547

TAG-Angolan Airlines
Reservations
Tel: 263-4911

TAP Air Portugal
International Airport
Tel: 398-3565/3455

Viasa
Reservations
Tel: 224-5345
International Airport

Tel: 398-3808

Airlines Serving Both International And Domestic Routes

Transbrasil
Reservations
Tel: 297-4422.
International Airport
Tel: 398-5985
Santos Dumont Airport
Tel: 220-9278
262-6061

Varig/Cruzeiro
Reservations
Tel: 292-6600
Santos Dumont Airport
Tel: 220-7728
297-5141

Vasp
Reservations
Tel: 292-2080
International Airport
Tel: 398-5989

Santos Dumont Airport
Tel: 292-2112

Regional Domestic Airlines

Nordeste
Reservations
Tel: 220-4366/9652
262-2237
Santos Dumont Airport
Tel: 262-3580

Rio-Sul
Reservations/Santos
Dumont Airport
Tel: 262-6911

Taba
Reservations
Tel: 220-2529/2649

Tam
Santos Dumont Airport
Tel: 262-6311
International Airport
Tel: 398-3271

ART/PHOTO CREDITS

Photos by H. John Maier Jr. and

INDEX

surf competitions, 160
surfing, 103, 165
swimming, 102, 103, 167
swimwear, 195, *see also* bikinis

T

Tamoio Indians, the, 18
tennis, 48, 165
Teresópolis, mountain resort of,
  67, 147, 152-153
theaters, 108
Tijuca Forest, **67, 117**
Tijuca Mountain, 125
topless sunbathing, 48
tourism, 23
tranvestite ball nights, 188
tranvestites, 185
Trinidade, fishing village, 171
trolley ride, the, 79, 117, *see also*
  cable car
Tunel Alaor Prata, Copacabana,
  98
Tunel Engenheiro Marques

Porto, Copacabana, 98

U

umbanda, 41, 42, *see also*
  religions

V

Valeria, Isis, writer, 180
Vasco, soccer team, 49 *see also*
  futebol
vegetable markets, *see* markets
Vespuccio, Americo, discoverer,
  17, 18
Vidigal, 38, 139, 143
Vila Riso, sugar plantation, São
  Conrado, 140
Villegaigono, Admiral Durant de,
  17
Vinicius, disco, Copacabana, 112
Visconde de Piraja, Ipanema,
  196
Vista Chinesa, 117

volleyball games, 34, 102

W

Welles, Orson, writer, 26
works of art
  A Grande Cidade, 81
  A Barca, 80
  Asas, 81
  Café, 71
  O Sapateiro de Brodowski, 80
Retrato de Maria , 71
wealthy, the, 52, 53, 55
wines, Brazilian, 47
women, 47, 48
working class, the, 55, *see also*
  favelados
windsurfing, 160
wood carvings, 197

Z

Zona Norte, Rio, 188
Zona Sul, Rio, 188